Politics, Archaeology and the Creation of a National Museum in Ireland

An Expression of National Life

Elizabeth Crooke

IRISH ACADEMIC PRESS
Dublin • Portland, OR

First published in 2000 by
IRISH ACADEMIC PRESS
44, Northumberland Road,
Dublin 4, Ireland
and in the United States of America by
IRISH ACADEMIC PRESS
c/o ISBS, 5824 NE Hassalo Street
Portland, OR 97213-3644

Website: www.iap.ie

British Library Cataloguing in Publication Data

Crooke, Elizabeth M.
  Politics, archaeology and the creation of a national
  museum in Ireland: an expression of national life
  1. Archaeological museums and collections – Ireland
  2. Archaeology – Ireland 3. Ireland – Antiquities –
  Collection and preservation 4. Ireland – Politics and
  government
  I. Title
  936.1
  ISBN 0-7165-2729-4

Library of Congress Cataloging-in-Publication Data

Crooke, Elizabeth M., 1971–
  Politics, archaeology and the creation of a national
  museum in Ireland: an expression of national life
    p. cm.
  Includes bibliographical references and index.
  ISBN 0-7165-2729-4 (hb: alk. paper)
    1. Ireland–Antiquities–Collection and preservation.
  2. Archaeological museums and collections–Ireland.
  3. Museums–Political aspects–Ireland. 4. Ireland–
  Politics and government. 5. Archaeology–Ireland.
  6. Nationalism–Ireland. 7. Museums–Ireland. I.
  Title.

DA920.C76 2000
936.1–dc21   00-063357

Printed by
Creative Print and Design (Wales) Ebbw Vale

Contents

FOREWORD   v

PREFACE   xi

LIST OF ILLUSTRATIONS   xii

Introduction   1

Chapter One:
The Politics of Interpreting and Valuing Museums   9

   Museums and Nationalism   9
   The Politics of Valuing Museums and their Collections   11

Chapter Two:
Nationalism and the Development of Cultural Institutions   17

   Understanding how Nationalism uses the Past   17
   Irish Cultural Nationalism   22

Chapter Three:
The Use of the Past in Irish Politics   32

   The Political Appropriation of Archaeology   33
   Variations in Political Ideology and Appropriation of
   the Past   49
   Archaeology and the Nationalist Narrative   58

Chapter Four:
Antiquarians and their Political Role in Nineteenth-Century
Ireland   68
   Nineteenth-Century Archaeology as a Function of the
   Political Context   69
   George Petrie and the Popularisation of Archaeology   82
   Antiquarians and the National Endeavour   91

Chapter Five:
The Establishment of a Public Museum in Ireland   100

    Museums in Nineteenth-Century Dublin   100
    The Department of Science and Art in South Kensington
    and the Imperial Influence   105
    Building the Dublin Museum of Science and Art   115
    The Dublin Museum of Science and Art: Early Years   123

Chapter Six:
From the Dublin Museum of Science and Art to the National
Museum of Ireland   129

    A Battle of Two Nations: The Case of the Broighter Hoard 129
    The Beginning of Change for the Dublin Museum of
    Science and Art   134
    Partition and Museum Provision   139
    The *Lithburg Report* and the Redefinition of the
    National Museum   141

Chapter Seven:
Museums, Archaeology and Politics: Links and Legacy   148

    Links between the Centuries   149
    Legacy: Can We Learn from the Past?   155

Notes   164

Appendices   181

Bibliography   185

Index   205

Foreword

The history of the National Museum of Ireland indicates that the institution has reflected more than led political, cultural and administration trends over the past century and a half. Dr Crooke's book shows how the institution evolved from two often conflicting sources – an imposed British administrative perception of the need to improve the industry of the citizens by exposing them to arts, instruction and self-education and a native mostly nationalist empathy with antiquities and archaeology which was sometimes romanticised and, in various ways used politically by public figures from Daniel O'Connell and Thomas Davis through to William O'Brien and John Redmond to Arthur Griffith and Eoin MacNeill. Her book traces both the national and archaeological politics from which the museum emerged and is particularly useful for the middle and later nineteenth century before tailing off from around the 1916 Rising. Although she deals with the museum in the Free State era up to the end of W. T. Cosgrave's government, it is hoped that she will return to the story of the museum under the new state where it mainly languished for eighty years. The accession by the museum of the Collins Barracks site which was opened by Sile de Valera in 1997, the imminent opening of the folklife branch at Castlebar, Co. Mayo, the refurbishment of Kildare Street and Merrion Street and the passing of the new Museum's Act all make this the ideal time for Dr Crooke's study and, it is hoped, for a sequel.

It would not be fully correct to see the origins and development of the National Museum solely in terms of an increased interest in archaeology and related pride in antiquities which was used for political and cultural ends. Neither in its remote Dublin Society origins back in the 1730s nor in the more proximate middle and later Victorian period can the museum be seen as exclusively or even primarily concerned with archaeology. While Irish Antiquities may have been brought to the fore in the museum firstly by the Broighter hoard controversy, then by Count Plunkett in a new prioritising of the exhibition galleries which took account of things ancient and Irish and especially by Dr Adolf Mahr and others after the establishment of the Free State, the original nucleus of what is now the National Museum of Ireland revolved around the natural history collections while the core educational concern and actual *raison d'être* of the institution were based on the decorative or applied arts collections. That the museum was known as the Dublin Museum of Science and Art under the South Kensington department of the same name and that, to this day, one of the major departments of the museum is known as the art and industrial division betrays a background with concerns which were primarily neither national nor archaeological. You only have to look at photographs of early displays in the centre court and rotunda of the Kildare Street building to realise the emphases which prevailed at the close of the nineteenth century. Pride of place at the centre of the rotunda was first given to a pair of six pounder field guns captured by the British from the Sikhs in India in 1845. This was replaced by the Lord Chancellor's and a circle of other coaches. It was well after independence that these were replaced by plaster casts of high crosses which, sadly in my view, were removed by Dr Raftery in the late seventies. The gradual Irishing or nationalising of the institution both in terms of staff, as well as collecting and exhibiting priorities as a consequence of the decline of the formal British presence in Ireland inevitably was to take longer than might have been at first thought to go by R. B. MacDowell's story of the museum attendant who had served with the Munster Fusileers and who, when asked what he thought of Patrick Pearse and his comrades being honoured in the museum, threatened to push the head of the questioner through a glass case!

As an archaeologist I have to be among the first to realise that Irish Antiquities is now close to the soul of the museum's essence and that this collection is high on the list of reasons why the Kildare Street premises attracts so many visitors every year. Irish Antiquities has been and continues to be closely bound up with the development of scientific archaeology and a responsible national collections policy fortified by necessary legislation, particularly the national monuments and other acts. Its staff carried out most of the excavation work in the Viking and medieval Dublin as well as the prehistoric sites at Lough Crew and Keenoge and the crannógs at Lough Gara. As well as monitoring the intake of acquisitions in an annual register and undertaking necessary fieldwork, its staff also supervise the intake of artefacts from all other excavations undertaken in Ireland. Not only that, our department of Irish Folklife which has found a home at Castlebar is the offspring of Irish Antiquities and, for older administrative reasons, the ethnographical collection with its celebrated South Seas material which will be housed in a later phase at Collins Barracks also belongs, for the present, with 'Irish Antiquities'.

For all its significance, antiquities is only part of the story of the museum and in any full history of the place we must be careful not to ignore the foundation collections and the work of the earliest directors, curators and administrators. The work of W. E. Steele the first director (1878–83) after the 1877 act and of his successor Valentine Ball (1883–95) who was present at the 1890 opening, especially of Colonel Plunkett who achieved so much with the inauguration of services like a circulating exhibition and the long-serving museum secretary Bantry White whose duties even included the design of show cases all have to be signalled. So have the earliest naturalists and geologists as well as to art historians like T. H. Longfield, J. J. Buckley and Archibald McGoogan (who helped design the seal of the new state).

I welcome Dr Crooke's book as a pioneering effort in investigating the development of the National Museum and Irish archaeology in the context of the political movements of the nineteenth and early twentieth centuries. That museums are reflective of the politics of the time in question is not new but to see Ireland's great museum and its archaeological collections against a background of the various strands of nationalism and with British attempts to administer the arts and heritage of later nineteenth-century Ireland also in focus is instructive. Far from being peripheral to the political life of the country, the very establishment of the museum, the initial choice of a non-native architect, and the eventual acquisition of the Celtic Iron Age gold hoard from Co. Derry which originally was requested by the British Museum were all hotly debated topics of national interest in their day. This was the time of the Home Rule debate, the establishment of the Department of Agriculture (and Technical Instruction) and of several progressive attempts by the British to kill off Home Rule with kindness. It was also the time of the foundation of the Gaelic Athletic Association, the Gaelic League and of the national theatre society – a cultural and political milieu outside which the Dublin Museum of Science and Art was to remain (at least officially) until the Broighter debate. This and the philosophy of Count Plunkett, who was made Director in 1904, brought the museum's role as the national repository of objects of Celtic heritage into play. It had already come to be regarded as the National Museum even by people like Sir Thomas Esmonde and was finally accorded that status by the Free State Government when Eoin MacNeill as minister for education asserted the museum's national role.

Dr Crooke's story ends with Cosgrave's government. She must continue the story. Eamonn de Valera's support for scientific archaeology and his interest in it to the very end of his life are worthy of study. So are the various museum commemorations of the 1916 Rising beginning in 1941 with a display, which probably has to be seen as a morale booster during the emergency, progressing to the comprehensive 1966 version opened by the then Taoiseach Sean Lemass culminating in the present arguably more toned-down 75th anniversary version. Coming towards the end of the recent troubles this subject was still regarded as too sensitive by at least one civil servant who enquired of the relevant curator whether the title of the exhibition, 'the *Struggle* for Independence' might be amended to the '*path*' and the guns left out altogether! For the record, we settled for the *road* and used guns sparingly!

Proving Dr Crooke's thesis correct that even when politics and politicians interfere in museum exhibitions, and only rarely (as apparently in the case of D. B. O'Malley and Rosc'67) do they ever do, the museum and its concerns still manage to reflect the political climate of the time. Our plan to have a military gallery at Collins Barracks commemorating all Irishmen and women in whatever army they served as well as having a fully comprehensive history gallery in the former equestrian centre at the same venue incorporating the present 1916 exhibition to deal with Irish history in a comprehensive way more appropriate to the prevailing perception of the political evolution of modern Ireland will be but the latest instalment in a reflective rather than a too obviously formative role vis-à-vis political developments.

Having said that politics and politicians have only rarely played an indirect role in the museum's recent history, I have to acknowledge that the award of Collins Barracks to the museum and indeed the decision to locate the folklife branch at Turlough Park, Castlebar were both political decisions. While no director can afford to be unaware of politics and of course few subjects are as consuming in Ireland, the active involvement of museum professionals in politics can have unfortunate consequences, not least for the professionals in question. It may have been all right for the archaeologist George Coffey to have been a Home Ruler, but the active involvement of Count Plunkett's family in 1916 when his son Joseph Mary was executed for his part in the Rising resulted in the director being sacked though he was to go on to win the first by-election for Sinn Fein and later to become minister for the arts in the first Dáil, a position not deemed worthy of filling by subsequent dáils until the appointment of Michael D. Higgins in 1992. Less happy was the outcome of the political involvement of another director, Dr Adolf Mahr, who left his position in the museum to help the German cause in the Second World War only to suffer later as a prisoner of war and after heated discussion in the Dáil never to return to his desk in Kildare Street. Among curators with the strongest political involvement were Michael O'Heaney and Liam Gogan. If there is a lesson in all this it is that curators and especially directors should not meddle in politics. There is the lesson of another director, Colonel Plunkett, who not gauging properly the political winds of change that were blowing across Ireland advised that the museum continue to be administered from South Kensington when, as Dr Crooke shows, local pressure resulted in the museum being made responsible to the new Dublin Department of Agriculture (and Technical Institution). Not altogether ironically, this was also the museum's greatest period of expansion probably until its relatively recent transition to the new Department of Arts, Heritage, Gaeltacht and the Islands. Showing that some things never change, there is the present parallel dilemma of whether the museum should continue as part of the department with its finances and staffing closely overseen by the Department of Finance or move out as a semi-state agency as is possible under the 1997 Museum Act with its financial and staffing considerations monitored as closely as ever by the same Department of Finance!

For opening up the academic discussion on the origins of the museum and recognising the importance of archaeology both to the museum and to the various strands of nationalist politics we are indebted to Dr Crooke.

Her study is mature in its approach and generous in its assessment of the personalities. As with all best commentators I think the reader will find it difficult to detect the writer's own bias. I hope that she will be suitably complimented when I say in tribute to her work that I feel her sympathies might not be too far from those of that pioneering archaeologist and scholar George Petrie for whom I suspect she has, understandably and properly in my own biased view, an empathy and fascination which I trust will one day result in a full-scale modern biography. This work shows that he deserves no less. But Dr Crooke must also tell the post-1916 story of the National Museum of Ireland. This book shows that she is the scholar for what on present evidence promises to be a most exciting and instructive undertaking.

PATRICK F. WALLACE
National Museum of Ireland
November 2000

Preface

This book began as a doctoral dissertation at the Department of Archaeology University of Cambridge and I owe special debt to those who through their guidance inspired my interest in the political and social aspects of museums and archaeology. I particularly wish to thank my supervisor, Dr. Marie-Louise Stig. Sørensen and my examiners, Dr Gabriel Cooney and Prof. Colin Renfrew. In its various stages, this work has benefited from discussion with many people. I am grateful to Patrick Wallace, Keith Jeffrey, Ray Ryan, John Carman, Robin Boast, Catherine Hills, Ann Hamlin and Andrew Vance who all read various drafts of this book. I would also like to extend my appreciation to all of those in libraries and archives who made finding my source material easier. This includes the staff of the Rare Books Room in Trinity College Dublin, those who helped me in the National Museum of Ireland, the National Library and the National Archives in Dublin, and those in the Official Publications Room and Early Printed Books in Cambridge University Library. I am also indebted to Dr Michael Ryan for introducing me to the Royal Irish Academy Library.

I would like to thank the National Museum of Ireland for giving me permission to use an image from their archive for the dust jacket of this book. I would also like to acknowledge Enniskillen Library who allowed me to photograph images in their collection and the group A Journey of Reconciliation Trust for allowing me to reproduce their photograph of the round tower at Mesen, Belgium.

Completing this book would have been more challenging without the kindness and generosity of my family and friends. I would like to extend my appreciation to the members of the Cambridge Group for Irish Studies for providing a stimulating forum for discussion of Irish issues. My interest in current museum provision is fed by my friends working in museums in Ireland, especially Robert Heslip, Vivienne Pollock, Pat Cooke, Helen Lanigan-Wood and Bronagh Cleary. I would also like to thank those friends who have accompanied me on innumerable museum visits, and those who remind me there is more to do! Above all, I am deeply grateful to Ceallach Levins for his constant encouragement and support and to my family in County Fermanagh for their love and attention. This book is dedicated to my parents, for their continued care, encouragement and interest in my endeavours.

Elizabeth Crooke
Paris, 20000

List of Illustrations

Figure 1   The 'monster meeting' at Tara   35

Figure 2   Detail of the cover of the National Repeal
           Association membership card   39

Figure 3   Frontispiece of *The Spirit of the Nation*   40

Figure 4   Frontispiece of *The History of Ireland Ancient
           and Modern*   43

Figure 5   Frontispiece of *Popular History of Ireland*   44

Figure 6   Dust cover of *And so Began the Irish Nation*   61

Figure 7   Postcard labelled The National Museum of
           Science and Art, Dublin   66

Figure 8   'National Emblems'   75

Figure 9   O'Connell Monument, Glasnevin Cemetery
           Dublin   89

Figure 10 Aerial plan of the site of Dublin's Museums   116

Figure 11 'Proposed Science and Art Museum. Design
           submitted by Mr G. P. Beater, Archt'   120

Figure 12 'New Science and Art Museum Buildings,
           Kildare Street'   120

Figure 13 The 'Peace Tower' Mesen, Belgium   160

Introduction

No community, however small and insignificant, considers itself properly provided for unless it has a museum. To my mind a museum is more than a system; it is part of the national life, it is an expression of the national life and of the higher qualities of the people to whom it belongs. It is something which locally has struck its roots, and we may expect from it such flowers and fruit as belong to the nature of the place.[1]

GEORGE NOBLE Count Plunkett, Director of Dublin's chief museum, made the above statement when he delivered his Presidential Address to the Museums Association in Dublin in 1912. For the purposes of this book Plunkett's statement is valuable in two ways. In the first place, the poetic account of the importance of museums reflects characteristics of the writings of nineteenth-century cultural nationalists. Secondly, Plunkett emphasised some of qualities about museums that many have considered central to understanding their value. Museums have been conceived as creating a sense of belonging, as emerging organically from the community and, since museums grow from the people, they become something greater. In the Irish context this is a representation of the nation. Adding to the effect of Plunkett's statement, the Dublin newspapers of the time, such as the *Irish Times* and the *Freeman's Journal*, reported his sentiments, thus bringing them into the public sphere. The *Irish Times* declared the Irish antiquities collection in the museum as not only 'a source of pride, but a source of inspiration'.[2] This occasion effectively sums up a century of events which made it evident that the subject of museums and archaeology in nineteenth- and early-twentieth century Ireland was intensely politicised. This was largely derived from the ideological force of nationalism which dominated the Irish political scene and through which a particular understanding of the relationship between the past and political endeavour evolved.

It is the relationship between archaeology, antiquities collections and politics that forms the subject of this book. This book is founded on the belief that nationalism produces a self-legitimising 'national' interpretation of the past, which will have an impact on how archaeology is valued and the character of museums. As a result of this, museums can be seen as the product of a certain political relationship with the past.

There has been a great deal of recent research that has shown that cultural activity and nationalist aspirations were closely linked in nineteenth-century Europe.[3] The joint production of the nation through nationalism and museums has been discussed in Flora Kaplan's edited volume, *Museums and the Making of 'Ourselves'*, as well as being the main theme of an edition of the *Museums Journal* which opened with the title: 'National Museums. Treasure Chest or Political Symbol?'[4] These studies, of cases in Greece, Spain, Denmark and central Europe, emphasise that knowledge of the past provided the aspiring nation with historical realism and material representation. They recognise that museums which are designated as 'national' must have a political and symbolic dimension and therefore any discussion of a national museum should take into account the issues of nationalism and national identity. Though there is a broad body of material, the emphasis of this work can be broadly grouped into two areas: those archaeologists and historians who recognise that their discipline has been used as a political tool, and others who emphasise the role of politics as instrumental for the very development of the discipline and its related institutions.[5]

The works referred to above are an important introduction and, indeed, it is fair to say that research into the ideological basis of archaeology and museums is in its infancy. An overview of the history of museum development in Britain and Ireland is provided in the Museums Association's *Manual of Curatorship*[6] and in volumes with a wide geographical area of interest.[7] Those volumes, which do consider the history of archaeology or museums in more detail, are mostly conventional institutional histories, often published as commemorative volumes. Two examples are those published to mark the founding of the Society of Antiquaries of Scotland[8] and the centenary of the Museums Association.[9] Such publications rarely consider the value systems that underpin their development. Recent work, which placed museums in their social context, has consisted of short articles in edited volumes that have raised many interesting questions, for instance those concerning gender issues, the politics of the past and of seeing, and the concept of collecting.[10] However these works cannot boast major historical depth. The research in this book represents the first attempt to offer a substantial account of the links between archaeology, the creation of a national museum and political aspirations.

Traditionally Irish archaeology has regarded itself as an objective science not needing to consider the theoretical debates, such as processualism and post-processualism, which have dominated archaeology elsewhere.[11] In addition, the subject of this study has had little attention: 'Irish archaeologists have shown little or no desire to engage in discussion about the influence of politics or nationalism on their work'.[12] This is also the case in the Irish museum profession, where there has been little or no consideration of the theoretical or socio-political basis of the field. The history of the development of Irish archaeology and museums has been restricted largely to that produced in connection with the commemoration of significant dates, such as to mark the bicentenary of the Royal Irish Academy,[13] and that in the introduction of volumes on the archaeology of Ireland.[14] No significant work has been published on the history of the National Museum in Dublin or its ideological roots. H. Bantry White[15] produced some short essays on the links between the museum and industrial education and a pamphlet was published in 1977 to mark one hundred years since the passing of the Science and Art Museum Act.[16] A. T. Lucas, former Director of the National Museum, produced two papers that linked the ideas of nation and national museum in their titles, but which did not engage with the concepts in their content.[17] The history of the Ulster Museum in Belfast is limited to a booklet published to mark the fiftieth anniversary of the opening of the museum at Stranmillus[18] and the history of the Ulster Folk and Transport Museum has only received brief exploration.[19]

Gradually, journals and volumes are beginning to publish short articles on Irish antiquarians. Many of the nineteenth-century antiquarians were polymaths. George Petrie (1789–1866), pronounced as the father of Irish archaeology by Myles Dillon,[20] was considered in a volume of the *Proceedings of the Royal Irish Academy* for his contribution to Irish music, numismatics, manuscript collecting and archaeology.[21] George Victor du Noyer (1783–1866) was considered by Petra Coffey as both an antiquarian and an artist; however, Jean Archer chose to discuss his contribution to the study of Irish geology. Du Noyer was also considered by Maire de Paor who discussed his artistic contribution along with that of other nineteenth-century antiquarians, amongst whom George Petrie,

William Wakeman (1822–1900) and members of the Ordnance Survey in Ireland were included.[22] Despite this largely historical emphasis, research in Ireland is beginning to recognise that the interpretation of archaeology is a product of socio-political context. Issues central to heritage debates outside Ireland, such as the impact of tourism and the commodification of the past,[23] are beginning to penetrate the Irish heritage scene.[24] In Irish archaeology, Gabriel Cooney has produced important work on the application of theory in archaeology and the politics of Irish archaeology,[25] which has also been taken up in other writing.[26] These papers demonstrate the importance of the subject and the need for further research. Questions significant for the study of archaeology and the history of museum development in Ireland are being raised in Irish geography. Brian Graham, for instance, writing on the concept of 'heritage' has argued that the importance of a heritage icon does not depend on the artefact itself but on its interpretation and suggested that heritage is regarded as an essential component of the foundation of the myth of the nation-state.[27] Graham has also edited a volume that considered how a sense of place in Ireland, which was important for the creation of national identity, was founded in landscape, literature and language.[28] Geographers have been encouraged to ask 'why a theory is put forward, whose interests are advanced or retarded, and in what kind of milieu was it conceived and communicated?'[29]

These questions have been applied to appraisal of the interpretation of court tombs provided by the archaeologist Ruadhri de Valera and that of the geographer-cum-archaeologist Estyn Evans. De Valera stated that the stylistic influences on court tombs came from France; Evans argued that the origins came from Scotland, and suggested that de Valera was deliberately downplaying links with Britain.[30] Brian J. Graham has pointed out that the former interpretation may be seen as having a nationalist intent and the latter might be regarded as unionist.[31] In addition to this critique, Evans' other work that spanned from the 1930s to the mid-1980s, the most influential being published in the 1950s and the 1960s, has come under scrutiny.[32] Graham states that Evans' work in Irish geography generated five cultural 'motifs': regionalism, human society and environment; the commond ground; continuity; Ulster; and Irishness. Matthew Stout argued that Evans' interest in making social comments based on the geography of place was an attempt to justify the state of Northern Ireland. Thus providing a landscape-myth for unionist nationalism.[33] Evans' widow Gwyneth Evans, in a detailed and passionate essay, has since challenged Stout's analysis.[34] The nature of the debate regarding Evans' legacy illustrates some of the complexities inherent in investigating the social and political contribution of research into the history and geography of a place. In addition, the very labeling of interpretations of history and archaeology as 'nationalist' or 'unionist' illustrates the ingrained and almost innate nature of political considerations running though the Irish academic world. Such analysis, which highlights the possible influence of political values on Irish archaeology and heritage development, links to the ongoing revisionism debate in Irish historical studies.[35] This debate considers the purpose of the past, the influence of historical texts on the formation of national identity and the contemporary function of writing history. Though the significance of these issues is not dependent on place, the nature of the debate in Ireland reveals the highly sensitive and political nature of creating history and it brings to light considerations pertinent to the practice of archaeology and material culture studies in Ireland. In addition, the intensity of the debate in Irish historical studies may be used as an indication of what may arise in Irish archaeology and museum studies as the disciplines begin to engage more fully with the political dimension of heritage interpretation and management.

Recent research on the relationship between museums, archaeology and nationalism are an important beginning, but a detailed exploration of the links between nationalism, archaeology and museums in Ireland is still to be undertaken. The aim of this book is to investigate how a 'national' antiquities collection in Ireland was formed in the context of a century of rising nationalism and how the collection changed in the early twentieth century according to the change in political conditions. By considering the significance placed on archaeology and collections in political texts, an insight both into nationalism as an ideology, and the nature of Irish nationalism specifically is provided. In addition, by the study of the writings and addresses made by members of the Royal Irish Academy it is possible to reveal how a certain vision of the Irish nation was brought into the evaluation and care of archaeology and the formation of a 'national' collection of antiquities. The social and political role of museum collections has been assessed by a consideration of the institutional records linked to museum provision in Dublin. For instance, the information held in the reports of the Department of Science and Art in London, annual reports published by the Director of the museum, and museum catalogues reveal various competing ideas of the purpose of a museum in Dublin. Through these sources one can track the foundation of the Dublin Museum of Science and Art and later the redefinition of the museum as it emerged as the National Museum of Ireland in the early years of the Irish Free State.

The majority of the political sources used to trace the links between archaeology, collecting and the legitimisation of the Irish nation have not been previously used for this subject. This research is therefore the first documented discussion of those links and provides additional insights into the nature of Irish nationalism. This book also represents the first account of the political history of Irish archaeology and the establishment of the Dublin Museum of Science and Art, later the National Museum of Ireland. Furthermore, the insights provided with regard to the Irish example contribute to general theoretical work on the use of archaeology and museums as instruments to define and legitimise a political programme or national identity. Finally, this book makes an original contribution to the study of the links between Britain and Ireland in the nineteenth century. While this relationship has been considered through various channels, it has not hitherto been investigated in the museum context. The findings in this book should, therefore, be seen as an alternative lens through which to view the relationship between Britain and Ireland in the nineteenth century.

This book looks first at the political purpose of archaeology, museums and their collections. It establishes three important points: why the past should be of interest to nationalism; how political agendas may shape the construction of values concerning archaeological objects, collections and museums, and how these values are moulded to make them desirable and useful for nationalism. This is placed in context through a discussion of the role of the cultivation of the past and cultural institutions in various instances of nationalism in Europe generally and Ireland specifically. There is a discussion of the development of a distinct form of Irish cultural nationalism in which references to antiquity, traditions and museums formed an essential part. This is a necessary prelude to a consideration of the appropriation of archaeology and collections by Irish nationalism. Not only can evidence of this be easily traced throughout the century, but also the methods by which the past was adopted can be used as a subtle indicator of variations in political opinion. From this political background a nationalist narrative emerged which glorified the Irish past, popularised the material remains of antiquity and created a pervasive interest in archaeology and museums.

Political and social interests both inspired antiquarians to take an interest in the past and provided their activity with an agenda, and the instances of this are traced. It is shown that the history of the interest in archaeology is a reflection of the political context. Led by the antiquarian George Petrie, the involvement with the past changed considerably in the nineteenth century, beginning largely as a private pastime and later emerging as a public activity. Attention will be given to the ideological concerns which shaped the development of Ireland's premier archaeological collection, that of the Royal Irish Academy. It will be shown that the collection was formed, and gathered strength, in the context of nineteenth-century nationalism when its content was regarded as useful for defining the nation and national identity. Later, towards the end of the century, the collection was caught in a 'battle' between the 'Irish nation' and the influence of British institutions in Ireland. This was symbolised by attempts made both by the Department of Science and Art at South Kensington in London and by the British Museum to assert control over the collection. Gradually, in the early decades of the twentieth century, the British influence began to lessen. Further evidence of the museum emerging as a 'national' institution is provided in the discussion of the renaming of the institution and changes in display priorities. This was completed with the creation of the Irish Free State when the institution became known as the National Museum of Ireland and various internal changes took place. Finally there will be a discussion of the role of museums and archaeology in the contemporary political situation in Ireland.

CHAPTER ONE

The Politics of Interpreting and Valuing Museums

MUSEUMS AND NATIONALISM

THE DECLARATION made by Karel Sklenár in his study of the history of archaeology in central Europe exposed the political nature of museums. He argued that his research had shown that 'the national museum is the typical institution for the small nation fighting for recognition in the world; it is a psychological and ideological weapon, a centre for the committed historicism and often the centre of the intellectual and cultural life of the nation'.[1]

This is not unique to central Europe. The study of archaeology and the creation of museums worldwide have both been linked historically to political aspirations and developments. For instance, in 1834 the newly independent state of Guatemala sponsored archaeological research and declared that the 'history of the state shall be ennobled with the descriptions of the monuments and antiquities'.[2] The Greek War of Independence in 1821 was preceded by an intensification of cultural activity which included republishing and teaching ancient Greek memorials and an interest in the Greek language and antiquity. In this context it was presented as particularly unjust that the Greeks, heirs to such a legacy, should lack independence. Greece's first public museums, being mostly archaeological in content, were founded soon after the formation of the new state with the purpose to reaffirm the history of Greece.[3] A similar romantic-nationalistic vision of the past had an impact on perceptions of archaeology in nineteenth-century Spain. There the glorification of pre-Roman Spain and associated 'Celtomania' materialised itself in art, literature and the teaching of early history.[4] The promotion of the Iberian period as the 'Golden Age' was central to Celtic nationalism in Spain; furthermore, the period was also appropriated for competing versions of Basque, Catalan and Celtic nationalism there.[5] In Denmark, as a result of the loss of land through war and increasingly also its colonies through economic collapse during the nineteenth century, the institutionalisation of the past was associated with a need to legitimise and create a sense of commitment to the nation.[6] This association between archaeology and identity continues to be a contemporary concern. Michael Dietler in his study of Celtic nationalism in France traced its rise in the eighteenth century and its current relevance both for claims of Breton regionalism and for a pan-European identity that, he argued, aims to authenticate the European Union.[7]

Although in most cases the links between the institutionalisation of archaeology and politics has had a relatively harmless result, some more serious consequences can be identified. Knowledge of archaeology was, for instance, central to the cultural propaganda of the Nazi regime. A particular interpretation of archaeology was used to assert the racial purity and superiority of the Germans and so justify genocide.[8] This was also evident in the former Soviet Union where Ukrainian history, language and culture were suppressed and an 'official history', which excluded certain atrocities, was propagated.[9]

In each of these cases the institutionalisation of archaeology, within professions and museums, was associated with the increased awareness of the political value of the past. Because of the ideological grounds on which museums were founded, critical museum-histories make an important contribution to the history of the development of nations. For instance, evaluating the impact that the Nazi regime had, and still has, on archaeology makes an important contribution to the history of Germany. Museum projects were important to the Nazi regime, as was the use of archaeology to legitimise a belief in Aryan-Germanic superiority. Monika Puloy has observed that 'all national collections entail political perspectives, but never has there been a plan so systematically laid and carried out as that employed by Hitler to establish a controlling cultural focus for the Nationalist-Socialist German Reich'. This regime saw the engineering of art confiscations on the grounds of 'safe-keeping', 'forced sale' or as part of 'peace-treaties'. These items, collected together, were to form the basis of a planned 'super museum' at Linz in Austria. By this 'Hitler, Goering and a number of other leaders came to view the amassing of art works as an important expression of their expanding empire'. Hitler claimed that the Aryans were descended from the Greeks and ancient Romans and so Germany could claim a history of two thousand years of power over Europe. In this context, art of any excellence, especially that in the classical style, was deemed to be of Germanic origin. Furthermore, modern art was labelled 'degenerate': it was presented as lacking German 'clarity' as well as being 'un-German and dangerous'. It was regarded as 'cosmopolitan, deranged, "negrified" and considered to be inspired by Jews and Bolshevists'.[10] As a result, within a year of coming into power the Nazis had removed almost all modern art from public collections. With the de-Nazification of museums later in the twentieth century, contemporary art and design became the symbol of the Federal Republic; this is also a product of the political situation.[11] The legacy of the Nazi period continues to disturb, or even 'haunt',[12] the German museum profession. In a discussion of the role of museums in the creation of identity, Barbara Heuser demonstrated how, as a consequence of the 'bad history' of Germany's twentieth century, history was not a compulsory subject in schools. As a result, Germans suffered a deliberate 'loss of history'. A desire to regain a sense of identity led, in the early 1980s, to the proposal to found a museum of German history in Berlin. The museum's explicit purpose was to 'search for affirmation of political and social identity' to offer 'possibilities for identification' so that visitors would know 'who they are'.[13] This proposal led, as one would expect, to a debate amongst historians about what that history should be and a fear of the formation of a government-endorsed history.

The creation and dissemination of knowledge of the past in museums and similar institutions is an ideological process. As recognised by the archaeologist Stuart Piggott, 'it is clear that even what appears to be a simple antiquarian enquiry ... will be conditioned by the climate and the thought of the day, and this in turn by social, political and ideological factors which will vary not only from age to age, but from country to country'.[14] Museums get drawn into this process because of their role in the collection of information about the past and the display of the material remains that can represent that past.

THE POLITICS OF VALUING MUSEUMS AND THEIR COLLECTIONS

Not only the museum as an idea, but the objects they contain are themselves 'message bearing entities'; they are material around which signs and symbols are constructed.[15] Understanding the formation of 'messages' is essential to understanding how objects function. The importance of objects depends on a complex range of codes or signs that are created by the context. The value of objects will then vary – they have a chain of meanings and they are polysemantic. In other words, to paraphrase Susan Pearce, an object is a metonymic sign which is expressed as a metaphorical symbol.[16] This plurality of meaning, and hence the range of possible interpretations of objects, must be placed into our understanding of the creation of knowledge about the past. Useful for the purposes of nationalism, knowledge is not constant and, equally, how we value the past is not immutable. One may argue that the individual can freely and independently choose his or her own interpretation of the meaning of the material remains of the past. This, however, is not necessarily the case, as a number of other forces affect the interpretative process, interfering with the opportunity of free interpretation. Access to the past, in the form of knowledge of the past, is restricted. Not only does a fraction of the past survive to become history, but also the creation of knowledge from 'original sources' by archaeologists, historians and educationalists will employ acts of personal selection and interpretation. The creation of an interpretation and understanding of the past is, therefore, a continual act of personal judgement made within the context of the contemporary framework, which is itself inherently complex. As has been noted by Chris Tilley, 'the archaeologist is not so much reading the signs of the past as writing these signs into the present: constructing discourses which should be both meaningful to the present and playing an active role in shaping the present's future'.[17] This analysis recognises the highly subjective nature of the creation of knowledge and, as a result, the potentially political nature of the discipline. There is 'an increasing awareness of archaeology's place in the present and the refinement of a politics of archaeological interpretation in showing that archaeologists cannot just get on with a neutral study of the past'.[18] It is evident, therefore, that 'the past' is as much a product of present-day experiences as those of earlier times.

The importance placed on archaeology and cultural institutions is mostly derived from one's own experience, but just as knowledge of the past is taught, so too is how we value that past. In this sense, the past and the material remains of the past are open to multiple interpretations and it is likely that attempts will be made to impose certain interpretations, for particular purposes, on a population. For instance, the Monymusk reliquary, a shrine said to house a relic of the sixth-century monk and missionary St Columba, can be interpreted either as a religious icon or a symbol of a Scottish victory against the English.[19] In a similar sense, the Stone of Scone, claimed as an ancient coronation stone in both Ireland and Scotland,[20] has been adopted as a symbol of Scottish kingship and national identity. The stone was removed from Scotland by Edward I in the thirteenth century and placed under the coronation throne in Westminster Abbey in London, and it was returned to Scotland in July 1996. For some the stone had a magical quality and its return was preordained: in other words, 'Scotland's touch-stone fulfils its destiny'.[21] Other commentators regarded its return as an attempt to mollify demands for a Scottish parliament and independence. Critics in the *Daily Telegraph* declared that 'the return of such a potent symbol panders to Scottish nationalism' and as such was 'shamelessly political'.[22]

It is possible, however, also to present the stone as symbolising the opposite of this. It has also been argued that since the stone remains the property of the monarchy its presence in Scotland may also act as a reminder of the reality of the Union.[23] Whichever way the return may be interpreted, the details of this case demonstrate how objects become the recipients of additional layers of meaning and value that are often quite potent, and then they may be used to supplement a political agenda. Ideal for the cause of nationalism, archaeological artefacts can become signifiers of a belief or emotion beyond that of their function, and consequently they may be used to create or trigger personal or shared memory. When relating to an object it is necessary to put a certain amount of oneself forward to be scrutinised with it. In other words, 'the emotions articulated in a given museum will mirror the contexts and concerns of a given society at any given point of time'.[24] David Lowenthal, in reference to the Elgin Marbles, demonstrated this emotional power of the object when he argued that they have now assumed a meaning or function beyond that of a historical artefact. Using this example, he observed that 'it may better serve Greek pride to go on demanding the return of the Elgin Marbles than to get them back. Identity is more zealously created and husbanded by the quest for a lost heritage than by its nurture when regained'.[25] Objects, therefore, removed from their 'original' context may take on significance and value beyond that of use, and assume a symbolic meaning which may be derived from their historical association.[26] The value of the artefact is in what it *symbolises* not what it is in a functional sense.

At every stage, therefore, archaeology reflects values that are legitimised within and through institutions. This is evident both in the process of selection of the material evidence of the past and later through 'heritage management', which selects exhibits of that past. The recognition of this point is the first step in a critical review of our engagement with the past, while the second is the realisation of the implications of this pluralistic past. Knowledge of the past, which is filtered through the education system and ancillary institutions such as museums, acts as a framework which functions as a perpetuator of a central truth. Tony Bennett has investigated this idea of the inherent power in the museum message.[27] Bennett argued that museums are far from passive institutions; rather, through their display and architecture they attempt to impose order and self-regulation. As a result, museums in their different forms, from the sixteenth to the nineteenth centuries, displayed a message of power. Early museums were largely cabinets of private curiosities. They were used to display the power the owner had to accumulate such collections and to reserve it for his own use. With the emergence of public museums in the mid-nineteenth century, those overseeing the development were less interested in the bizarre than in the commonplace. In addition, within the ordered space of the museum the behaviour of the visitor was required to conform to an accepted norm. In these ways the public museum became a governing tool, a 'social script', which was both an educational and a civilising force. The past encapsulated in the museum provided the modern state with a deep and continuous ideological underpinning that could articulate either rhetoric of progress or of nationalism and imperialism.[28]

Within this framework museums select, conserve and reproduce knowledge in a seemingly impartial manner legitimised by their status. They 'come to procure for themselves a monopoly over the knowledge exhibited in their halls, and from this emerges a pedagogic authority that establishes an impeccable and unquestionable expertise which exercises a solitary reign over their empire of signs'.[29] The implication is that museums, because of their control of knowledge of the past and the value placed on the past for the creation of identity, are overtly political and powerful institutions. In this manner one may argue that 'museums have long served to house a national heritage, thereby creating a national identity that often fulfilled national ambitions. Often beginning with the private collections of elites obtained through conquest and exploitation, museums came to conserve cultural heritage and to educate the public.'[30]

The importance and power of the museum are formed by 'a series of allegiances, affiliations and attachments, built up in a nested hierarchy like a set of Chinese boxes',[31] each contributing to a sense of place and identity.[32] At the centre is the museum as a keeper of the past, on the second level are the objects within the museum, which are the material evidence, and on the third level is the scale and presence of the museum as an institution. Each level legitimises the existence of the museum and sanctions the museum message; as such, objects, collections, institutions and their buildings are expressions of power relationships. Therefore, 'reconstruction [such as in museums] involves repowering the object, investing it with the authority and privilege of those currently possessing it, who then impose upon it (and upon those whom it represents) their own histories'.[33]

In this context, the overall significance of the museum is not only dictated by its role as an institution and a storehouse of objects, but also in its architectural presence. Museum buildings specially constructed in the eighteenth and nineteenth centuries to house national collections were often given a grandiose form of architecture and placed in prominent positions overlooking the city (such the National Museum in Prague). The significance of the museum building is evident from the fact that the palace of the overthrown monarchy provided a location for France's first public museum. The British Museum building was inspired by the Greek revival in the eighteenth century, with the result that the 'museum building was itself a museum, the essential image of the museum idea'.[34] Within Britain and Ireland a combination of the museum, gallery, library and/or government offices located together provided the educational, cultural and administrative core of cities (for example in Liverpool, Dublin and Cardiff). In addition, the symbolic meaning of architecture and place may create positive and negative emotional responses in the present. A debate revolved around the accommodation of South Korea's National Museum in the Capitol building, the former seat of the Japanese government that ruled in Korea from 1910 to 1945. Some people regarded this building as an inappropriate home for the national treasures; their belief was that 'the building [wa]s a constant reminder of the humiliation of colonial occupation and the Japanese disregard for everything Korean'.[35] For this reason when the decision was made to demolish the Capitol building it won approval, despite its potential usefulness as the home of the museum and its importance as an example of Japanese colonial architecture. Demolition began in 1995, on the fiftieth anniversary of Korea's liberation from Japan, and 'many interpreted the ... decision as an authoritarian measure and an obvious play on the people's nationalism for political gain. The well-being of the Museum and its collection did not seem to be on [the] agenda.'[36]

This chapter has established some of the issues central to this book. In the first place, knowledge of the past is not given but is a product of the social context. Secondly, it is clear that as a result of the power gained from the cultivation and ownership of knowledge, and the value placed on culture and inheritance, the past is often used as a political tool. Therefore those disciplines involved with the creation and dissemination of knowledge about the past, such as archaeology, history and the museums they generate, need to consider the purpose of their engagement with the past, and the implications of this activity.

In order to determine the full importance of museums one must look beyond the whole and consider the values associated with the individual elements that compose the museum: the objects, the collection, the museum building and then, finally, the institution as a whole. Each has its own import, its own message and its own pedagogic authority. The importance of the museum is not gained from any one factor; rather it is derived from the accumulation of symbolic frameworks. In order to 'calculate' the importance of the museum, one must deconstruct the whole and consider the value of its parts. One must then rebuild the museum and recognise that its value as an institution is greater than the sum of its collections. It is the contemporary impact of the perception of the past, and the value placed on the past for future needs, which have an influence on the practice of archaeology and museum provision. It is therefore necessary for archaeologists and museologists to consider the implications of such political influences on knowledge of the past, to challenge the reasoning behind individual or state involvement with the past and to question the basis on which national identity is formed.

CHAPTER TWO

Nationalism and the Development of Cultural Institutions

UNDERSTANDING HOW NATIONALISM USES THE PAST

THE READERS of the Young Irelanders' newspaper, the *Nation*, which was dedicated to the repeal of the Union with Great Britain, were asked to 'develop the materials of nationalisation'. These were outlined as 'the food to nourish a healthy and permanent knowledge and love of country in the minds of all the classes', which should be accompanied by:

> *National* books, and lectures and music – *national* paintings and busts, and costume – *national* songs, and tracts, and maps – *historical* plays for the stage – *historical* novels for the closet – *historical* ballads for the drawing room – we want all these, and many other things illustrating the *history*, the resources, and the genius of our country, and honouring her illustrious children, living or dead. These are the seeds of permanent nationality and we must sow them deep in the People's hearts. These are the weapons with which we may take by assault the bosom of the young student in his library and the merchant in his relaxation. Let us be then asked – When shall we have Repeal?[1]

This extract is an example of nationalist writing published in Ireland in the mid-nineteenth century. It demonstrates some of the ways by which the past gets drawn into political rhetoric. Nationalism was one of the most powerful forces in nineteenth-century European politics. As the above statement shows, and the various cases discussed in the previous chapter demonstrated, nationalism formed a certain relationship with the past and cultural institutions in order to further its ideals. The past, represented by history, archaeology and references to 'culture', was used to create the idea of a national space, heritage and identity in order to legitimise political ideals. It is important to consider how this has been practically demonstrated by examining the processes that linked cultural activity to nationalism. For this it is necessary to both understand the emergence of nationalism and the nature of the ideology itself.

Miroslav Hroch's model of the co-development of nationalism and cultural institutions in nineteenth-century Europe draws attention to the pivotal role of cultural activity in the development of nationalism. In his model, nationalism and the importance of cultural activity passed through three phases of national revival. The first phase was one of scholarly interest in the culture of the nation. This phase developed the ideas that 'make the nation', that is a sense of the history of the nation. The second phase was characterised by the involvement of the intelligentsia, which gave rise to political agitation that was often linked to issues of an agrarian, modernising or industrial nature. The third is typified by the popularisation of the movement by involvement of the masses, for 'the peasants, as the natural repositories of the nation's linguistic and cultural tradition, were an indispensable condition for the success of any national movement'. Though each phase has unique characteristics for each particular nation, varying in timing and length, high value was frequently placed on history and culture.[2] Such consideration of the development of nationalism in Europe, including Ireland, has inspired many definitions of what constitutes a nation and creates nationalism.[3] The nation as a product of the crisis of culture, as a result of the impact of modernisation, is a major theme in the work of Ernest Gellner.[4]

A. D. Smith, on the other hand, emphasises the pre-modern foundations of the nation[5] and E. J. Hobsbawm the political nature and 'inventedness' of nations.[6] Variations in interpretation of nationalism evident in their writing has served to illustrate the diversity of theories regarding the origins of nations and concludes that there can be no scientific definition of the nation or nationalism.

With regard to the concept of 'nationalism', Smith has established a core doctrine, which he argues conveys the convictions that are common to all forms of nationalism. This is the belief that

- humanity is naturally divided into nations
- each nation has its own peculiar character
- the source of all political power is the nation

- the nation creates freedom
- nations can only be fulfilled in their own states
- loyalty to the nation overrides all other loyalties
- global freedom will be achieved through the strengthening of the nation-state.[7]

Furthermore, nationalism can be said to create the nation via 'maps' of history, destiny and moralities for a 'regenerated community'. These are created by the way of 'poetic space' of the nation: the historic sites and sacred places and the 'Golden Age', a point in the nation's history on which it can now model itself. In this context, 'historical events and monuments of the homeland can be "naturalized". Castles, temples, tells and dolmens are integrated into the landscape and treated as part of its special nature.' This can be illustrated by the use made of Stonehenge during the romantic revival of the eighteenth and nineteenth centuries when it became a symbol of Britain, or by the adoption of the Early Christian Period as the Golden Age of Irish nationalism in the 1890s. A parallel example can be found in Finnish history in 1835 where there was a revival of interest in the people of the first millennium AD. In addition, Smith defined the nation as 'a named human population sharing an historic territory, common myths and historical memories, a mass, public culture, a common economy and common legal rights and duties for all members'.[8]

The 'core doctrine' presented by Smith considers the past as essential to nationalism. The past is used to form the character of the nation, to define the territory and to legitimise the political ideology. In this way one can argue that history is essential to the nation. However, though the political theorists agree that the past is essential to nationalism, it is interesting to reveal the differences that have been attributed to the role and form of this significance. According to Gellner the nation is presented as a representation of the culture and heritage of the people: it is a *product of nationalism*.[9] In his interpretation, nationalism arises out of a need to legitimise and create identification with the state that is itself presented as the modern reincarnation of the historically rooted nation. Nationalism, therefore, occurs with the creation of the conditions of the state. This has also been recognised by George Boyce who has identified nationalism as the doctrine deployed by people who consider themselves a nation and who, by that doctrine, assert autonomy and self-government, solidarity and fraternity in the homeland and a distinctive history and culture.[10] Nationalism is presented as the belief that the national unit (the nation) and the political unit (the state) should be congruent and so, under such conditions, 'ethnicity enters the political world as nationalism'.[11]

The desire to create ethnic boundaries that would coincide with political boundaries, according to Gellner, evolves from the conditions of modern industrial society. The uneven spread of industrialisation and modernisation brings about the widening of cultural cleavages between groups that leads to discontent. The nation is then necessary to present modern society as predestined. As such, the nation is created as a consequence of modernisation and, furthermore, is dependent on the conditions of modernisation. According to Anderson, the fruits of modernisation, such as a standard language and print media, are necessary to construct the fields of exchange between people, thus helping to create a mass movement and laying the basis for the development of national consciousness. To develop such a bond between the people and the nation (and since one can never interact with the nation in its entirety), the sense of unity and common identity must exist in the imagination, and this creates the 'imagined community'.[12]

What creates this desire that is at the core of the 'imagined community'? Having posed this question, Hobsbawm explored the concept of 'proto-national' bonds, which he argued create a sense of identity associated with the nation. The bonds are the characteristics of a community, such as language, ethnicity or religion. They are the elements that form our identity and which are then reinterpreted to form a national identity and commitment to the nation. Such 'bonds' are introduced as having roots in the past which, via communication, common usage and consciousness, are reinterpreted and presented as being of the nation. If not already in existence these bonds may be invented: for example, a standardised national language will be created out of language dialects.[13] The authenticity of the claim is not necessarily of interest to the nationalist; what is important is that the bonds create a sense of perceived common inheritance and community, which brings the population together as a coherent unit. The nation is here established as a modern creation rather than, as the rhetoric would suggest, a primordial reality: 'nations as a natural, God-given way of classifying men, as an inherent though long delayed political destiny, are a myth; nationalism which sometimes takes pre-existing cultures and turns them into nations, sometimes invents them, and often obliterates pre-existing cultures: *that* is a reality'. Gellner's theory presents a transformed past as essential to nationalism: 'dead languages can be revived, traditions invented, quite fictitious pristine purities restored'.[14] The nation will forget its culture and create a new definition of the past and under these conditions 'what ultimately matters is not what is but what people believe is'.[15]

Gellner presents the national past as *created* by politics and Smith presents it as *used* by politics. However, to understand the political nature of the nation one must consider aspects of the theories of both Smith and Gellner. One cannot dispute the basis of Smith's argument that regions have unique characters that have been expressed through language, tradition and culture. However, it must also be noted that the combination of these characteristics is not, alone, enough to create the nation. There must be an awareness of an idea of the national unit that is greater than the regional unit. Similarly, there must be a sense of the national identity that is greater than the sum of individual identities; in other words 'there is no modern nation without national consciousness'.[16] Though the language and tradition of a place may have antiquity, the notion that the antiquity is necessarily shared across a political space is an invention. In the case of Ireland, Kevin Whelan has shown that nationalism distorted the existing regional music, language and dancing traditions to create a national style.[17] The County Antrim version of hurling, for instance, was standardised in the early twentieth century and banners and costumes were specially designed for the Gaelic festival held in 1904 in the Glens of Antrim.[18] Nations and 'national traditions' are therefore a product of the past, but only when it is channelled through the political process. It is important to recognise that nationalism moulds the characteristics of the nation to create a popular and simplified ideology that better complements the political process. The theories discussed agree that the need for the nation comes from a time of political upheaval and discontent. Therefore, whether the traditions are historically rooted (as argued by Smith) or an invention (as claimed by Gellner and Hobsbawm) is not as important as the realisation that national tradition *per se,* and the jealous preservation and propagation of a 'national past', is derived from the political process.

IRISH CULTURAL NATIONALISM

Throughout the nineteenth century much Irish political nationalism, as expressed by the Young Irelanders for instance, was broadly based on the fundamental belief in providing power and self-government for the country's population. This aspiration was presented as a civic duty as well as an issue of constitutional law. Against this background, O'Connell, the Irish Republican Brotherhood and the Home Rule movement utilised references to the past as political rhetoric as well as inspiration. O'Connell held political meetings at archaeological sites;[19] the popular name of the IRB, the Fenians, was taken from legend,[20] and the Irish Parliamentary Party made use of symbols with historical associations.[21] However, these expressions of nationalism involved predominantly political tactics and may be defined as instances of 'political nationalism' that can be distinguished from other cases of 'cultural nationalism'. The role of culture in Irish nationalism has had much investigation.[22] In this work cultural nationalism has usually been seen as deliberately promoting the relationship between politics and an interest in Irish history or archaeology. It is, however, important to distinguish the objectives of this form of nationalism and establish how it relates to other forms of political and cultural activity. It is imperative to address three essential questions. How may one define Irish cultural nationalism? What is its relationship with political nationalism? How does cultural nationalism relate to cultural revivalism? It is crucial to have a clear understanding of these terms since they are frequently used in discussions of Irish nationalism.

There is a very close relationship between politics and culture. As suggested by George Boyce the links are 'not only the arts, music, philosophy, but also as constituting a nation's "design for living, handed down from generation to generation", expressing the characteristics by which people assert their identity'.[23] Using this definition, Boyce presented culture in Ireland as almost inseparable from politics in its different forms. In association with the rise of nationalism, interest in Gaelic games, literature, language and antiquities gained political connotations, some of which have endured to present-day Ireland. This interest can be grouped into three stages of heightened cultural awareness that have been termed the 'Gaelic revivals'. The first revival, in the 1780s, was signified by the establishment of the Royal Irish Academy (1785) and ended with the failure of the 1798 Rebellion and the Act of Union. The second revival arose in the early nineteenth century and is identified with the foundation of various learned societies such as the Gaelic Society of Dublin (1806), the Iberno-Celtic Society (1818), the Celtic Society (1843) and the Ossianic Society (1853), as well as the activity of individuals such as George Petrie and Samuel Ferguson, both antiquarians. This cultural activity was expressed politically though the Young Ireland movement. The third revival came in the 1880s and has been associated with the establishment of the Society for the Preservation of the Irish Language (1877) and the Gaelic League.[24] The collective activity associated with the latter movement both brought together the leaders of the 1916 Rising and provided them with cultural inspiration.

It is this cultural interest that is frequently labelled as 'cultural nationalism'. The discussion of theories of nationalism above highlighted how the 'national past' and references to tradition and culture as 'of the nation' are drawn into the ideology. Gellner and Smith both recognised the usefulness of the past to nationalism, but they each placed varying emphasis on the how the past was drawn into the process. Gellner emphasised a political process which created an invented past while Smith defined nationalism as a movement which revived a pre-existing or 'true' past or culture. Considering their two different approaches will add to an understanding of how Irish nationalism has been analysed. Many of the critics of Irish nationalism identify different expressions of nationalism: one that is political nationalism and the other that is cultural nationalism. One such is John Hutchinson who argued that two forms of nationalism, 'political' and 'cultural', co-exist in Ireland.[25] Hutchinson began his study by placing cultural nationalism in its European context. Drawing on the work on nationalism by Elie Kedourie, and using instances of nationalism in Europe as examples, Hutchinson defined political nationalism as a philosophy with the idea of a civic polity of educated citizens united by common laws (the manmade state) as its ideal. Though the civic polity may be mobilised into a political unit through historic and ethnic ties, reason is used as its ethical source. This can be distinguished from cultural nationalism that, Hutchinson argued, perceives the state as accidental, believing that the essence of the nation is to be found in its distinctive civilisation. By this, 'nations are primordial expressions of this spirit; like families, they are the natural solidarities. Nations are then not just political units but *organic* beings, living personalities, whose individuality must be cherished by their members in all their manifestations.' In order to further their cause, proponents of a specifically cultural nationalism will:

> Establish informal and decentralised clusters of cultural societies and journals, designed to inspire a spontaneous love of community in its different members by educating them in their common heritage of splendour and suffering. They engage in naming rituals, celebrate national cultural uniqueness and reject foreign practices, in order to identify the community to itself, embed this identity in everyday life and differentiate it against other communities.[26]

However, though cultural and political nationalism are different philosophies or methods, they will have the same ultimate goal: the autonomous state.

Applying this to the Irish case, Hutchinson argued that the three revivals of the 1780s, 1830s and the 1890s revealed shared characteristics: each passed through common phases of preparation, crystallisation and articulation. The first phase, preparation, was encapsulated in antiquarian activity that played an important part in laying a foundation of historical knowledge. This triggered the second phase, crystallisation, which was frequently led by historicist intellectuals who created and disseminated knowledge of Ireland's early history. This was then harnessed for the third phase, articulation, which found expression in a socio-political programme led by intellectuals who aimed to form an ideological movement that would be a vehicle for a revolutionary campaign. Applying this to the mid-nineteenth-century cultural revival, its first phase was marked by the activity of antiquarian scholars of the 1830s that 'crystallised' into the production of popular newspapers, such as the *Dublin Penny Journal*. In turn this influenced the political world and found expression in the cultural politics of the Young Irelanders in the 1840s. In a similar manner, the revival of the 1890s was, in part, inspired by the historical writing of the previous decades; this crystallised into the activity of the cultural groups, such as the Gaelic League, and later the politics of Arthur Griffith, Patrick Pearse and others.[27]

John Hutchinson's argument illustrates the links between cultural activity and political movements and in this aspect has much in common with Hroch's European model discussed earlier. As Hroch's analysis indicates, and as various European cases discussed in the previous chapter demonstrate, museums are public institutions within which the elite and competing social groups may express their ideas and define the 'self'. The cases given emphasise three important points: the dependency of political projects on the past for legitimisation, the power implicit in the ownership and control of the past, and how political systems use the past to endorse their agendas. In both cases antiquarian activity provided the knowledge of the past from which nationalists could glean information about the 'ancient and heroic nation'. Links between the generation of such knowledge and its use in the political sphere clearly exist, but the nature of the relationship is more complex. Though antiquarian knowledge will be a product of the political context within which it is created, the pursuit of such knowledge will vary in political intent. For instance, antiquarian activity may have been undertaken in such a way that it was unrelated to popular politics. This antiquarian activity must be distinguished from, in the first instance, that which had a revivalist motive (in other words cultural revivalism), and secondly, from that which can be labelled as cultural nationalism. If this is the case, one can argue that nationalism will have varying consequences for archaeology, both in the form of investigation of the past and preservation of the material remains. For instance, if culture is only important to political nationalism in order to aid the immediate movement, once the nation is achieved the past may not play an important role. However, one would expect cultural nationalism to have a more lasting interest in archaeology, culture and the creation of museums. The remainder of this chapter will establish the nature of cultural nationalism in the Irish context by comparing it to instances of 'political nationalism'.

The Irish-Ireland ideal at the heart of Irish cultural nationalism, as it materialised in the early twentieth century, is recorded in the essays of those involved in the Gaelic League. Douglas Hyde, the first President of the Gaelic League, regarded culture as an essential part of nationality and attempted to present this as separate from politics. Hyde portrayed the activity of the League as part of the 'struggle of the Irish race to preserve their national identity'. He claimed that this was not driven by a hate for England but rather a love for Ireland. For Hyde cultural nationalism was not sectarian, but something by which the entire population should unite. He claimed:

> we are no clique, we are no faction, we are no party. We are above and beyond all politics, all parties and all factions;

offending nobody – except the anti-Irishman. We stand
immovable upon the bedrock of the doctrine of true Irish
nationhood – an Ireland self-centred, self-sufficing, self-
supporting, self-reliant; an Ireland speaking its own language,
thinking its own thoughts, writing its own books, singing its
own songs, playing its own games, weaving its own coats, and
going for nothing outside of the four shores of Ireland that can
possibly be procured inside them.[28]

Hyde, in the style of Thomas Davis before him, was straining to
create a form of nationalism that would unite the Protestants and
Catholics of Ireland through the common appreciation of Irish
culture.[29] Hyde, and those like him, appealed to a remote Irish past,
on the fringe of Christianity, free from sectarian prejudices. Together
they 'colonised the past, misrepresenting it in a nationalist mode as
a kind of pre-Norman Utopia of comely maidens and chivalrous men
of song and story'.[30] This cultural activity was, however, not 'above
and beyond politics' as wished for by Hyde. Rather, involvement
with culture was, for many, an expression of their political ideology,
one that was using culture to create national consciousness. This is
most evident in an essay by George Russell in which he accepted that
conditions had now arisen in Ireland that made it essential for those
involved with culture to engage in politics. He wrote:

> the literary man, who is, or ought to be, concerned mainly with
> intellectual interests, should only intervene in politics when
> principles affecting the spiritual life of his country are involved.
> To me the imperial idea seems to threaten the destruction of the
> nation being which has been growing through centuries.[31]

The history of the Irish Literary Theatre (re-established as the
Abbey Theatre in 1904) provides an example of how such cultural
institutions were drawn into political conflict. The theatre was
formed in 1899 to produce Irish national drama, but from the outset
it was involved in public controversy, primarily because some of the
plays it staged were considered non-Irish or anti-Catholic. The most
famous incident was the rioting on the streets of Dublin by people
objecting to the storyline of the play *The Playboy of the Western
World*. For some political nationalists cultural activity was only
important if it had a national consequence. For instance, in reaction
to the style of plays produced at the Irish Literary Theatre a member

of the Irish Parliamentary Party asked: 'how is it to help the national cause?' Arthur Griffith believed the theatre was not playing the role of a national institution, but simply one of an art institution. Therefore he argued it should abandon the misleading title of 'Irish National Theatre' and adopt the name 'Art Theatre'. The appropriate function of a national theatre was obviously one of a 'nationalist theatre'; therefore 'it was art, not for art's sake, but for propaganda'.[32]

The nationalist D. P. Moran, who popularised his ideas in support of an independent Ireland in his paper *The Leader*, argued that political ideals should go hand in hand with those of a cultural nature. In his essay 'The Battle of Two Civilisations', he wrote that achieving a Republic by 'a hundred thousand English corpses with Irish bullets or pike wounds' would be pointless if Ireland were not a nation. He maintained that Ireland would only be a nation if it had nationality. He argued that 'Ireland will be nothing until she is a nation, and as a nation a civilisation, she will never accomplish anything until she falls back on her own language and tradition, and, recovering there, her old pride, self-respect'.[33] For Moran culture was paramount to the creation of an Irish national identity, which he considered useful for the creation of a progressive modern nation.[34] Engaging in cultural activity, such as the Irish language, was therefore a political endeavour for many. The examples given above demonstrate that the links between culture and politics are subtly interwoven. For some forms of nationalism culture itself was not the driving force; rather it was important as the material for the political process. The fact that culture may only be important as a political tool is demonstrated by the way in which some members of the Gaelic League attempted to draw the society away from chiefly cultural interests and to adopt more extreme tactics in pursuit of political ends. This was to the exclusion of those, such as Douglas Hyde, who wished to distinguish between revivalist activity and separatist politics.[35]

Patrick Pearse was one of the central figures in this politicisation of the Gaelic League. His significance to the national movement began as predominantly revivalist and ended as a leader of the 1916 Rising. At the age of sixteen Pearse became a member of the Gaelic League, three years after its formation. In this early part of his career Pearse considered the cultural activity of the League, such as the promotion of the Irish language, as more important than party political matters. For him culture was the ideal tool through which to create the nation-state. Political autonomy, he wrote, 'can be lost and recovered, and lost again and recovered again. It is an accidental and an external thing – necessary, indeed, to the complete working out of a national destiny, necessary, in many cases, to the continued existence of a people, but not in itself an essential of nationality.'[36]

Pearse demonstrated his distinct philosophy of cultural nationalism; that is, the belief that the state is a manmade creation, that the essence of the nation is found in its culture and that the nation-state, as the ideal way to nurture culture, is the ultimate goal. Pearse argued that once culture was restored independence would follow:

> When the position of Ireland's language as her greatest heritage is once fixed, all other matters will insensibly adjust themselves. As it develops, and *because* it develops, it will carry all kindred movements with it. Irish music, Irish art, Irish dancing, Irish games and customs, Irish industries, Irish politics – all of these are worthy objects ... when Ireland's language is established, her own distinctive culture is assured. ... All phases of a nation's life will most assuredly adjust themselves on national lines as best suited to the national character, once that national character is safeguarded by its strongest bulwark.[37]

At this point in his career, Pearse's principal driving force was the prospect of re-establishing the culture of the historic nation; the independent state would then develop as a result. This contrasts greatly with the tone of political nationalism as already defined. In the first place, political nationalism presented the independent nation as a civic right based on principles of reason, rather than heritage. For example, the nationalist politician John Redmond argued that 'the demand for Home Rule means no less and no more than this: Ireland asks for an Irish Parliament, with an executive responsible to it, to deal with purely Irish affairs, subject to Imperial supremacy'.[38]

Political nationalists also exhibit an aversion to cultural tactics and this is evident in their rejection of revivalist activity. Hutchinson cites the example of the clash at a National Convention of the United Irish League between Douglas Hyde and John Dillon, future leader of the Irish Parliamentary Party, as indicative of 'a classic confrontation between the cultural and political nationalist'.[39] The issue was the status of the Irish language in the Irish education system and particularly whether the language should be necessary for matriculation to the National University. Dillon did not believe so. He regarded the Irish language issue as divisive and therefore standing in the way of achieving national self-government. Hyde, on the other hand, regarded the Irish language as essential for the creation of the Irish nation. Cultural nationalists considered the Irish language as a reflection of the national identity. It was at the core of the ideology of the Young Irelanders and central to the revival at the end of the century led by the Gaelic League. The writings on the Irish language in the *Nation* are particularly representative of those written throughout the century. Here the Irish language was depicted as having great antiquity, providing a linguistic link with the past and a native tradition that could be nurtured only by self-government. Revivalist activity was then necessary in order to return to this natural condition. Readers of the *Nation* were told that their past was integral to their very being. Language, the readers were told, 'grows up with a people, is conformed to their organs, descriptive to their climate, constitution and manners, and is mingled inseparably with their history'. Therefore:

> to impose another language on such people is to send their history adrift among the accidents of translation – is to tear their identity from all places ... to lose your native tongue to learn that of an alien, is the worst badge of conquest. How unnatural – how corrupting it is for us, three-fourths of whom are of Celtic blood, to speak a medley of Teutonic dialects. ... how can the language be restored, now ... through the labours of the Archaeological and lesser societies.[40]

However, the Irish Parliamentary Party did attempt to create a sense of nationality by methods associated with cultural nationalism. Peter Alter, for instance, has shown that the party was active in the creation of historic symbols of the nation, including a national flag, anthem and festivals, the erection of public monuments and the renaming of streets (often with some form of historic reference), which they used to attempt to introduce political integration.[41] Furthermore, those political activists who did not hold the revival of culture as a predominant policy, such as Daniel O'Connell and the IRB, did employ the past for political means. Therefore, though one can refer to instances of cultural nationalism in Ireland, it is necessary to regard them, and political nationalism, as two sides of the same coin. Each expression of nationalism had its own distinct relationship with the Irish past and had the same ultimate purpose – the restoration of a Dublin parliament. In the long term, however, they may have quite different effects on the care and preservation of archaeology.

The terms 'cultural nationalism' and 'cultural revivalism' should not be taken as synonymous. The strength of the term 'cultural revivalist' becomes most apparent when one attempts to understand the contribution of unionist patriots to the promotion of Irish culture and the creation of a popular and shared interest in Irish archaeology. Samuel Ferguson and Standish O'Grady, both of whom promoted an interest in early Irish writing, have been referred to as revivalists rather than nationalists since both were unionist in their politics. Samuel Ferguson is of particular interest as he combined his literary work with antiquarian activity and it will be useful, in later chapters, to consider the political intent of the activity of other antiquarians who may also have been pro-union. Robert O'Driscoll has argued that Ferguson had a political agenda derived from his belief that 'the most effective way of dissipating the prejudices of his countrymen was by turning their thoughts from narrow political interests to the study of their country's history, antiquities and literature'.[42] Therefore Ferguson's interest was one of a 'self-regarding action', by which he hoped to maintain a socially and politically influential position. With this in mind, he 'sought to stimulate all Irishmen, but more especially Protestants, to take an interest in the history and antiquities of Ireland in order to develop a distinctively Irish way of life and thought', in order that Protestants should evolve as 'natural leaders of the nation'.[43] The cultural activity of such individuals, therefore, 'was not meant to foster Irish nationalism' but rather 'it was meant to bring Irishmen to a sensibility of what great literature they had produced'.[44] Since Ferguson was not inspired by nationalist goals it is inappropriate to label him as a 'cultural nationalist', but since his antiquarian activity did have a political objective it is useful to think of him as a 'cultural revivalist'.

Similar overlaps in interest in Irish culture with varying political allegiances were evident in the twentieth century. Jonathan Bell, in his study of the impact of the Gaelic League in County Antrim at the turn of the century, has shown that the first Gaelic festival in the Glens of Antrim in June 1904 had both nationalist and unionist support.[45] Horace Plunkett, speaking at the festival, stated that the

Gaelic revival could unite the people under the understanding of a shared past because its search after a national life and character went 'beyond the bitter centuries when class was divided by class and creed against creed. It went back to the time when Ireland was united'.[46] Despite this confidence, cultural revivalism was likely to cause political upset: 'once [the Protestant revivalist] dipped his toe into the waters of culture, he was confronted with a dilemma ... how far should he go to popularise his appeal?'[47] This tension can be traced throughout the century and is an inevitable result of the politicisation of the past for the needs of nationalism.

The popularity of Irish nationalism, as it grew through the nineteenth century, culminating in the republican movements of the early decades of the twentieth century, was linked to an understanding of the cultural significance of the nation. Knowledge about the past achievements of the nation came from many sources and was brought about by a variety of political and social aspirations. The understanding employed in this book differentiates between cultural revivalism and cultural nationalism; it still provides both with a political purpose but establishes the goals of the former as distinctly separate from those of the latter. This chapter has also established the place of culture in Irish nationalism, but it has identified that there are subtle variations in the extent to which it was adopted. It is important, therefore, for any consideration of the political nature of archaeology, collecting and museum development in Ireland to establish whether this was for the purposes of nationalism or revivalism. Both ideologies were linked in method, materialisation and sometimes consequence, but could be quite different in motivation. The remainder of this book will establish the importance of archaeology, collecting antiquities and the formation of a public museum for the creation of an understanding of the nation in Ireland. As will be seen, this interest had a complex relationship with nationalism. For some it was justified as a method to gain support for the restoration of a Dublin parliament, while for others the past did have a social and political role but it was not necessarily one that was nationalist in foundation.

CHAPTER THREE

The Use of the Past in Irish Politics

IN ORDER TO succeed, nationalism needs to create a sense of commitment to the nation. This was emphasised by E. J. Hobsbawm who explored the concept of 'proto-national bonds' that created the idea of a shared identity central to the 'imagined community'.[1] Since nationalism relies heavily on the imagination, archaeology has been used to create a sense of the nation being natural and predetermined and also to provide material legitimisation for the myths of the nation. Hutchinson has identified a number of myths that were particularly potent in nationalist thought in Ireland, all of which recur through writing about archaeology. Examples include the myth of descent from a Celtic people; the idea of a Golden Age, considered as a time of intellectual, social, political and ethnic integration; the myth of degeneration, triggered by the arrival of the English; and the myth of regeneration, made possible by a return to the values of the Golden Age.[2] By such appropriation, the past provided the intellectual context for an improved present, and in doing so 'celebrating the glories of the Irish past ... compensate[d] for a fraught inglorious present'.[3] As a result of this, archaeological sites and landscapes became the 'poetic space' of the nation and artefacts the material evidence of a political concept.[4]

In some instances one can argue that commitment to the culture, traditions or history of the nation was the principal driving force behind Irish nationalism, while in other cases the past was simply a political aid. It is apparent, however, that in each case the past was considered to be useful to give historical legitimisation to the idea of the nation.

THE POLITICAL APPROPRIATION OF ARCHAEOLOGY

The idea of archaeological remains encapsulating 'memories', whether real or fanciful, is a continual theme in nationalist writing about archaeology. In a powerful lecture delivered to the Cork Young Ireland Society in 1885 by the nationalist William O'Brien entitled 'The Irish National Idea', the entire Irish landscape was presented as a historic entity 'woven inextricably around the Irish heart'.[5] O'Brien presented Irish patriotism as emanating from the archaeological remains scattered over the Irish landscape and the nation as still existing, though in a spiritual form and waiting to be brought back to life. The passion of Irish patriotism, he told his listeners, was:

> the weird voice we hear from every graveyard where our fathers are sleeping, for every Irish graveyard contains the bones of uncanonised saints and martyrs. When the framers of the penal laws denied us books, and drew their thick black veil over Irish history, they forgot that the ruins they [the martyrs] had themselves made were the most eloquent school masters, the most stupendous memorials of a history and a race that were destined not to die. They might give our flesh to the sword, and our fields to the spoiler, but before they could blot out the traces of their crimes, or deface the title-deeds of our heritage, they would have had to uproot their last scrap of sculptured filigree, the majestic shrines in which the old race worshipped; they would have had to demolish to their last stone the castles which lay like wounded giants through the land to mark where the fight had raged the fiercest; they would have had to level the pillar towers. And to seal up the sources of the holy wells, and even then they would have not stilled the voice of Ireland's past.[6]

This extract contains some of the key uses of archaeology in fuelling nationalist sentiment. The material remains of the past were ascribed special power or talismanic charm. The remains of Ireland's Golden Age, the shrines and round towers, emerged above historic events to demonstrate the glorious nature of the Irish race, thus providing political inspiration. The archaeological monuments were represented as more than ruins: they were 'eloquent school masters', 'stupendous memorials' and 'wounded giants'. The presence of such symbols, or totems, on the landscape was taken as indicative of past martyrs and a race 'destined not to die'.

Such themes recurred in political speeches and writings in a number of ways. In the first place one can trace repeated reference to the value of certain archaeological sites and monuments. Irish nationalism attached itself to these monuments in order to create a political landscape integrated with the archaeological landscape. This association used archaeological monuments to signify the political ideology, so providing nationalism with a sense of precedence and authority. In a similar fashion, certain archaeological artefacts were used as political symbols and regarded as important subjects for collections. Interestingly, out of the vast material remains of the past only a handful of artefacts were chosen to become political icons. In other words, the past in its entirety was reduced to a national past of particular periods, monuments and artefacts that were useful for the political process. As part of this, institutions that preserved the material remains were claimed as essential to the nation. Finally, certain characteristics, such as the Irish language and folklore, were declared to be 'national traditions'. By associating archaeological monuments with national traditions, the former was provided with live and active representation and the latter was granted ancient precedence. In this context, the ancient remains and the 'still living traditions' became symbolic of the magical and enduring quality of the nation.

In nationalist writing, archaeological sites and monuments became 'remarkable witness[es] of the greatness of the Irish nation'.[7] It was on such a basis that the Hill of Tara, part of which is known as *Ráth na Ríogh* (the fort of the Kings),[8] was the site in 1843 where 500,000 people gathered for a 'monster rally meeting' of O'Connell's National Repeal Association. Such meetings were highly opportunist; they drew on the already established popular pastime of visiting historical sites[9] and were manufactured as 'political spectacle'.[10] The Tara meeting was a symbolic display, with the archaeological site as the stage and the political event dramatised by speeches and various other adornments, such as banners, costumes and flags (as evident in Figure 1).

The *Ráth na Ríogh* enclosure, which is part of a wider archaeological landscape, contains a passage tomb that dates from the Neolithic period. However, it was its reuse in the Early Christian Period, and its associations with Irish kingship, which were of interest to the proponents of nationalism. These aspects of Tara,

Figure 1: The 'monster meeting' at Tara (*The Illustrated London News*, 26 August 1843). Notice the banner in the background with a harp, wolfhound and round tower. In the foreground, a man is depicted in costume with a harp.

rather than its Neolithic origins, became fixed in the popular memory. The language in O'Connell's address intended to rouse and inspire the crowd to political action. He gave the site a contemporary political value by his reference to Ireland independent from English rule and by his emphasis on a 'public mind' which could unite through a 'pledge of honour'. He declared:

> It is impossible to deny that Tara has historical recollections that give to it an importance, relatively, to the other portions of the land, and deserves to be so considered by every person that comes to it for political purpose (hear) [*sic*] and gives it an elevation and point of impression in the public mind that no other part of Ireland can possibly have. History may be tarnished by exaggeration, but the fact is undoubted that we are at Tara of the Kings (cheers). We are on the spot where the monarchs of Ireland were elected and where the chieftains of Ireland bound themselves by the sacred pledge of honour and the tie of religion to stand by their native land against the Dane, or any other stranger (cheers).[11]

In this example, the value of the archaeological site and the political event became intermingled. Since independent Ireland, which is what the site symbolised for the movement, could only be recaptured by the way of politics, the political act was presented as being of equal, if not greater, value than the archaeological site. In the report of the meeting in the *Nation*, the editor revered Tara and used the associations as a springboard to elevate the status of the political event. In this manner he wrote: 'the history of Tara is proud and old, but it never saw so proud a sight as this meeting'.[12] Through the rousing and romantic language that was characteristic of the Young Irelanders, Tara became a vessel in which to forge the emotions that would bring the Irish nation to bear. The readers were informed that 'the tear glistened in the eye of the stranger when he looked on that scene and thought of our history; and many a heart was too full to restrain the big drop which, joy and grief, and hope, and sympathy, made to trickle down the cheek'.[13]

By the time of O'Connell's meeting, Tara had already been established as a political symbol,[14] and this endured throughout the nineteenth century. In the 1890s the *Irish Builder* claimed that the 'memory of the great banquets in the halls of Tara' had never died out and as a result 'will foster yet for many generations to come the feelings of independence'.[15] In a similar fashion, the readers of the *Irish Nation* were told of the desire for an independent parliament that could even govern from Tara. The editor hoped that the 'the ancient glories of Teamor' would be revived so that he would see:

> a Parliament of a free Ireland legislating amid surroundings rendered sacred by the memories of a dead past. In this venerable and hallowed spot the spirits of departed legislators would be there to inspire and encourage their successors to emulate the great example and devote their talents to the noble and patriotic task of remaking the modern Ireland.[16]

Though it may have been the most evocative, Tara was not the only ancient site that was used by Irish nationalism. In 1843 the Repeal Association also met at the Rath of Mullaghmast and planned a meeting at Clontarf, the site of the death of Brian Boru, a hero to nationalists. In 1883 the Gaelic League, in a manner reminiscent of O'Connell's Repeal Movement, made a 'pilgrimage' to 'the fine historical ruins' of Monasterboice, a sixth-century monastery with a round tower and high-crosses. At this meeting the chairman asked the crowd to 'show by their actions their thorough nationality as identical to those who inhabited the ancient edifices around them'.[17] This practice of holding political meetings at ancient sites was an act in foreshortening time, for by bringing temporally distant events together the impact of the past was increased.

References to the Irish past made by nationalists shifted between history and prehistory according to how that past was to be used to bolster their argument. The Rath of Mullaghmast was significant to the Repeal Association as the location of a historical event.[18] In his speeches at the rath, O'Connell spoke of the death of the Irish chiefs at the hands of English colonists and the suppression of the Irish through British law, giving the Treaty of Limerick and the penal laws as examples.[19] The readers of the *Nation* were told that the rath was selected for the 'great meeting' as the 'scene of a massacre atrocious event [by] the Saxon' where, in the sixteenth century, 'the Earl of Sussex shortly after the reformation having invited FOUR HUNDRED CHIEFTAINS of Leinster to a conference on this hill, murdered them in cold blood'.[20] There was a qualitative difference in the employment of Mullaghmast as a historical location and the Hill of Tara as an archaeological site. Tara was important as a representation of the glorious nature of the Irish nation, a trigger to evoke pride and self-respect. On the other hand, Mullaghmast was a context in which the people could be united under the idea of a trampled nation, and a method to form an impression of the bad behaviour of the English in Ireland. History, therefore, was playing a distinctly different role to that of archaeology. The recent past had negative connotations, whereas Ireland in antiquity was distant enough to evoke confidence.

It is also useful to note the method by which the sites were harnessed. As is usually the nature of battlefield sites, no actual material remains of the event were evident on the Mullaghmast landscape. Furthermore, the evidence used by the political figures at Tara was derived from mythological tales or medieval texts, rather than remains on the ground. Despite meeting at an impressive archaeological site, it was not the archaeology that was important. It was the associations or feelings that could be ignited that were of greatest worth. At both locations, the imagination of the past played the principal role and the places were important for what they could conjure up in the mind. The imagination can be far more vivid than archaeological and historical sites, yet these, with their slight ambiguity, were ideal for moulding the concept of the nation – what it was and what it could be again. The activists were therefore able to revive an idea of the past in the style and manner they wished to have it remembered, so creating an atmosphere suitable for their political actions.

The many ways in which archaeological sites were imbued with political value are also evident in another stirring and romantic oration delivered by William O'Brien in 1892 to the National Society of Cork, reported in the *Gaelic Journal*. This address, like so many others he published in *Irish Ideas*, is heavily laden with nationalist sentiment, violent rhetoric and archaeological symbolism. It is quite striking that these were all brought together in one address, revealing that such employment of the past had become frequent and acceptable. O'Brien began by preaching on the importance of archaeological sites with an attempt to present the nation as natural. He then claimed that Irish people should find reverence of such sites intuitive, and he stated that 'every Irishman of finely strung nature loves to piece together the stones of the cloisters of Cong where the last High King of Ireland found a more durable rest than his earthly kingdom'. O'Brien also emphasised the value of the places associated with events when the Irish were triumphant over the British. He went on to declare 'our pulses quicken as we trace amidst the vestiges of the old town wall of Limerick the breach where King William's Brandenburg Regiment was blown into the air'. Finally, in romantic and inspirational language, he asked his audience to venerate archaeological sites. He claimed:

> We follow Dr Petrie's[21] footsteps reverently among the mounds on Tara Hill, while he proves to us where stood the Mead-circling Hall, once glittering with the revelry of kings, and the Chamber of Sunshine ... A broken column, a place-name, a mere mound glorified with the dust of heroes, may enable us to live over again THE FEASTS, THE ROYAL JOUSTS, THE ROMANCES which lit up the land a thousand years ago (applause).[22]

As well as referring to some of the most prominent archaeological monuments in Ireland, such as the burial mounds in the Boyne Valley and at Tara, O'Brien also made reference in this address to the most important archaeologist of his century, George Petrie. Taken together, it is clear from this, and the other examples given above, that political activists used archaeology to increase the political significance of their meetings. Furthermore, as will become evident in later chapters, the awareness and value of the practice of archaeology was also increased by this coalescence.

In this political context, archaeological monuments and artefacts became symbols of Irish nationality and as such were frequently used in nationalist iconography. One may consider, for example, illustrations of archaeological artefacts and monuments in the printed propaganda of political groups, such as pamphlets, newspapers and membership cards, as well as references made to archaeological artefacts in political speeches and writing. The high circulation and readership of newspapers, as well as the quantity of membership cards issued, gave easy and multiple access to the images. The membership card of the National Repeal Association, for instance, was decorated with a crown, a socketed axe, a brooch and a harp (Figure 2). With the possession of a membership card a sense of shared ownership of the archaeology symbolised on the covers could be created.

Figure 2: Detail of the cover of the National Repeal Association membership card. The symbols of Irish nationalism are evident: the harp, shield, Irish crown, socketed axe, horn and brooch.

Figure 3: Frontispiece of *The Spirit of the Nation*. Drawn by Frederic Burton (republished in Flood 1911).

Images of antiquity were also brought together in the frontispiece of a book entitled *The Spirit of the Nation* originally published in 1845 as a collection of writings from the *Nation* newspaper (Figure 3). The image is composed of a harpist, a bard and two figures standing against a fictional landscape of a standing stone pictured in a Hiberno-Romanesque arch. This is framed by four images of Hibernia, one for each province of Ireland, and examples of Celtic interlace. This powerful illustration was made even more potent because Thomas Davis chose to dedicate an essay to its subject.[23] This essay, written for the readers of the *Nation*, described a 'young bard, harp bearing' depicted with 'the hills of Ireland behind him, he has come down full of strength, and wisdom, and faith'. An old bard listens to the young 'minstrel of the Nation'. Two brothers also listen, both of whom are in Irish costume, one wearing the gold torque of 'an Irish knight' the other with a sheathed sword which, according to Davis, 'will be drawn'. Davis claimed that the design represented the 'hopes and passions of the Irish people'. Above these figures are an *Irish* eagle and a serpent. The former is 'soaring' from the serpent 'vast, wounded and hissing'. Davis added 'the bird is safe – need we translate the allegory?' For Davis the eagle and serpent symbolised the relationship between Ireland and Britain. He celebrated the national characteristics of the design and the inherent political message in its artistry. For him the illustration was the 'most beautiful' and 'national design' with 'more poetry in it than in any poem'. The example of this illustration, complemented as it is by Davis' description, demonstrates the political narrative that developed out of nationalist iconography. In this context archaeological features became symbols and were used to communicate the political message and portray the myths of the Irish nation: the glory of the Golden Age, the degenerate impact of the English and the potential for regeneration.

Archaeology was also used in illustrations in popular magazines and books on Irish history. Here again the editors involved themselves in, and helped cultivate, the rising sentiment concerning the 'national' past and the raised status of archaeology, and the examples are numerous. The cover of *Duffy's Hibernian Magazine: A Monthly Journal of Literature, Science and Art* (1846) depicted Hibernia standing by a harp framed in a stylised snake, in the manner of the art in the Book of Kells. As well as romantic scenes from Irish life of a harpist, a monastic scribe and a storyteller, this illustration included other national symbols, such as a Celtic cross, shamrocks and a round tower.[24] The *Irish National Magazine* (1846) illustrated its header with a round tower, a harp, an Irish crown and an axe. Later, the cover of the first number of the *Irish Nation* (June 1916) was illustrated with Hibernia (the female embodiment of Ireland) adorned in a cloak with penannular brooches. She is pictured walking on water with the sun rising behind her and the slogan 'the spirit of Ireland is eternal' circled with shamrocks.

Romantic nationalist images of the past are also found in popular volumes on Irish history. The frontispiece of Haverty's *The History of Ireland Ancient and Modern* (Figure 4), published in 1860, was dominated by the three Irish saints, Patrick, Bridget and Columba, and recreated a mythical landscape combining a round tower with a monument in the style of Stonehenge. The frontispiece of the volume *Popular History of Ireland* shows Hibernia sitting at a Celtic cross and a round tower in the background (Figure 5). The artefacts that were repeatedly illustrated in this context, such as the 'Tara' Brooch and the Ardagh Chalice, date from the period before the arrival of the Normans in Ireland in the twelfth century and they were used as examples of the art that an Ireland free from English power could produce. A round tower was the most frequent monument to be used as a nationalistic symbol. It was particularly useful because, as will become clear in the following chapter, the towers were enigmatic and inspired diverse interpretations. The significance of the round tower could therefore be easily manipulated to indicate the greatness of the Irish nation. The very nature of the monument was also of political value; the tower recurs throughout Ireland and is characteristically Irish.[26] As a result, the monument was recognisable to the entire population and therefore could easily become a medium through which to create a sense of a unique and shared heritage. This aided the creation of a group identity that could be used for the purposes of nationalism. The frequent use of such imagery secured the idea of the antiquity of the Irish nation and, in a cumulative effect, added veracity to each example. Their reuse bred familiarity with archaeological remains and naturalised their use as symbols as well as the ideology they were taken to represent. The use of archaeology in such illustrations helped give nationalist ideology authenticity and historical realism in a manner similar to images of the Celt found in popular historical writing in late-nineteenth-century France.[27]

Against such a background, the preservation, collection and display of antiquities was of concern, as evident in the political

Figure 4: Frontispiece of *The History of Ireland Ancient and Modern* (Haverty 1860). Notice the depiction of Stonehenge in Glendalough, Co. Wicklow at the base of the drawing. This draws on the Arthurian legend of the wizard Merlin who used his magical powers to bring the stones from Ireland to England.[25]

Figure 5: Frontispiece of *Popular History of Ireland*. 'Hibernia' is mourning at the foot of a Celtic cross, notice a round tower in the background.

statements that made reference to the value of artefacts and the importance of forming collections of antiquities. In addition, the cultural institutions that would nurture archaeology and Irish traditions were perceived by political activists to be of immense value. It was because of the importance of having the past managed for nationalism that poor management or neglect of the remains came under attack. Once the readers were reminded of the glory of the past they were also informed that proper management of their national heritage was only possible under a native and independent government. Thomas Davis, for example, in an essay on Newgrange stated that the site was both 'a thing to be proud of, as a proof of Ireland's antiquity' and one 'to be guarded as an illustration of her early creed and arts'. Moreover, it is 'one of a thousand moniments of our old nationality, which a national government would keep safe'.[28] William O'Brien, in his address to the National Society of Cork, also spoke of the importance of preserving archaeology. He described the 'public indignation' directed 'to the vandalism of the men who should carry away the delicate stone traceries of our cathedrals to build his cabin walls, or turn the royal cemeteries of the Boyne into quarries to mend roads with'.[29]

In this context, an antiquities collection was regarded as a powerful representation of the glories of the nation. Davis wrote that in order to nurture nationality one must preserve the monumental record; in other words the past was linked to the future. He suggested a holistic approach to the preservation of the past by posing the question: 'why shall we seek for histories, why make museums, why study the manners of the dead, when we foully neglect or barbarously spoil their homes, their castles, their temples, their colleges, their courts, their graves? He who tramples on the past does not create for the future.'[30] A similar appeal was made in the *Nation*. The paper asked its readers to 'collect all the manuscripts and books of the neighbourhood ... copies of any old histories or surveys ... subscribe to the Irish Archaeological Societies'.[31] This was with the ultimate purpose of forming a 'NATIONAL SCHOOL OF IRISH HISTORY AND LITERATURE AND A MUSEUM OF IRISH ANTIQUITIES, on the largest scale'.[32] The readers of the *United Irishman* were reminded of instances of neglect of Irish material remains by the British administration, attempting to adopt this as cultural evidence in their case against British rule. If Ireland was governed by Irishmen, 'instead of being occupied by an enemy's garrison, the Book of Rights', the *United Irishman* claimed, was 'precisely one of the Public Records of the island which should long ago have been collected and purchased by the state'.[33] The lack of funds from Britain for Irish institutions involved with the preservation of Irish heritage was presented as having a political purpose. It was depicted as yet another example of British suppression of Irish nationality. The *Nation,* for instance, described this as part of a process of 'discouraging national institutions as well as national men'. Many of those who were involved with institutions such as the Royal Irish Academy or the Royal Dublin Society, and senior in the Ordnance Survey, were loyal to the Crown. With this in mind the *Nation,* in hope, suggested that the 'mismanagement by the Foreign Parliament' of the Dublin Society would lead to a decline in support for the union amongst its largely pro-union membership. The editor wrote:

> The sway of a stranger has a kind of impartiality in its wickedness. Here was a body consisting nine-tenths of men arrayed in favour of English supremacy. Still the curse of Swift was upon them and their institution – they were Irishmen – it was Irish in origin and objects – away with it said the centralizer, it was not managed by Englishmen – away with it said the assimilator and imperialist, it is a relic of nationality.[34]

Because of this 'gross mal-treatment of that Irish institution by a Foreign Parliament' the editor wrote 'who knows how soon they [the pro-unionists] will see the necessity of going the one step further, and demanding National Government as the only means of national posterity and fame'.[35]

Political interest in cultural institutions continued through to the end of the nineteenth century. The *Irish Nation* emphasised both the importance of collections for the development of the nation and the lack of such advancement. Its readers were told 'it is deeply to be regretted that as yet we have not adequately explored the numerous valuable monuments and the great abundance of natural records, which have been bequeathed to us by our Celtic ancestors'. The paper also suggested a remedy to this situation:

> By the Irishman of the present day it ought to be felt an imperative duty, which he owes to his country not less to himself, to learn something at least of her history, her literature, and her antiquities, and, as far as existing means will allow, to ascertain for himself what

her position was in past times when she had a name and a civilisation, a law and life of her own.[36]

A similar interest is also to be found in the cultural politics of the Gaelic League and of the activist Arthur Griffith, who based his cultural and political policies on the Hungarian example. He believed that Irish people should reject foreign culture and embrace native language, dress, songs and pastimes. Griffith, moreover, claimed 'greater than all the patriotic resolutions of Ireland are the monuments of Hungary's patriotism that today stand in the capital of Free Hungary – the National University, the National Museum, and the National Theatre'.[37] Similar proposals had already been outlined by Griffith in the objectives of *Cumann na nGaedheal* in 1900 and in his address entitled 'The Sinn Féin Policy' delivered in 1905. Paramount to the establishment of Sinn Féin institutions was, according to Griffith, the formation of a National Academy of Sciences 'devoted to the resuscitation of the [Irish] language as the language of literature, science, and industry'; a National Theatre 'where all the plays were acted in the National language and dealt with the past, present and future', and a National Museum 'designed to inspire reverence and pride in the past ... and to educate the people in the possibilities of its future'.[38]

The *Gaelic Journal* argued along similar lines. In an issue published in 1909, the readers were told that if Ireland were 'in national health', the publication of Irish manuscripts would be more prevalent.[39] What is interesting is that these individuals were asking for the collections and institutions to be established. Even though these institutions had yet to be formed, the effect of their writing was to create an image of vast accumulations of rich remains, a charge that helped further the nationalist goal. For nationalism, as we have seen, is a powerful force which depends as much on the imagination as action or reality. Referring to potential collections was useful because it evoked the idea of a rich nation on the brink of recreation. A similar appropriation of the past was can be seen to have been practised by Douglas Hyde. In an essay he told his readers of his own interest in Ireland's early history and he stated that he believed in 'going here and there throughout the entire island and gathering together, here and there, every relic of the past upon which we can lay our hands and gathering them together into one great whole and building and enshrining everyone of them in the temple that shall be raised to the godhead of Irish nationhood'.[40]

This powerful statement elevated Irish antiquities collections to the status of a sacred entity. Rather than continuing with any practical advice, Hyde idealised collecting as one of many ways of nurturing the notion of an 'Irish Ireland', composed of the return to the Gaelic language, music, habits and customs. In fact, Hyde is not recorded as having formed an antiquities collection.[41] Hyde's interest in archaeology, on this particular issue, was actually more rhetoric than reality. The collection had, in other words, all the qualities of existence, except existence.[42]

A further example of how the past was used by Irish activists can be illustrated by their reference to those traditions that were deemed a reflection of national identity, such as folklore and language. More importantly they were depicted as having great antiquity, sanctioned by being associated with archaeological sites and periods. The message inherent in the political sources was that tradition revealed the uniqueness of the Irish nation, which itself legitimised independence. Such sentiment is found throughout the sources cited above and it is neatly summed up in the pages of the *Irish Builder*. In an essay headed 'Archaeology and its Bearing upon Irish Affairs' the evidence of Irish tradition was used as an aid for defining who had the right to govern Ireland. It read:

> The Irish are in fact a Celtic race with purely Celtic traditions, traditions that are still full of life. Our English rule, founded on an entirely different set of traditions, finds, therefore, the utmost difficulty in gaining any hold on the people proper. ... The researches of archaeology prove to us that many of the features of the original Celtic organisation of Ireland lasted till comparatively recent days; the memory of the great banquets in the halls of Tara, which has inspired us so often to muse of the Irish poets has never died out, and the traditions of those days will foster yet for many generations to come the feelings of independence.[43]

Monuments, artefacts, cultural institutions and traditions were identified and used by activists to define the Irish nation in different ways. The idea of 'the nation' is a vague and tenuous notion, so nationalists used archaeology to provide a tangible and seemingly objective representation. The use of the past was twofold: on the one hand political activists made blanket statements about the 'heroic past' while on the other they made frequent reference to specific objects, sites and periods. In doing so they gave their political argument greater legitimisation and actual material evidence. Their rhetoric, by referring to the archaeological landscape of mounds, round towers and crosses, created the imagined space of the nation. Since these monuments were found throughout Ireland they were useful as recurrent symbols by which to create a unified space and a sense of shared community identity. By a similar method archaeological monuments, such as the round tower, and artefacts, such as the 'Tara' brooch, were highly evocative and therefore continually reused in political illustration.

Though such use of archaeology was frequent, the monuments, sites or artefacts referred to were relatively few. These features selected from the vast record of the past became the symbols of the nation. Therefore, though nationalist rhetoric raises the profile and awareness of archaeology itself, the actual knowledge of the archaeological record generated is narrow. The past is selectively imagined in a manner that will suit the political end. In other words, to quote the archaeologist Chris Tilley, 'the interpretation of the meaning and significance of material culture is a contemporary activity. The meaning of the past does not reside in the past, but belongs to the present.'[44] What is chosen are the features of the past that can be easily used to convey the political idea. Those elements are used to portray the people as of the nation, as subject to their own past and as custodians, obliged to both the past and the future. The people as a unit are reminded of their inheritance, their responsibility and the necessity of creating a political future both in imitation and worthy of the national past. This aspiration is, however, created and led by present day perceptions. Their ideology is inspired by their notion of the past rather than having any ancient foundation.

VARIATIONS IN POLITICAL IDEOLOGY AND APPROPRIATION OF THE PAST

The relationship established between archaeology and Irish nationalism becomes more meaningful with a consideration of the nature of the links established by different forms of Irish nationalism. The extent of dependency on the past, the method of appropriation, and the detail of the references to archaeology, reveal subtle differences in political opinion and programme. The nature of the different relationships illustrates that the value placed on the past will vary within a particular socio-political context as dictated by many other issues, such as one's background, identity and specific political purpose. Therefore one can argue that the past is a flexible political tool, which is used according to various needs.

In the first instance one can contrast the relationship with archaeology as expressed by the constitutional movement of Daniel O'Connell and the cultural nationalism of the Young Irelanders, the two most popular voices of mid-nineteenth-century Irish nationalism. For O'Connell the gathering on Tara Hill was a symbolic gesture – it was a political instrument which was only significant for so long as it served its purpose. 'O'Connell was perfectly capable of calling on Irish history as evidence for the prosecution, as proof that Irishmen were brave noble creatures whose rights had been filched from them by settlers and Englishmen'; however, 'he stood firmly in the modern world, and was concerned with the present, not the past'.[45] References to the past do not, therefore, dominate the anthology of O'Connell's speeches published by his son.[46] On the other hand, for the Young Irelanders archaeology was the material evidence of the Irish nation and inspiration for their romantic form of nationalism. Nearly every number of their paper, the *Nation*, considered subjects of an antiquarian or cultural nature. In addition Thomas Davis, the most popular Young Irelander, wrote extensively on the subject in essays on such topics as 'National Art', 'Irish topography', 'Irish music and poetry', 'Irish antiquities and Irish savages', 'Irish history', and 'The Round Towers of Ireland'.[47] This more striking role of the past in the rhetoric of the Young Irelanders can be argued to be a consequence of their political position. Daniel O'Connell was able to popularise his campaign through the establishment of the Catholic Association and the 'Catholic rent'. Since Thomas Davis and the other Protestants of the Young Ireland movement could not appeal to Catholicism to unite the people of Ireland, they needed some other shared characteristic which would also provide them with a form of self-legitimisation. Therefore they recreated the Irish past, and 'the nation' which it would inspire, in their own image with their own particular style of mythology.[48]

The Young Irelanders appealed to an identification with Ireland that was immaterial of religion: 'what matter that at different shrines we pray unto one God? ... By fortune and in name we're bound by stronger links than steel.'[49] Therefore, for them involvement with the Irish past was part and parcel of involvement with the Irish present:

'it was because the Protestants believed themselves to be the Irish nation that they involved themselves in Ireland's past, and sought to shape her political future'.[50] This is demonstrated in an essay by Davis in which he regretted the state of neglect of historical monuments in Ireland. He included the material remains of *all* lines of descent, 'our Scotic or Milesian, or Norman, or Danish sires', as worthy of preservation. This is a reflection of his definition of Irish nationalism and nationality: his desire to unite everyone, irrespective of religion, interested in an independent Ireland. Therefore he appealed to everyone to come together for this purpose:

> The Clergy, Protestant, Catholic and Dissenting, if they would secure the character of men of education and taste – we call on the gentry, if they have any pride of blood, and on the people if they reverence Old Ireland, to spare and guard every remnant of antiquity. We ask them to find other quarries than churches, abbeys, castles, and cairns – to bring rusted arms to a collector, and coins to a museum, and not to iron or goldsmiths, and to take care that others do the like.[51]

The newspaper of the Young Irelanders had a similar inclusive concept of the nation, and the past was again established as a tool to bring the people of Ireland together. Their readers were told that 'every party, and every creed of Irishman' should 'unite for objects generally circulated to elevate the character of their native land in the eyes of the world, there can be no subject more worthy of attention, than that of the ancient history and literature of the country'.[52] Davis praised the contribution to Irish archaeology of the largely Protestant and Ascendancy institutions, such as the Royal Irish Academy. He also paid tribute to their members, he made reference to George Petrie in the pages of the *Nation* for instance.[53] He celebrated the 'noble and national' Irish Archaeological Society which 'independent of every party, embracing all creeds … continues to prepare and publish the materials of our national history, so long neglected – so essential to a nation'. Because of this good work, he claimed:

> It is discreditable for any Irishman of tolerable income to neglect joining the society. It is giving us what we never had before - copious and genuine materials for our national history, both civil military and literary: and it is *rapidly reviving the study of the Irish language in the middle and upper classes*. The man who does not wish them success is a brute, a slave, or an alien enemy.[54]

The *United Irishman* published in 1848 exhibited a far more violent form of nationalism. The paper was founded by John Mitchel, who also wrote for the *Nation*, in order to provide him with a context in which to propagate his more extreme approach.[55] This was revealed in attitudes to the activity of the Royal Irish Academy and similar Ascendancy institutions as expressed in the paper. The societies were presented as a spin-off of occupation by the 'enemy's garrison'. The readers of the *United Irishman* were told that an Irish State would be a better collector of Irish antiquities and manuscripts, but until that end, and in a direct reference to the work of the Ordnance Survey in Ireland, the paper read 'we must rescue such of our records as we can out of the clutches of British engineers and military officers'.[56] Contributors to the *Nation* and the *United Irishman* both recognised the importance of antiquarian activity; however, as in their politics, the *Nation* was prepared to embrace anyone Irish, Anglo-Irish or British taking an interest in Irish archaeology, whereas the *United Irishman* wanted to keep Ireland, and ownership of the Irish past, exclusively for the Irish people.

A later movement, the Irish Republican Brotherhood, exhibited its own particular notion of the nation and the role of the past within it. The IRB's common name, the Fenians, had historical roots: it 'reflects the movement's intermittent historical nostalgia; the name evokes a legendary warrior order of pre-Christian Ireland'.[57] The IRB had a distinctly different relationship with the past from that evident in the *Nation* cited above. The IRB presented the past and archaeology as important only in so far as they were an illustration of the oppressive nature of English rule in Ireland. Thus, they preached to their readers: 'we are enthusiastic admirers of the warriors and chieftains of the olden time ... we love the godlike men of other days ... we respect and admire, then, the old chieftains of our land, especially those who fought against English rule'. The *Irish People* considered excessive engagement with the past as diverting people's minds and actions away from the true route to independence, by the way of revolution. The paper rejected cultural tactics and informed its readers 'true national independence never was and never will be anywhere achieved, save by the sword'. Though the past was of value, the *Irish People* did not see the usefulness of attempting to create an independent Irish nation by a revival of interest in Irish literature and the collection of Irish manuscripts and antiquities. It threw scorn on such activity:

Some amiable and enlightened young men still fondly imagine that they are surely regenerating their country, when they are pushing about in a drawing-room society, and busying themselves in setting up academies and unions for artistic purposes, creating an Irish national literature, schools of Irish art, and things of this sort ... A branch of these specially cultivate archaeology as an infallible means of national rejuvenescence ... For our part we think it idle for a prostrate and trampled subject-province to dream of a national literature or a national school of art. Let her regain her independence, and these things will follow as a matter of writes [*sic*] ... your lost independence ... can be won by but one method ... the sword.[58]

Two matters are likely to have been significant here. In the first place, such nationalists only had a rhetorical interest in archaeology and investing energy in cultural projects would have been regarded as not having immediate enough results. Secondly, many of the developments in Irish archaeology were being led by Anglo-Irish revivalists, some of whom were pro-Union. Because of this connection extreme nationalism would have doubted the long-term contribution of such activity for achieving independence from Britain. James Stephens, the founder of the IRB and the *Irish People*, turned away from the upper classes; he believed the heart of Irish nationalism 'beat only in the breasts of the common people, the men of no property'.[59] The readers of the *Irish People* were told that it was a waste of time and labour to make an 'appeal to the aristocracy' because it was impossible 'to arouse the upper and middle classes to a sense of duty they owe their country. Whatever is not thoroughly rotten in these classes will follow the people.' Rather, 'the real Irish gentry are to be found in the lanes of Dublin'.[60]

To add to the proposition that the form of engagement with archaeology is a reflection of one's national ideals, it is interesting to refer to the writing of Standish O'Grady at different points in his career. O'Grady was one of the chief cultural revivalists of the 1890s, and he has been labelled as the 'father of the Irish literary revival', though he remained unionist throughout his life.[61] Since he held such significance, how O'Grady wrote about Irish archaeology is of interest. O'Grady did not become familiar with Irish history until he was in his mid-twenties when he came across Sylvester O'Halloran's *History of Ireland* in a country house library where he was a guest. From thence O'Grady consulted the manuscripts in the Royal Irish Academy library and works on Irish history, such as

Eugene O'Curry's *Manners and Customs of the Ancient Irish* and *Manuscripts of Irish History* in which he was introduced to 'the wonder-world of Irish heroic and romantic literature'.[62] Subsequently he popularised this work and 'filled a generation of young writers with the proud consciousness of a nationality divorced from mere politics, and sent them back to the sources of national thought and national literature'.[63]

In one of his most popular works, O'Grady presented the legends and archaeology of Ireland as a reflection of Irish nationality. O'Grady valued antiquity: he stated that 'the history of Ireland clings and grows out of the Irish barrows' and argued that the existence of the monuments on the Irish landscape triggers an interest in the Irish past. The legends were established as a method to unlock the mystery attached to the monuments because 'the history of one generation became the poetry of the next'. For O'Grady they brought life to archaeology by providing the 'names, pedigrees, achievements and even characters of these ancient kings and warriors over whom [the] massive cromlechs were erected and great cairns piled'. The legends and antiquities of the past were therefore important to O'Grady but only in a romantic sense – he shunned the development of a scientific archaeology as less worthy than legends. In a manner that was typical of Irish literary revivalism, O'Grady made the claim that Irish legends 'represent the imagination of the country; they are the kind of history that a nation desires to possess. They betray the ambition and the ideals of the people and, in this respect, have a value far beyond the tale of actual events and duly recorded deeds, which are no more history than a skeleton is a man.' His interest in legends, in preference to 'actual events and duly recorded records', is revealing. He regarded the practice of 'scientific' archaeology as unnecessary and unrewarding; the legends of Ireland were held as a more vivid portrayal of the past. He argued that archaeological sites and monuments should be left undisturbed. Moreover, he damned conventional archaeological practice as an unromantic and pseudo-scientific activity. He claimed:

> For after the explorer has broken up certainly, and perhaps destroyed those noble sepulchral raths; after he has disinterred the bones laid there once by pious hands, and the urn with its unrecognisable ashes of king or warrior and the industrious labour of years hoarded his fruitless treasure of stone celt and arrow-head, of brazen sword and gold fibula and torque; and after the savant has rammed many skulls with sawdust,

measuring their capacity, and has adorned them with some obscure label, and has tabulated and arranged the implements and decorations of flint and metal in the glazed cases of the cold gaunt museums, the imagination, unsatisfied and revolted, shrinks back from all he has done ... an antiquarian museum is more melancholy than a tomb.[64]

This is an example of revivalist sentiment which did not require the verification of actual, 'factual', history; it was only interested in a version or idea of history which would further a particular agenda. Through his writing O'Grady formed a popular idea of Irish history. His inventive rhetoric aided the definition of the Irish nation and inspired Irish nationalists, thus creating the 'imagined community' useful for nationalism. As a result, O'Grady's writing was more popular than contemporary scientific work in archaeology.[65] This is, in essence, a demonstration of the point made by the French thinker Renan in 1882: 'to forget and – I will venture to say – to get one's history wrong, are essential elements in the making of a nation; and thus the advance of historical studies is often a danger to nationality'.[66]

O'Grady popularised early Irish history, but in a piece of his earlier writing one will find a different emphasis on the value of Irish legends and archaeology. In an introduction to a collection of O'Grady's essays, E. A. Boyd makes reference to O'Grady's previously 'unilluminating' journalism published under the pseudonym 'Arthur Clive' prior to his work on the Irish legends that made him so renowned. This writing was considered by Boyd as 'an interesting proof of what the author was, and might have remained, but for a certain accident'. (This was the accident of finding O'Halloran's work of history in the country house library, which O'Grady stated triggered his interest.)[67] One may assume, therefore, that the essay published by 'Arthur Clive' in the *Dublin University Magazine* (December 1876) was written by O'Grady. In this essay, 'Irish Archaeology', the history of Ireland is introduced as a 'hopeless puzzle', with the comment 'the whole of ancient history is chaotic and obscure' and a tangle of myth and misinterpretation. After this, some the chief figures of nineteenth-century archaeology were attacked and presented as being influenced by their nationalist politics. He referred to the work of history written by O'Halloran and that on Irish legends by Eugene O'Curry and John O'Donovan, as well as the collection formed in the Royal Irish Academy. O'Curry, he wrote, 'read all the ancient muniments of the country with a mind prejudiced in their favour ... and stricken with intellectual blindness'. Further on in the essay, O'Grady argued that the Royal Irish Academy did not make a major contribution to Irish studies but 'did much more to advance antiquarian science generally, than contribute anything distinctive to the accumulation of specially Irish antiquarian learning'. The Stone and Bronze Age antiquities of the Royal Irish Academy collection, rather than being remarkable, had 'nothing distinctive'. In his opinion, pride in the collection was appropriate only if one heralded it as 'a poor thing, sir, but my own', and the Academy museum housed 'gaunt and chilly collections [which] numb and clip the imagination'.

It is quite remarkable that O'Grady could be the author of 'Irish Archaeology' in the *Dublin University Magazine* and the later works in which he celebrated Irish legends. In 1876 O'Grady's writing would have been useful for anyone wishing to dispel pride in Ireland's legends and material remains; in 1881 his writings would have instilled such pride. In the passage written in 1876, O'Halloran's work was presented as 'wild and theoretical';[68] however, in 1899 O'Grady described his volume as 'scholarly, eloquent and impassioned; reason seemed to govern all his statements'. The legends that O'Grady read in the library of the Royal Irish Academy were subsequently described as the history of a 'race of conquerors' and 'divine dynasties'.[69] These contrasting interpretations of the same evidence by the same individual, but at different points in his career, show how history can be given different emphasis. In addition to this, the example of O'Grady demonstrates the highly subjective style of interpretation of archaeology applied by one of the most popular authors during the literary revival of the 1890s. This is significant because his writing both as Arthur Clive and later under O'Grady would have influenced perceptions of Irish archaeology, antiquarians and museums. This was amongst two quite different audiences – the pro-union subscribers to the *Dublin University Magazine* and the popular and often nationalist readership of his volumes on Irish history. In a manner, both essays would have endorsed the preconceptions of their readership.

As the political movement intensified in the early twentieth century, particularly during the negotiation of a 'political settlement' between Britain and Ireland, the past was moulded as evidence either for or against proposed changes. The third Home Rule Bill was passed in the Commons in 1914 and, when the Westminster government went on to debate options linked to Home Rule, political newspapers took an opportunity to comment. The *Irish*

Nation demanded complete separation from Britain, refusing to accept the proposed inclusion of a British figurehead. According to the paper, the past provided evidence of how unacceptable this would be to the Irish people. The paper claimed:

> Ireland is a Nation, one of the oldest in the world. She cannot, even if she would, part with her birthright by accepting the position of a Colony. The present generation of Irishmen cannot mortgage or otherwise dispose of the inheritance of their children. No Irishman worthy of the name would consent to such a degradation. If through the accident of birth there are living amongst us men who call themselves Irishmen but who are not of our race or our blood, such men have not the right to barter away Ireland's nationhood which is our independence.[70]

Historical evidence was also used as an argument against the notion of Ireland being partitioned. The idea of partition was introduced by Unionists, most of whom were from the north-east of Ireland, who were using it as a method for the counties of Ulster to opt out of Home Rule and maintain their links with Britain. To the annoyance of the editors of the *Irish Nation*, some nationalist politicians were discussing the feasibility of this. For Eoin MacNeill partition was an anathema. In an essay in the *Irish Nation* he pleaded to his readers: 'for the sake of your country with the memory of the men who have fought before you – unite'. He presented 'the heritage of an Irishman' as 'one of the grandest in the world', and asked the question: 'what son of Ireland, realising it, would willingly do ought to mar it? Yet, these frequent dissentions are doing it. They are the chinks in our armour, and they must be repaired now, if we would again have "Ireland a Nation".'[71]

As shown, references to antiquity were not only used in general statements of political rhetoric but also used in various ways by different shades of nationalist political opinion. One can argue, therefore, that the past is consistently used across the political spectrum, but the manner in which the past is adopted is not fixed and will vary according to time and the specific expressions of nationalist ideals. This demonstrates that though nationalists may wish the same end, an independent state legitimised by references to the 'historic nation', nationalism, and hence the past of the nation, is variable. This suggests the subtle nature of the relationship between politics and the past. Each reference to the past made in addresses or newspapers, whether brief or more extensive, contributed to a national interpretation of the history and prehistory and a shared relationship with antiquity. As was noted in Chapter One, knowledge of the past is taught, and this dictates how the past is valued. Such teaching created and fed a common narrative of history and prehistory that aided the nationalist cause.

ARCHAEOLOGY AND THE NATIONALIST NARRATIVE

Popular newspapers provided an ideal context within which to propagate a particular interpretation of Ireland's past. Much consideration has been given above to the writing about Irish history in nineteenth-century material such as penny journals, the pages of the *Nation* and political addresses. Now we turn to material that was important in laying down a 'national history' in the early twentieth century. The early history of Ireland was, at that time, particularly important because the 'ancient nation' became the independent state that was so desired.

In the first Presidential Address delivered to the Royal Society of Antiquaries of Ireland in post-independence Ireland, the archaeologist Robert Macalister informed his audience of the role newspapers took in disseminating popular accounts of Irish prehistory. He claimed that on sending copies of his lectures on antiquarian subjects to be reported in Dublin newspapers they had been read with 'distorting glasses' and reinterpreted and reprinted to endorse the papers' political prejudices. From his experience the editors of the different newspapers were either 'anglophilic' or 'anglophobic'. He explained:

> The Anglophile extends his energies in displaying England to us as an all-wise, all-ruling, and all-bountiful Province, incarnate in a superior race before which we in Ireland are less than nothing ... The Anglophile looks back to the dim ages of the [Irish] past ... and he can describe nothing but hordes of naked savages, living mere animal lives, and expending their whole time and energies in devastating tribal wars: a savagery from which England has raised us ... The Anglophobe scans the same horizon and sees the cloud-clapped towers, the gorgeous palaces, the solemn temples, of a cast and imposing civilisation, devoted to letters and learning: a civilisation which England has destroyed.[72]

Such competing interpretations of the Irish past are examples of what has been identified by Bruce Trigger as 'colonialist' and 'nationalist' archaeologies. Colonial archaeology was defined as a form of archaeology which is active in 'emphasizing the primitiveness and lack of accomplishments of these peoples to justify ... poor treatment of them'. On the other hand, nationalist archaeology aims to 'bolster the pride and morale of nations or ethnic groups'.[73] Trigger gave examples of both kinds of archaeology in the experience of different countries. The simplicity of this approach is demonstrated by the complexity of the Irish experience. Not only do different expressions of nationalism form individual relationships with the past, but also colonial and nationalist interpretations of the past occurred contemporaneously.

In Ireland a popular and shared perception of the past was developed in two ways: through volumes of work from historians, most of whom had an impeccable nationalist record, and through political newspapers. At a time of heightened political activity, contributors to such papers as *Nationality*, published between 1917 and 1919 and edited by Arthur Griffith, and the *Irish Nation*, published between 1916 and 1918, wrote many articles on historical subjects. For instance the *Irish Nation*, which claimed a readership of eighty thousand, ran a series headed 'The Irish Race'. This was in seven parts starting with 'The Irish Race' and continuing to trace 'The Birth of Ireland', 'The First Irishmen', 'The Germanic Wave', 'The Coming of the Celts' and 'The Danes'. The series ended with 'The English Plague'.[74] The newspaper also produced many occasional pieces such as those with the titles 'Ancient Irish History and Tradition' and 'The Ancient Race' and 'Ancient Milesian Customs'.[75] This writing was supplemented by short books on historical subjects like those produced by the Catholic Truth Society, such as a pamphlet on the history of Irish art, or which formed the basis of a historical introduction in political pamphlets, such as *What Sinn Féin Stands For* or *The Case for Home Rule*.[76]

These overviews, frequently spanning from prehistory to the modern period, were made up of what one may describe as 'soundbites' that were becoming the key elements of a standard interpretation of the past according to Irish nationalism. They also represented 'an instructional history' providing lessons in Irish history that were a mixture of historical fact and fiction.[77] As noted by Richard Kearney, the development of such a narrative (which he defined as stories, myths or other forms of dramatic representation) was essential for the creation of communal or 'national' identity, providing the political imagery that would legitimise the self and delegitmise the other.[78] The key themes established in nineteenth-century writing also emerged from these texts, the most significant of which are given further consideration below. These included the idea of the ancient nation and the 'noble Celt' as well as the belief in the superiority of a people who were not invaded by the Romans. These works propagated notions of the 'saints and scholars' of the Early Christian Period who spread a civilising influence throughout Europe. Furthermore, they emphasised the negative impact of invasions from England on Irish culture and creativity. These foremost themes provided the material for volumes on Irish history with such evocative and politically charged titles as *The Indestructible Nation* and, in post-independence Ireland, *The Story of the Irish Nation, And so Began the Irish Nation* and *Ireland a Nation*.[79] The titles of these works, as well the language used in the newspaper articles, are significant. With the English in Ireland described as a 'plague' and the Irish race as 'ancient' and 'indestructible', the reader immediately knew what to expect. Illustrations on the cover or the opening pages of the volumes summarised the political message. In many cases, illustrations in volumes from this period included Celtic style motifs used on the initial word of each chapter, or archaeological monuments or figures from mythology on the frontispiece. The dustcover of *And so Began the Irish Nation* is a particularly striking example; it is dominated by the silhouette of a portal tomb against a rising sun with a round tower in the background (see Figure 6).

The academic Eoin MacNeill and the more popular historian Alice Stopford Green both produced significant volumes of work on Irish history in the early decades of the twentieth century. MacNeill was one of the founders of the Gaelic League and he edited its official organ, the *Gaelic Journal*. He became the Professor of Early and Medieval History at University College Dublin in 1909. In the political context, MacNeill was chairman of the council that formed the Irish Volunteers and later was their chief-of-staff. As a result of his links with the 1916 Rising he was arrested and given a life jail sentence. However, he was released after a year. In the new Free State government he was Minister for Education (1922–25).[80] His work on Irish history included *Phases of Irish History* (1901), *Celtic Ireland* (1921) and he also wrote the chapter on history in *Saorstát Éireann*, the official handbook of the Irish Free State.[81] Green was

Figure 6: Dust cover of *And so Began the Irish Nation* (Seamus MacCall 1931).

described by her biographer as a 'fervent nationalist'.[82] Though she was born in Ireland, her family moved to London and she lived most of her life in England. While there she wrote two important works *The Making of Ireland and its Undoing* (1908) and *Irish Nationality* (1911). After the 1916 Rising she returned to Ireland and wrote other pieces, including her last major work *A History of the Irish State to 1014* (1925).[83] Her writing, which she claimed drew from that of MacNeill, had the overriding aim to further Irish nationalism by establishing the highly developed nature of the political institutions in pre-Anglo-Norman Ireland that could be revived by drawing from the 'Irish national memory'.[84]

In her 1911 volume, *Irish Nationality,* Green wrote on the history of Ireland from the arrival of the Gaels to the English invasion. In this she furthered a 'national idea' of antiquity. For her the arrival of the Gaels in Ireland marked the beginning of a 'heroic period', as recorded in the legends of 'Conor Mac Nessa, Cuchulainn and Queen Maeve' and 'King Ceallachan of the lovely cups'. Green, in the style of O'Grady before her, associated the legends with actual antiquities. In her work the remains preserved in the 'Dublin Museum' became 'the relics of the heroic time' and were considered of equal value to mythology. Continuing on this theme, she described 'the hearth of Tara' as the 'centre of all the Gaelic states ... where kings and chiefs sat each under his own shield, in crimson cloaks with gold brooches, with girdles and shoes of gold, and spears with golden sockets and rivets of red bronze'. The quantity of these artefacts was as significant as their quality. Green, quantifying the remains, told her readers that 'some five hundred golden ornaments of old time have been gathered together in the Dublin Museum in the last eighty years, a scanty remnant of that have been lost or melted down, their weight is five hundred and seventy ounces against the weight of twenty ounces in the British Museum from England, Scotland and Wales'.[85] This was presented as evidence of the richness of the Irish nation that far exceeded that of her neighbour.

Green's source for the quantity of gold remains in the Dublin museum collection may well have been the calculations made by the archaeologist, and active nationalist, George Coffey. In 1898 Coffey estimated that the Dublin collection had 570 ounces of prehistoric gold, which far exceeded collections held in any other country.[86] Green presented this volume of Irish antiquities as a demonstration of the wealth of the Irish nation. That such material should be in greater abundance in Ireland than in England was interpreted by

Green as evidence that Ireland was superior. By emphasising the glories of the past, Green also implied that the people owed it to Ireland to resurrect the state, so looking to the past and the future simultaneously, a skill often associated with nationalism. Therefore she would remind her readers of their debt: 'the peoples who created Irish civilisation have bequeathed ... a heroic tradition and literature, which has assured to this island an eminent place, one of singular distinction among the nations of Europe'.[87] Green described Irish heritage as one of 'an enduring state or nation', with 'an instinct of national life' which had existed since the time of the Gaels. Green's political desire was the recreation of a Gaelic nation wherein one would find the ideal of the 'joint spiritual inheritance' described as 'the union of those who shared the same tradition, the same glorious memory, the same unquestionable law and the same pride of literature'.[88] This was the utopian state, quite different from the unwanted and industrial influence of the British state in Ireland.

Similar arguments are found in other popular writing about the past.[89] J. E. McKenna's volume, *Irish Art*, provided a romanticised nationalist version of Irish history. He referred to the 'dreamy, Celtic mind' which, in the Early Christian Period, produced the Book of Kells, reliquaries such as the Cross of Cong and precious artefacts like the Ardagh Chalice and the 'Tara' Brooch, some of which could be seen in 'wonderful variety' in the 'National Museum Dublin'. Again, the Irish nation was presented as one of the superior nations of Europe and the material remains provided the evidence. McKenna wrote:

> The Psalter of Columbcill [*sic*], the Book of Dimma and the Book of Armagh are monuments of which all Irishmen may be justly proud, and may excitingly produce as evidence of the civilisation and literary requirements of their country, produced when other nations of Europe, if not in utter ignorance and barbarism, were in their primers, in their hornbooks.[90]

The antiquarian Francis Joseph Bigger told his readers that 'the ruins of Ireland are her proudest monuments. ... The shrines and gospels, the reliquaries and missals, the crosses and bells that are all still existent ... attest beyond any dispute that Irish art workers held a pre-eminent place.' This essay by Bigger was published with a collection of thirty-four essays by different authors in a volume titled *The Glories of Ireland*, produced for the Irish-American market. A number of the other essays were also on antiquarian subjects, such as: 'The Islands of Saints and Scholars', 'Irish Metal Work' and 'Irish Manuscripts'. Other essays included that on 'Irish Nationality', 'The Sorrows of Ireland' and 'Irish Wit and Humor'.[91]

In his essay Bigger named a select number of antiquities: the Book of Kells, the Book of Durrow, the Cross of Cong, the Shrine of St Patrick's Bell, the 'Tara' Brooch and the Ardagh Chalice. No other antiquities are mentioned, as those named were firmly established as the symbols of the Irish nation. However, the entire landscape of Ireland was adopted into his project. 'Every portion of Ireland,' he claimed, 'has its ruins. Earthworks, stone forts, prehistoric monuments, circular stone huts, early churches, abbeys, crosses, round towers, castles of every size and shape are to be found in every county, some one in every parish, all over Ireland.'[92]

Robert Lynd writing in 1936 repeated many of the interpretations presented in these earlier texts. In his volume *Ireland a Nation*, he made almost identical statements to those presented by Green in *Irish Nationality*. This is interesting in itself as it reveals that the same interpretation of the past was being continually recycled in nationalist writing. The same arguments, the same language and the same evidence recur. Clearly new research was unnecessary – nationalist sentiment had found its niche. In a similar fashion, therefore, Lynd described pre-invasion Ireland as a 'luxurious civilisation' evident in the wealth of her material remains. Ireland was also depicted as superior to Britain. In a passage particularly reminiscent of Green, Lynd wrote that 'indeed by the fact that, while the weight of the gold ornaments in the British Museum collected from Great Britain is about 50 ounces, the weight of a similar Irish collection in the National Museum in Dublin is about 570 ounces'. In common with earlier writers, Lynd also presented Ireland as 'a land of schools lay and monastic', arguing that Ireland's 'schools and scholars were celebrated throughout Europe'. Therefore, Lynd argued, the Irish should be respected as the 'makers of Europe'. As before, the Book of Kells, the Ardagh Chalice, the Cross of Cong, the 'Tara' Brooch and the legends of Cuchulainn were all presented as evidence of a 'richly imaginative national life'. The prosperity of the Irish past was interpreted as greater than that of her neighbour and Irish tradition was deemed superior in its purity because it was able to resist a Roman invasion. Again, the cultural and artistic productivity of the Irish nation was presented as having been thwarted by the Norman invasion.

Pursuing this, Lynd argued that 'it is now impossible to say along what lines this most promising Irish civilisation might have developed if it had not been interfered with by invaders'. Most importantly, self-government would result in returning to the ideal of Gaelic rule, when 'Ireland was a nation with one code of laws, one language and one King'.[93] All of this sentiment, and the main political themes, are well summed up in the following extract, written for the readers of the *Irish Nation*:

> The history of Ireland shows that the Gael possessed, as well as valour, other greater qualities. The brains to evolve elaborate laws and establish great schools; the piety and courage to Christianise parts of pagan England and the continent; the ear to make entrancing music; the artistic mind that produced workers on vellum and workers in metal, the beauty and perfection of whose works can be seen in the National Museum today; the imagination to create a marvellous Heroic literature. We walk down the steps of the centuries and salute great figures as we pass. We salute the generations.[94]

Such sentiment involved the Dublin museum and its contents in a symbolic sense. By the time of the production of this postcard (Figure 7) (*c.*1910) the harp and shamrocks were firmly established as popular symbols. Presented in this way the buildings are drawn into nationalist iconography.

The many popular nationalist histories of early Ireland written at the turn of the century had one unavoidable message: by the way of self-government Ireland would be returning to its natural state, to that which existed in antiquity. This is made clear in Lynd's extract above that has all of the characteristics of nationalist prose. In it the ancient people of Ireland were presented as heroic, skilful and pious. Importantly, their archaeological remains, as evident in the museum, were deserving of respect. Clearly, political activists in Ireland used archaeology to legitimise their programme. In addition, as a partial result of this link, a certain interpretation of the early history of Ireland became popular, may be labelled as nationalist and was, therefore, imbued with political consciousness. Against the political background of the nineteenth and early twentieth centuries, Irish archaeology was consistently used to provide the material evidence of an ideal past that, through political change, could be resurrected. References to antiquity, archaeological sites, monuments and artefacts, as well as to museum collections, were used to reinforce

Figure 7: Postcard labelled the National Museum of Science Art, Dublin. The photograph is of the National Library, which is a mirror-image of the museum. This may have been a simple mistake on behalf of the photographer, but it is interesting for the purposes of this study. It illustrates the point that the accuracy of the image was not important – what was of value was the notion of the Irish nation symbolised by the harp, shamrocks and the (museum) buildings which was evoked by the combination.

and legitimise the need for political change and to create a sense of an organic and emergent community bound to the past. In this context archaeology was of a political-rhetorical value. A single object or monument was used to 'speak' many words, and the material remains were taken to symbolise the richness of antiquity that had been passed down to the present. One may argue that these objects had their own cultural life that varied with the contemporary context.

Reflecting on the links between archaeology and politics, Robert Macalister declared in the foreword of *The Archaeology of Ireland* that 'the Archaeology of Ireland is worthy of a better fate than to become the playground of the Politician'. In this volume, Macalister declared his wish to dispel the 'myth of Early Irish civilisation' that he believed to be untenable. Other key myths were also described as 'no less pernicious', such as the 'legend of a primitive civilization' that presented Ireland as 'the most ancient nation in Europe'. In a timely remark, given the events in Germany, Macalister announced that 'in Ancient Europe there were no "nations"' – in his mind 'patriotism which closed its mind to the facts is a false patriotism'.[95] Macalister's attempt to revise 'nationalist' interpretations of Irish antiquity must also be seen as political judgement. One needs only to refer to the current revisionist debate in Irish historiography to illustrate the point that there seems to be no way of excluding the continuing impact of politics on historical interpretation. For instance, the concept of national ownership of the past, which appears so natural today, developed in association with the rise of nationalism. The following chapters trace this growing sense of the past as having a national purpose amongst those active in antiquarian and museum circles. It illustrates the mutual influence and dependency of *both* spheres in seeking legitimisation for their endeavours.

CHAPTER FOUR

Antiquarians and their Political Role in Nineteenth-Century Ireland

THE INFLUENCE OF politics on archaeology and museums was both internal and external. Antiquarian activity in nineteenth-century Ireland (as expressed in societies, their publications and research) was not immune to the impact of nationalism. In addition, the political process did not passively influence antiquarians. Many were aware that their researches were instrumental in feeding nationalist interests by contributing to a sense of the historic nature of the nation and providing its material representation.

Evidence of how archaeology and the creation of collections linked to the outside political field can be found in various sources, such as addresses made by members of the Royal Irish Academy, publications dealing with archaeological sites or artefacts and public statements made by antiquarians. It is important, however, to consider precisely how language was used in these sources and compare this with how it was employed in the overtly political sources cited in the previous chapter. The antiquarian world of the Royal Irish Academy provided a sharp contrast to the cultural activities of political activists such as Thomas Davis, Arthur Griffith or Patrick Pearse. For the latter the political goal of Home Rule, or the creation of an Irish Republic, was the political ideal. Their use of the terminology of nationalism, such as 'the historic nation' or the 'national people', had this intent. Antiquarians made similar allusions to the 'nation', but one must consider whether their references to archaeology as a reflection of 'nationality' incorporated a different understanding of the word 'nation'. E. J. Hobsbawm has argued that the words 'nation' and 'patria' are used with significantly different purpose today compared with what they would have meant in the eighteenth and early nineteenth centuries. In former times they indicated place and home while more recently they have become linked with ideas of the state or government.[1]

However, as the nation-building aspirations of the mid-nineteenth century began to take hold across Europe, the term 'nation' may well have begun to take on greater political meaning.

Rather than being able to generalise about how 'nation' was used, one must accept that different groups would have had their own understanding of the word. Antiquarians in Victorian England were fascinated with the past and their interest has been described as deriving from a 'strong sense of national duty and national pride, revelling in the bygone feats of their country'.[2] One may argue, therefore, that similar references to the nation made by antiquarians and political activists in the Irish context may not necessarily carry matching political meaning. Joep Leerssen has argued that 'the pursuit of cultural projects like the cultivation of the Irish past or of the Irish language – something which is so very obviously political to the latter-day observer – was considered apolitical at the time'.[3] However, while recognising variations in etymology, it is important also to acknowledge that there was a great deal of awareness about the political role of the past. Because of the political tensions, Irish antiquarian activity took place in a far more sensitive political context than for example in England. One should not doubt, therefore, that the leading Irish antiquarians were aware of the possible political implications of their activity. However, it is important to distinguish between antiquarian interest and the regard shown for Irish archaeology by those interested in the creation of an independent Ireland.

NINETEENTH-CENTURY ARCHAEOLOGY AS A FUNCTION OF THE POLITICAL CONTEXT

In parallel with the changes in political life in nineteenth-century Ireland, the management of Irish archaeology altered considerably between the beginning and the close of the century. In Ireland, as in Britain, antiquarian institutions of the late eighteenth and early nineteenth centuries, such as the Dublin Society (1731), the Royal Society of Arts in London (1758), and the Royal Society of Edinburgh (1783), were primarily the domain of the privileged.[4] In the Irish case this interest was at the core of both eighteenth-century patriotism and nineteenth-century nationalism. These two ideologies, though using similar tools, were fundamentally different. Patriotism was the politics of the Anglo-Irish. It was about the affirmation of their distinct place in British politics and their right to the same political power and privileges within Ireland as policy makers had within Britain. It was about asserting the place of Ireland within the British political system, not outside it, which was the later goal of nineteenth-century nationalism. Many of the Anglo-Irish, including those active in the politics of patriotism, had their own cabinets of Irish curiosities and were instrumental in the establishment of antiquarian societies. Their influence laid the foundation for the practice of archaeology in the nineteenth century. In the eighteenth century the activity of Irish antiquarians was brought together within 'philosophical' societies. A number of societies were formed, many of which only survived for a few decades. One of the earliest was the Physico-Historical Society of Ireland (1744–52). It was typical of its time in that it formed as a club for 'Lords and Gentlemen'. It met in the committee room of the Irish House of Lords and its purpose was to be 'a voluntary society for promoting an inquiry into the ancient and present state of the several counties of Ireland'.[5]

Two societies that came from similar origins and have survived to the present day are the Royal Dublin Society and the Royal Irish Academy. Both expressed an early interest in the investigation of Ireland's history. The former was established by a group of men who met in Trinity College Dublin to discuss the formation of a society which would develop Irish husbandry and other 'useful arts ... for the benefit of the country'.[6] In 1772 the Society formed a committee for enquiry into 'the antient [*sic*] state of arts literature and antiquities', the function of which was the promotion of science, literature and antiquities. At the end of the same decade another 'select society of gentlemen', formed for the investigation of the antiquities of Ireland, emerged as the Irish Academy (later to become Royal) and shared many of its members with the Dublin Society.[7] The Academy, however, went on to lead antiquarian research in Ireland and to found a significant archaeological collection, which was later housed in the National Museum.

Both of these institutions, the Royal Dublin Society and the Royal Irish Academy, were functions of the enlightenment thinking of eighteenth-century Europe. Enlightenment philosophy materialised in Ireland as a sense of 'disinterested service to one's country' with the purpose of being 'the good citizen, the loyal, responsible member of society'.[8] This social agenda is well demonstrated in the records of the archaeological associations and the writings of the antiquarians.

The purpose of the Academy was, for instance, defined according to such an ideal. It was stated as being to 'civilize the manners and refine the taste' of the people through 'the elegance of polite literature'.[9] The political power of the Anglo-Irish in Ireland was at its height during the period of legislative independence gained in 1782 until its demise as a result of the Act of Union in 1800. The development of societies and their collections at this time was a reflection of the confidence of this class. Later, with the Act of Union and the administration of Ireland then coming from Westminster, it was important for the private societies in Dublin to feel that they were still leaders of Ireland's cultural and industrial development. Dublin may have lost its own parliament, but its antiquities collections could still hold a prominent and respected place within Europe. The Royal Irish Academy and the Royal Dublin Society, therefore, went on to develop their own collections and declare them as having European status.[10]

The management of the past within the early societies and their collections was largely the reserve of the privileged who had the income and the leisure time to enjoy such pastimes. What inspired the interest of this class in the Irish past? Was the Irish past, enclosed in glass cabinets in their homes, a symbol of control over the past and consequently over the present? One can argue that the relationship the Anglo-Irish had with the past was much more complex than a representation of their power; the Anglo-Irish needed a sense of the past to naturalise their position in Ireland. John Hutchinson gives the example of Samuel Ferguson for whom the past, and the Celtic revival, 'provided a means by which to attach the Ascendancy firmly to the Irish soils as leaders'.[11] Certainly this seems to be the case if one considers Sir William Rowan Hamilton's Presidential Address delivered to the Royal Irish Academy in 1838. Hamilton claimed that 'societies such as ours if they do their duty well and fulfil ... their own high purpose [will] become hereditary counsellors of crown and nation'.[12] Indeed, Samuel Ferguson in his own Presidential Address, delivered almost fifty years later, claimed that the Anglo-Irish had now earned their place in Ireland. Employing an inventive method more characteristic of nationalism, he provided the Anglo-Irish with an ancient lineage by linking them with the mythical settlers in Ireland of *c.*1300 BC. Ferguson declared that they were now:

At least as far as birth on Irish soil goes, most of them by many centuries more Irish than were the great-grandsons of Milesius ... all of them have been here long enough to take root, and they have no intention of going out. They have imbibed ... an Irishism of their own ...The works of the Academy can testify to what they have been able to achieve in that direction during nearly a century of patriotic endeavour.[13]

Though these individuals may well have been confident of their place in Ireland, there is a sense from the Presidential Addresses that the members were earning their place and position in Ireland through the creation and dissemination of knowledge about antiquity. One can argue, therefore, that the Anglo-Irish needed to share in Ireland's heritage and that the material remains created a sense of Irishness for a people insecure about their national identity. F. S. L. Lyons, for instance, has referred to the 'schizophrenia' which was the 'natural condition' of the Anglo-Irish, since they belonged neither to Irish nor English society.[14] L. M. Cullen considered them as having a 'crisis of identity',[15] and George Boyce wrote of the Anglo-Irish as being conscious of themselves as a 'middle nation'.[16] As observed by Joep Leerssen, 'Anglo-Ireland decided to write itself out of its English-oriented ancestral history and instead to trace its cultural origins in a nationally Irish, and therefore aboriginally Gaelic, frame of reference'.[17] So, rather than saying that the Anglo-Irish were attempting to own and control the past, we could say that the past 'owned' them.

Though the institutionalisation of the past was largely the domain of the Anglo-Irish, they did not have a monopoly on interest in archaeology. As noted by Charles O'Conor, 'there were undoubtedly many Irishmen in that century who manifested a genuine interest in Irish antiquities, but the political and social disorders of the country placed them at a great disadvantage'.[18] After the passing of Catholic Emancipation Act of 1829, and the establishment of the National Education Board in 1831, there was a potential for political and social change – Catholics in Ireland had more rights and opportunities. Through the activity of Daniel O'Connell and his 'monster meetings', often held at archaeological sites, and Thomas Davis writing in the *Nation*, the profile of Ireland's early history was raised and brought into the lives of those who previously would not have engaged with the past in this way. In addition, access to the past in the form of societies and availability of reading material on historical subjects began to broaden. As a result, by the end of the nineteenth century 'the past' was less of a private concern and had entered into the public sphere. An interesting example of this shift is demonstrated by the history of the Irish Archaeological Society, which was formed in 1841 by members of the Royal Irish Academy for the purpose of collecting and publishing Irish manuscripts.[19] The society was established predominantly as an Ascendancy institution and this is reflected in its membership. The first report of the society recorded its members as being the Archbishop of Canterbury, the Lord Primate of Ireland, three dukes, five marquises, thirteen earls, ten viscounts, five lord bishops and six lords. In addition, those voted in after the first meeting were mostly members of the Royal Irish Academy, Fellows of Trinity College Dublin, members of parliament and Church clergy.[20] However, also instrumental in the formation of the Irish Archaeological Society were the Gaelic scholars John O'Donovan and Eugene O'Curry. Their involvement represents a form of collaboration between the 'native' and 'Ascendancy' traditions at an institutional level, as was also evident in the Ordnance Survey work of the 1820s and 1830s. Greater social mixing occurred when the Archaeological Society later merged with the more pro-Catholic Celtic Society, which had been founded in 1845 and included nationalist politicians such as Daniel O'Connell and William Smith O'Brien in its membership.[21] This created the Irish Archaeological and Celtic Society,[22] thus lessening, but by no means eliminating, the Ascendancy identity of the institution.

Though greater opportunities were available as a result of Catholic emancipation and the establishment of national education, widespread knowledge of the past developed most successfully as a result of the increased popularity of the printed word. Newspaper publishing increased in the mid-nineteenth century, partly as a result of the success of the medium at spreading the doctrine of Irish nationalism. What is interesting is that archaeological topics featured highly in this political context. In addition to the official organs of political groups, many other newspapers of an antiquarian, historical or literary nature appeared, such as the *Dublin Literary Gazette* or *Weekly Chronicle of Criticism, Belles Lettres and Fine Arts* (1830-1831). Within this period, the *Dublin Literary Gazette* was renamed the *Irish National Magazine* in order to 'represent the country's new prevailing mood', suggesting 'a possibility of a national unity, above polemics and religious bickering'. Many of these newspapers, such as the *Dublin Penny Journal* (1831–37) or the *Irish Penny Journal* (1840–41), became popular, aided by their low price. Journals for the pockets of the intelligentsia were also established, such as the *Dublin University Magazine* (1833–77) founded by a group of 'very Conservative and very Protestant' members of Trinity College Dublin. A new voice was later heard in the establishment of the pro-nationalist *Dublin Review* (1836–1969, in three series), which set upholding Irish Catholicism as its task. In addition to these, journals also formed which specialised in arts, such as the *Amateur* (1849–50) and the *Irish Quarterly Review* (1851–60). The stated purpose of many of these journals was to foster nationality and they did so through reference to Irish culture and, though many claimed to be apolitical, few escaped the 'purple prose of polemics'.[23] The success of these popular journals can be taken as a reflection of the growing awareness of nationalism generated by the activity of the Young Irelanders and the National Repeal Association.

The popular journals, with their many articles of a historical nature, would have increased the profile of archaeology and antiquarian activity. The most influential was the *Dublin Penny Journal* which was headed by two members of the Royal Irish Academy, Caesar Otway and George Petrie.[24] The paper pledged to cover the topics of 'history, biography, poetry, antiquities, natural history, legends and traditions of the country'.[25] It embraced all social, financial and geographical groups[26] with the purpose to animate 'minds zealous for the moral improvement of the country'.[27] The paper aimed towards 'the exclusion of politics and sectarian religion, and the general desire to be instructive, the *Penny Journal* start[s] on new and exclusively national ground, and with national as well as useful objects in view'.[28] To this end almost every number of the journal contained an article on a historical or archaeological subject, as well as occasional series. The second number of the *Dublin Penny Journal* published an illustrated article on 'national emblems', which included the round tower, the ancient Irish crown and the harp.[29] The stated aim of the journal, to 'excite the attention and obtain the good will not only of the humbler classes ... but also of the higher and better informed who had generally a deep-rooted prejudice against what was home-bred and national',[30] would have been well served by the illustration below. The idea of depicting archaeology as a national symbol was part of the same revivalist interest, that resulted in a similar iconography being used in both the popular and the political context. The illustration of 'national emblems' in the *Dublin Penny Journal* (see Figure 8) is similar in theme and style to that later illustrated on the membership card of the National Repeal Association.

Figure 8: 'National Emblems' illustrated in the *Dublin Penny Journal*, 7 July 1832.

In addition to the generation of interest through newspapers, the establishment of the Ordnance Survey of Ireland in the early nineteenth-century was signicant both for the academic development of archaeology and the popularisation of the subject. The history of the Survey is an example of the importance placed on archaeological research in the nineteenth century and the political tensions that may arise from it. The Survey was a British institution established in Ireland in 1823 and funded by the British Treasury with the aim to provide a set of local and general maps on which to base land valuation.[31] Because of this administrative purpose, the

Survey has been interpreted as an attempt to secure British dominance in Ireland by controlling knowledge of the landscape through maps.[32] However, the activity of the Survey was beneficial for Irish archaeology. In the first place, it brought together individuals from diverse backgrounds. It was directed by British Army officers, primarily Colonel Colby and Lieutenant Larcom. It involved members of the Protestant Anglo-Irish class, such as William Wakeman, together with Catholic Gaelic scholars, the chief of whom were John O'Donovan and Eugene O'Curry. In addition, George Petrie was involved as head of the historical division. The Survey is best remembered for the production, in addition to the maps, of extensive 'memoirs' of Irish parishes. The memoirs were to be composed of information on the nature of the buildings and antiquities of the area as well as population and employment data, the guidelines for which were outlined in a thirty-seven page pamphlet issued by Larcom. The information was so extensive that the first, and only, memoir published, of Templemore Parish in County Londonderry, ran to three hundred and fifty octavo pages.[33]

The production of the memoirs led to political upset. In the first place, the area that was the subject of the first publication was 'a notorious flashpoint' in Irish political history. Because of the sensitive nature of the history of the area, some objected to the content of the memoirs: 'for readers of a strongly Protestant and loyalist persuasion, it must have been irritating to find the charge of fanaticism levelled against Scottish settlers in northern Ireland and to see it suggested that cultural life in Derry had deteriorated as a result of the union'. Discord also arose because of other factors. In 1842 objections to the political sympathies of those carrying out the historical research were brought to the attention of the British Government in an anonymous letter signed by 'a Protestant conservative'. The letter stated that most of the Survey topographical staff were 'Catholics and opponents of the government' who were collecting and spreading 'historical' information in order to challenge the rule of the government. Referring to the members of the historical division of the Survey, the letter stated:

> Their bigotry and politics ... are carried to all parts of the kingdom, where we find ... persons sent from this office engaged in taking down the pedigree of some beggar or tinker and establishing him the lineal descendent of some Irish chief, whose ancient estate they most

carefully mark out by boundaries, and they have actually in several instances as I have seen by their letters, nominated some desperate characters as the rightful heirs to these territories.[34]

It is not clear whether this was actually the case or not, nor whether this opinion was widely held. However, what the letter does reveal is the contentious nature of historical investigation. The case led to the establishment of a Parliamentary Commission to consider the matter of the Ordnance Survey memoirs, held in July 1843.[35] Its aim was to report on the history of the memoirs and recommend on the wisdom of their continuation, considering the fact that no investigation of that nature was being undertaken in Britain. Two issues were revealed as important to the British establishment. The first of these was the need for considering the reasons for writing Irish history. The second was whether the revival of knowledge about the past could foster republican feeling. Speaking for the continuation of the memoirs both George Petrie and the Reverend James Todd, representing the Royal Irish Academy, emphasised their value, both in social and political terms. For Todd it was a matter of enabling the writing of a 'correct' history. He stressed two key points: the malleability of the past and the negative impact of dubious and potentially dangerous interpretations of history on relations between Britain and Ireland. He argued:

> I do not believe that any harm can ever result from the publication of truth on any subject, least of all on such a subject as the history of a nation: but besides this, nothing can be more mischievous than the present vague state of our knowledge of ancient Ireland. The political events of former times may now be quoted by any party and turned with equal facility to their purposes, while from the general ignorance that prevails of the real character of those events, the public are unable to detect the fallacy. The popular notions of ancient grandeur and independence can now be propped up with almost any evidence, but if the original sources of history were better understood, and correct views properly disseminated, it would gradually come to be as impossible to make use of the ancient Irish history for the propagation of political animosity as it is to make use of English history, which is only less dangerous because it is better known.[36]

Indeed, those of different political opinions were united over the issue of the Survey. The *Nation* newspaper had already declared its support for the Survey.[37] To Thomas Davis its activity was a reflection of his political ideal, an example of people from diverse backgrounds brought together for the same purpose. The unionist paper the *Dublin University Magazine*, in an article that may have been written by Samuel Ferguson,[38] described the Survey as being of 'great national importance' and evidence of 'pure patriotism'. In the style of Davis, the magazine continued: 'is it not a delightful spectacle, now perhaps for the first time exhibited in Ireland, to see Irishmen of all parties and creeds, the most illustrious in rank and the most eminent in talents, combining zealously for an object of good to their common country?'[39] Despite this support for the Ordnance Survey memoirs, the provision of Treasury funds for their production ended in 1844. On the one hand this was presented as a result of the high cost of maintaining the memoirs. This reasoning was based, according to the antiquarian William Wakeman, on 'a miserable system of false economy'.[40] On the other, ending the memoirs was interpreted at the time as an indication that the British administration was no longer oblivious to the nationalist power of historical scholarship that gathered information on the glories of Irish civilisation.[41] Later, some nationalists regarded the 'suppression' as 'a deliberate act of cultural warfare'.[42]

Though the work of the memoirs was brought to an end, its legacy continued because a seed of romantic and patriotic engagement with the past had been germinated in the minds of the scholars. This is evident in the letters of John O'Donovan written during the Survey in which he described the work as 'romantic mediations among ruins'.[43] Likewise, William Wakeman wrote of the surveyors as living in 'such an atmosphere of antiquarianism, that a thousand years ago seemed as familiar to us as the time when we first donned breeches'.[44] The most important implication of the memoirs was, however, that it provided George Petrie with the material that formed the foundations of his influential essays on the antiquities of Tara Hill and the ecclesiastical architecture of Ireland.[45] This is significant because Petrie's work went on to gain a high public profile and consequently raised awareness of Irish archaeology (as evident in the many references made to Petrie's work in political addresses). The establishment of the Ordnance Survey, the products of its research, as well as the reactions to it, contributed to the development of popular appreciation of Irish prehistory and was 'an important ingredient in the strong national awareness of the 1840s and 1850s'.[46] As pointed out by William Thompson, thenceforth 'an *idea* of history [began] to emerge in Irish archaeology'.[47]

A further significant development, which also raised the public profile of Irish archaeology and the notion of exhibiting to the public, was the development of industrial exhibitions. Following on the Great Exhibition in London in 1851, an exhibition was held in Cork in 1852, and in 1853 an international exhibition was held in Dublin organised by the Royal Dublin Society.[48] The 1853 exhibition was held in an 'Exhibition Palace' erected on Leinster House lawn in the heart of Dublin. Though it was supposedly held for the purposes of encouraging Irish industry, because of a lack of industrial exhibits the collections of fine art, sculpture and oriental art came to dominate.[49] The hall of Irish antiquities, loaned from the Royal Irish Academy, was amongst the more prominent exhibits. *The Times* doubted the relevance of antiquities to an industrial exhibition. In an article in the paper the collection was described as 'a very curious and highly interesting but extremely useless collection of Irish antiquities', and the article continued with the question: 'how is it that when Mr Dargan offers them [the committee in charge] a building in which to collect everything that may stimulate the industry and develop the resources of the country, the committee appropriates a very considerable portion of it to such objects as the harp of Brian Boroihme and Rorie More's horn?'[50] However, the collection was, according to the *Atheneum*, useful for encouraging the art industry[51] and the exhibition handbook described it as 'altogether most interesting, a monument to the glories of ancient Ireland'.[52] This suggests that *The Times* did not appreciate the appeal and value of Irish antiquities and the importance of those objects that were emerging as symbols of the Irish nation. Since the exhibition was taking place in the post-Famine decade, the glories of Ireland's ancient history, captured in the material remains, could only improve confidence in Ireland. The provision of an antiquities collection for public viewing was also entirely in keeping with the cultural revival of the time. In many ways, it seems the power of cultural nationalism, which raised the appeal of antiquities, was of equal if not greater importance than industrial interests.

The success of the various Irish exhibitions was also influential in creating interest in the idea of a permanent public museum in Dublin. In order to make further use of the building erected for the exhibition, a local committee was founded for the establishment of a 'Royal Irish Institute of Science and Art'. It was proposed that this would be an educational institution, for the benefit of industry in

Ireland, which would include a permanent exhibition of Irish products and also a national museum, managed by a 'board of resident gentleman' possibly as a 'Royal Commission of Irishmen'.[53] Provision for science and art instruction lay at that time with private bodies such as the Royal Irish Academy and the Royal Dublin Society, both of which made annual reports to the London-based Department of Science and Art. In the 1860s the Department of Science and Art in London held a number of commissions to accumulate information on the provision of science and art instruction by the Irish institutions receiving government aid. The members resolved that science and art instruction in Ireland should be provided by a public institution in the style of the Science and Art Museum in South Kensington, rather than predominantly by private societies in Dublin. The new institution was formed with the passing of the Science and Art Museum Act 1877 and was established to house the collections of the various Dublin museums, including the antiquities collections of the Royal Irish Academy, the industrial collections of the Museum of Irish Industry and those of the Natural History Museum. The first stone of the Dublin Museum of Science and Art was put in place in 1885, and the building was opened to the public in 1890. The history of this development is discussed in detail in Chapter Five, but the main issue from this period is relevant to this section. The foundation of the Dublin museum was very much a product of the political context. Its very establishment was an opportunity for London to exercise its influence, while later it was a place for those in Ireland to implement their own authority and to affirm an Irish national identity.

The history of the practice of archaeology in Ireland in the nineteenth century, as expressed in societies, publications and management, is one of a transfer from the private to the public. In other words, there was a move from the learned academy to the popular society, from the pastime of the Protestant gentleman to an universal interest. A consideration of this transfer provides some of the material for a small volume by Reverend Patrick MacSweeney of St Patrick's College, Maynooth. Published in 1913 in the sensitive political atmosphere of the third Home Rule Bill, MacSweeney's essay provides a history of the activity and discipline of Irish archaeology from the 1830s to the 1860s, tinged with a nationalist hue. MacSweeney may have had to credit the beginning of interest in Irish archaeology with the Anglo-Irish, but he went on to provide the reader with a scathing interpretation of these eighteenth-century origins. Of the Anglo-Irish interest in Irish antiquity he wrote: 'the Celt began to win sympathisers amidst the families of the Pale ... The stuccoed mansions of a cultured tyranny — cemented, as they were, with the sweat and blood of a Celtic people — were to become the homes of the priceless manuscript collections of the Royal Irish Academy.' In the foreword, MacSweeney introduced the idea of three 'battles', each of which he said was fought in the nineteenth century and one of which involved archaeology. Firstly, there was the battle for the freedom of religion, secondly that for the ownership of the land and thirdly the battle for free access to intellectual life. According to MacSweeney, research into Ireland's early history, as well as the popularisation of the findings, contributed to the third battle. MacSweeney argued that those archaeologists who contributed to this endeavour deserved the title of 'national heroes'. He claimed that such individuals:

> Loved Ireland and the Irish people with a lasting love. They cherished the Past of Ireland, they reverenced it, and they believed in it. They determined that the Ireland of the Future should be bound to the Ireland of the Past by the strong links of knowledge and of Love. They forged these links in the white-heat of patriotic research. They were, in every true sense of the word, Nation-builders; and we should not forget them.[54]

George Petrie, John O'Donovan and Eugene O'Curry, the three people principally involved with the Historical Section of the Ordnance Survey were named as 'nation-builders'. Roy Foster has claimed that none of the three would have recognised themselves under such a title. Whilst this may have been the case, their writing on antiquarian subjects reveals a commitment to a sense of the nation (see for instance Petrie's work in the *Dublin Penny Journal* and the *Irish Penny Journal*). Nevertheless, as Foster also argued, this title of nation-builder represents an important retrospective opinion that linked antiquarian activity with political aspirations.[55] The concept of the hero, referred to by MacSweeney, is a timeless and important idea in nationalist writing, and in giving these individuals such status MacSweeney was paying them the highest compliment. MacSweeney's essay also reveals that no form of engagement with the past, whether it is writing about antiquity or the history of archaeology, can escape the political context.

GEORGE PETRIE AND THE POPULARISATION OF ARCHAEOLOGY

George Petrie contributed to all forms of 'institutionalisation' of the past. Petrie's father, a Scot who settled in Dublin, was a portrait painter and he introduced Petrie to the Royal Dublin Society's School of Art. Petrie began his career as a landscape artist and his interest in painting archaeological sites brought him to the Royal Irish Academy. He became a member of the Academy in 1828. In 1829 he took charge of the antiquities collection and set about arranging and expanding it. He was also a member of the Royal Hibernian Academy and was appointed head of the Placenames and Antiquities Division of the Irish Ordnance Survey in 1833. As well as being active .in the Dublin societies, he researched and wrote extensively about the archaeology of Ireland. He read twenty-eight papers to the Royal Irish Academy, contributed extensively to the popular journals of the 1830s and 1840s and illustrated many books.[56] With all this in mind, he has warranted the title 'the pope of Irish archaeology'[57] and the archaeologist Westropp named him the 'High King'.[58]

Petrie was also devoted to other matters of Irish culture, most famously music, numismatics, manuscript collecting and folklore.[59] His commitment to the collection of Irish music is evident in his declaration: 'Dear music of my country! I cannot speak of it without using the language of enthusiasm; I cannot think of it without feeling my heart glow with tenderness and pride!' His dedication to archaeology comes across in his disappointment in not being the one to complete the catalogue for the Royal Irish Academy collection: 'for a long period of my life it was my most anxious and cherished desire to undertake it'. It is also evident in the immense joy that he gained from archaeological trips with the Ordnance Survey which is recorded in his letters. In one such he described a region of Ireland, West Connaught, as a 'little region of fairy land'. Furthermore, the women of the region were deemed 'exquisitely beautiful and simple — exactly as if they had stepped out of the pictures of Raphael or Murillo'. Finally, in reviewing his own life, Petrie stated: 'my days have been passed in the quiet enjoyment of nature's beauties, in the cultivation of a taste for the fine arts, and occasional excursions into the distant regions of antiquity'.[60]

Petrie produced two major works, both of which considered sites that were emerging at the time as symbols of the Irish nation. These works were his essay 'On the History and Antiquities of Tara Hill' published in 1837 in the *Transactions of the Royal Irish Academy*, and the later essay on round towers published in 1845 under the title *The Ecclesiastical Architecture of Ireland*. Petrie's research technique reflected the beginning of the development of a logical and scientific method in Irish archaeology and a decline in unsubstantiated and fanciful theories that had been characteristic of late eighteenth-century and early nineteenth-century archaeological interpretation.[61] To this end he was successful: 'his clear-minded approach and his respect for Baconian logic helped to bring Irish antiquarianism from the extremes of the romantic phase into harmony with the more logical and scientific spirit of the nineteenth-century science'.[62] This can be demonstrated by the shift from the illogical functions formerly attributed to round towers, such as 'temples for the holy fire', 'astronomical gnomons' or 'phallic temples', to Petrie's reasoned theories which were based on archaeological evidence and the use of manuscript records.[63] This was first demonstrated in his Academy prize essay of 1832 where he suggested that the towers were of Christian and ecclesiastical origin, were erected between the fifth and thirteenth centuries, were used as belfries and a place of security, and may have been used as watch-towers.[64] This is the interpretation that is still largely held today.[65] In fact, regarding the extent of his influence, Petrie has been recognised, in retrospect, as having done 'as much in the long run for Ireland's self-respect as Daniel O'Connell'.[66]

At this point, it is interesting to consider how differently Petrie's contribution to archaeology has been interpreted. There are those who considered him simply as a great intellectual leader. This is evident in Petrie's biography, written by his long-time friend William Stokes and published in 1868, as well as the eulogy delivered to the Academy members on his death. The latter, delivered by Charles Graves, included a description of Petrie's legacy: 'his genius and learning had rendered him famous; and the charm of his noble and graceful character had made him equally beloved'. Graves celebrated Petrie's work as an artist, his contribution to the establishment of the Academy museum and his achievements in securing some of the most important objects in its collection, such as the Cross of Cong and the Tara Torques as well as many Irish manuscripts. He also praised Petrie's contribution to scholarship and described his essay on round towers as 'the most remarkable essay that was ever produced by an Irish antiquary'. This, taken with his leadership in the historical division of the Ordnance Survey, made him 'the

informing spirit, the great instructor, of a school of Archaeology'.[67]
Comparing this to the interpretation of Petrie's legacy provided in
the account of his career given by MacSweeney is revealing. Though
MacSweeney considered Petrie as a 'pioneer', he presented
O'Donovan and O'Curry as Petrie's equals, unlike Graves'
description of their relationship. MacSweeney emphasised Petrie's
reliance on O'Donovan's scholarship for translation of Irish
manuscripts which were one of his chief sources for his essay on Tara
Hill which earned him a Royal Irish Academy gold medal. This work
established his reputation, and MacSweeney argued that 'in the
praise which Petrie won, O'Donovan deserve[d] a large share of his
praise'. Such differences in emphasis in the interpretation of Petrie's
career, between MacSweeney and Graves, can be described as a
function of political interests. In the case of MacSweeney it was
imperative for him to place some of the credit for the advances of
Irish archaeology on native scholars; the glory could not all go to
members of an institution with its origins in the 'stuccoed
mansions'.[68] Despite these contrasting views, Petrie is appropriately
considered the 'father of Irish archaeology'. His influence extended
well beyond antiquarian circles. Hutchinson, for instance,
designated Petrie the 'intellectual linchpin' of the Celtic revival of
the mid-nineteenth century, citing his contribution to the
popularisation of archaeology and involvement in many of the
revivalist activities of the time.[69]

Part of what drove Petrie's interest in archaeology was inspired by
distinct social agendas. The first of these was his desire to make the
past and arts popular. To this end, Petrie contributed to the *Dublin
Penny Journal* and was editor of the *Irish Penny Journal*. As President
of the Royal Hibernian Academy he was an advocate of a two-tier
entrance fee into the art galleries, with those on a low income being
offered a reduced fee. He even went so far as to resign his position
when the decision to introduce such a system was overturned.[70]
Petrie's second and most influential interest was in improving the
interpretative process in archaeology. He considered that the bizarre
theories employed by past antiquarians had, under the guise of
'archaeological interpretation', left the past vulnerable to a range of
political abuse. As recorded by his biographer, Petrie believed that
such ill-treatment had been two-fold. On the one hand there had
been the interpretation of the past which 'sp[oke] of the civilisation
of the country, and the antiquity and splendour of its monuments, in
a spirit of exaggeration'. On the other hand was the interpretation

which 'h[e]ld that previously to the twelfth century the Irish people were utterly barbarous, and possessed of little, if any, knowledge of the arts — especially that of building with stone'.[71] The latter view was held by a number of English authors writing about Ireland who used it to legitimise English rule in Ireland.[72]

The archaeologist T. S. J. Westropp, in his Presidential Address to the Royal Society of Antiquaries of Ireland on 25 January 1916, presented a paper on the 'progress of Irish archaeology' that provided an overview of the changing interpretations of Irish archaeology from the seventeenth to the early twentieth century. The 'English school', rooted in thinking established in the seventeenth and eighteenth centuries, employed a 'mendacious and bitter' approach and presented the Irish as 'barbarians'. The contribution of Irish craftspeople in production of early art was dismissed. The opinion presented was that rather than the Irish, 'the Danes made the Irish round towers, forts, towns, ships, trade, Bronze Age ornaments, Hallstatt and La Tène ornaments, weapons, and, indeed, everything else from the stone age to the 10th or 11th century. Everything good that the Danes did not introduce was brought in by the Normans.'[73] In response to this attitude, Irish antiquarians of the time exaggerated the glory of the Irish past, thus providing the rhetoric for the romantic nationalism of years to come. This two-fold approach to Irish antiquity, and its political resonances, has been investigated by Clare O'Halloran[74] who argued 'as part of their defence against such imputations of barbarity, Irish antiquarians ... invented a glorious pre-colonial past which contrasted with their present perceived position as colonial subjects'. Furthermore, 'native Irish writers projected their desire for change on to a mythic past which was sophisticated politically and culturally, rather than primitive; and destroyed by outside aggression and not by its own inadequacies'.[75] Petrie wished to rationalise these interpretations of the past, both of which he believed were damaging. He told his readers that 'prejudices, springing chiefly from political feelings, have equally blinded both sides, and an able and impartial work on the ancient state of Ireland is still a desideratum'.[76]

Of particular interest to this issue of how archaeology has been interpreted is the seven-part essay written by Petrie titled 'Fine Arts: Historic Sketch of the Past and Present State of the Fine Arts in Ireland' published in the *Dublin Penny Journal* (between 8 September 1832 and 4 May 1833). In this passionate essay Petrie revealed his belief that collections of Irish antiquities illustrated not only cultural but also political history. He, like others, drew attention to a decline in the richness of the Irish antiquities between the fourteenth and sixteenth centuries. This, he argued, was a result of 'misrule and civil war [which] debased and demoralised the island from one extremity to the other; and the Fine Arts appear to have been reduced to a lower ebb'. Consequently the archaeology of that period 'presents a melancholy, but interesting commentary on the history of those times'. Petrie claimed that 'the progressive decline of the Fine Arts is equally observable in the productions of the inferior departments of the carver, jeweller, and die-sinker as will appear evident on an examination of the articles of *virtu* preserved in the cabinets of the few collectors of our national antiquities in Dublin'. By this interpretation, Irish antiquities were serving not only as an illustration of the richness of Irish culture before the arrival of the English, but also of the oppressive nature of that rule. In addition, with an example of the prejudice that he claimed to deplore, Petrie argued that the relics of Roman Britain 'are only monuments of barbarism'.[76]

Social comment was not untypical of Petrie, and a similar statement was made when he addressed the Academy about the 'Tara' Brooch shortly after it was discovered. According to Petrie, the 'exquisite delicacy and perfection' of the brooch was a demonstration of the fine craftsmanship of the people of Ireland. He named the brooch as an item that should be obtained for the Royal Irish Academy museum, the 'national depository', with some 'generous and patriotic zeal'. For Petrie the craftsmanship of the brooch would dispel any doubt about the state of development in Ireland in earlier times. Petrie continued by citing a Dr Brinkley who, in reply to one of Petrie's previous addresses, had said to him 'Surely, Sir, you do not mean to tell us that there exists the slightest evidence to prove that the Irish had any acquaintance with the arts of civilized life anterior to the arrival in Ireland of the English?'[77] This address, including the reference to Brinkley, was reprinted in newspapers published in Dublin and the regions, such as *Saunder's Newsletter*, the *Nation*, the *Newry Examiner and Louth Advertiser* and the *Anglo-Celt* of Cavan.[78] Resulting from the circulation of these papers, Petrie's profile was raised and his interpretation of prehistory made more popular. In addition the existence of the 'Tara' Brooch was made public, its excellence established and its national worth secured.

These interpretations of the remains of antiquity, in such a popular context, fed both the nationalist narrative of the time and of generations to come. Petrie must have been aware of the political context of his activity and it is likely that he was sympathetic to the political movements of the time.[79] As well as this, Petrie must have been aware of the public and political acknowledgement his work received. The *Dublin University Magazine* published an essay on Petrie in the 'Our Portrait Gallery' series.[80] Thomas Davis dedicated an essay to the subject of round towers and made reference to Petrie's Royal Irish Academy prize.[81] Petrie's other main work, on Tara Hill, was publicly recognised by both Daniel O'Connell and William O'Brien. In 1886 Douglas Hyde acknowledged his work on Irish manuscripts in an essay entitled 'A Plea for the Irish Language'.[82] In *Hibernia* the work of Petrie was directly linked to some of the most significant political developments of the century. The readers were told that the 'Irish Renaissance' was produced by 'Catholic Emancipation wakened into passionate life by the genius of Young Ireland, and nurtured by the labours of Petrie, O'Donovan and O'Curry'.[83] With the aid of the proponents of nationalism, Petrie was revered and his research was publicised.

It is also interesting that Petrie, who did so much for Irish archaeology in the nineteenth century, should have been regarded appropriate to design the graveside monument for the leading political figure of the time, Daniel O'Connell. O'Connell died in 1847, and in that year the committee in charge of Glasnevin cemetery, where he was to be buried, decided that a memorial should be put in place to honour his contribution to the Irish people. They agreed to approach Petrie to design the monument.[84] The committee requested that the monument should 'express [O'Connell's] character of Irish nationality', that it should be a 'temple-tomb' and include a round tower, cross and church in the style of Early Christian Period architecture in Ireland. Petrie wrote that he considered his involvement in this project of 'national interest' as being a 'great honour'. He assured the committee that his design would serve 'as a fitting and characteristic shrine in which to preserve the mortal remains of the lamented leader, and as a church in which the services of his religion, to his memory, could be worthily performed'.

There is no doubt that Petrie would have been aware of the importance of the round tower for Irish nationalism. However, he seems to have accepted the responsibility of designing the tower for reasons other than feeding the nationalist cause. In his reply to the committee he made it clear that he also considered building the monument as an interesting academic exercise, expressing his hope that the monument would be a scientific reproduction and thus preserve some of the features of one of the most important periods in Irish history. In Petrie's words, the design:

> With its accompanying round tower and cross, ... would present a monument in itself of great historical value, and which could not fail of being interesting to all cultivated minds, as well as to country-loving Irishmen of every class and creed. For, when every vestige shall have disappeared of those ancient ecclesiastical structures, in the possession of which any other nation would feel the highest national pride, but in which we take so little interest, and with a heartless indifference, so generally abandon to the wreck of time and the devastations of ignorance; it would secure to use for those better and more enlightened times to which the good look forward with hope, the forms and features of that simple ancient architecture, and be a typical memorial, to endure for ever, of that pure and ardent Christianity which gave it birth, and which, combined with learning and enthusiasm, for so long a period made Ireland illustrious, and still entitles her to the respect and gratitude of civilized Europe.[85]

This choice of commemorative monument is particularly interesting. Ecclesiastical architecture, most especially the round tower, had come to symbolise nationalist Ireland. Those on the cemetery committee were not interested in the O'Connell monument purely as an imitation of archaeology or in Petrie's involvement solely as an antiquarian. They were interested in what an archaeological monument represented about the Irish nation and what Petrie's involvement would portray. Their real interest became clear when the committee came to erect the monument. They exaggerated the part of the design which was the most potent symbol of Irish nationalism — the round tower (see Figure 9). As a result, the tower became the sole focus of the new design and was built out of proportion compared with Petrie's original 'scientific' plan. The monument towered over Dublin, elevated the memory of O'Connell and became a site of pilgrimage.

By creating a bond with the Early Christian Period, nationalist Ireland was presenting O'Connell's political ideals as historically predetermined. In addition, the 'father of Irish archaeology' was not asked to design the monument because he was regarded as an ideal representative of nationalist Ireland. Rather, George Petrie was chosen because of what his involvement would symbolise. It was Petrie's reputation as a popular antiquarian, an acknowledged expert

Figure 9: O'Connell Monument, Glasnevin Cemetery Dublin.

and the leader of the 'rational' school of archaeology that was of value. Because of Petrie's involvement in the design of the monument, O'Connell's politics were given greater respectability and veracity. The political process, therefore, used the antiquarian and his approach to the past in order to further a nationalist agenda.

Petrie's work may have provided some of the material for Irish nationalism and he himself may have been sympathetic. However, he was 'dedicated wholly to the good life as he saw it, and for him it meant the cultivation of Irish art, Irish history and antiquities, [and] Irish music'.[86] His interest in creating a popular understanding of the past is key to understanding his political role. Petrie did not actively go about attempting to create an independent Ireland through his work. Though he justified his interest in archaeology with a desire to create public interest in the past and all things 'national', he did not aim to inspire the formation of an independent Irish nation. John Hutchinson makes it clear: Petrie was 'a patriotic unionist'.[87] He was, however, first and foremost an antiquarian, though one can suggest that he had an agenda — to popularise archaeology and to write a history of the Irish past free from prejudice. In this sense one could claim that Petrie was a cultural revivalist and because, of the political context, his activity and findings were useful for the nationalist cause.

Therefore, though Petrie's activity was important and useful in the political context, the political significance of his work was the product of forces external to him. Petrie's political aspirations were the creation of mutual respect through culture, rather than anything of a party-political nature. This point also becomes clear in his essay 'Fine Arts', referred to earlier. It was originally published in the *Dublin Literary Gazette* in January 1830, eight months after the passing of the Catholic Emancipation Act.[88] In it Petrie referred to religious prejudice as having a 'blinding' influence and to his pleasure at the fact that 'brighter prospects appear to be at length opening: great changes have at length taken place in the political world'. In his mind, 'the Fine Arts must participate in the blessing'. Furthermore, and significantly, he wrote that since 'our minds are no longer engaged in the harrowing broils of political and religious strife, [we] will seek the soft and humanising enjoyments which the cultivation of the taste will alone impart'.[89] These are hardly the words of someone driven predominantly by political interest. This may be complemented by the description of Petrie given by his admiring biographer Stokes. Petrie was described as having 'a mind uninfluenced by national prejudices' and 'loving his country and feeling for her wrongs, he was a liberal in his politics ... at once a loyalist and a patriot'.[90]

ANTIQUARIANS AND THE NATIONAL ENDEAVOUR

The history of Irish archaeology through the nineteenth century is one of its increasing popularity as a function of the changing socio-political context of the activity. George Petrie was not the only antiquarian who seemed to have been aware of the ongoing political process. One can trace similar references in the published material of other antiquarians of the same period, many of whom were members of the Royal Irish Academy. These individuals were also not immune to the popular effects of nationalism. This is reflected in a number of ways. In the first place, the past in general, as well as some specific periods and material remains, was often labelled as 'national', thus introducing a manufactured concept into archaeological language. Secondly, the past was presented as having a distinct social role, such as reducing prejudice by increasing respect for the achievements of antiquity. These statements reveal that engagement with the past in Ireland involved motives and concepts in addition to the academic desire to accumulate information. Thirdly, one can also argue that the opinions exhibited by the antiquarians in their writing often mirrored the rhetoric of nationalism.

There are many references in the antiquarian sources to a specifically national past. One may consider, for instance, the Presidential Addresses delivered to the Royal Irish Academy. These are important records of the value assigned to archaeology. The first address to be published in the *Proceedings* of the Academy was made by Sir William Rowan Hamilton, the sixth President of the Academy. He insisted that 'the study of Antiquities [should] be regarded in its highest aspect, as the guardian of the purity of history — the history of nations and mankind ... the study is worthy to interest any body of learned men'.[91] This was endorsed by his successor who claimed, that 'the study of Antiquities, ... and especially of the Antiquities of Ireland, — has never been, and, I hope, never will be out of fashion here'.[92] The following President, Reverend T. R. Robinson, referred to the work of the Departments of Literature and Antiquities as 'the main sources of our national influence' and the activity as 'in truest harmony with our duty to our country'.[93] A later President, Reverend James Todd, believed that the study of 'our national antiquities' was important because it 'brings to light the manners and customs of our forefathers; it makes known to us the origin of our noblest institutions; ... it connects, as by a golden chain, the present and the past',[94] noticeably mirroring the language of romantic nationalism. The Presidential Addresses made in the remainder of the century reveal similar sentiment (such as that by Talbot de Malahide delivered in 1866 and Samuel Ferguson in 1882). So do other writings about archaeology produced outside the Academy, for instance an article published in the *Ulster Journal of Archaeology* concerning the interest in antiquities and monuments in the north of Ireland.[95] It was, therefore, quite in keeping for the members of the Academy to consider archaeology as having an important national role, considering themselves as the leaders of that influence.

Archaeologists were also aware of a popularising force which was influencing this interest in the past. Samuel Ferguson, in a letter written in 1847, wrote of 'the spirit of nationality which is touching men's minds, at the present moment, with its mysterious influence'.[96] William Wilde, who is best remembered for compiling the first catalogue to accompany the Royal Irish Academy collection in 1857,[97] made similar remarks. In his volume *The Beauties of the Boyne and the Blackwater*, first published in 1849, the collection of the Royal Irish Academy was described as 'our national collection' and the recent increased antiquarian activity of the Academy as being nationally inspired. A 'zeal and an enthusiasm' and, he argued, 'a nationality, unparalleled in the history of any other Irish institution' had infused amongst the members of the Royal Irish Academy and its Council. The Academy, Wilde commented, had 'amply redeemed its past indifference, by creating a museum of Celtic and early Christian antiquities unexampled in the British Isles'.[98]

Bringing out the same point, William Wakeman in his *Handbook of Irish Antiquities*, published in 1848, stated that Ireland was remarkable for the '*nationality* of its ancient remains'. He added that 'a new impulse, leading to the study of Archaeology in this country, has, for various reasons, steadily prevailed', as evident in the number of publications and interest in archaeology. In the same volume, and in keeping with popular politics, Wakeman also chose to cite an article written by the Young Irelander Thomas Davis and published in the *Nation*. The Davis essay was relevant to him because it mentioned George Petrie's work on round towers.[99] These examples suggest that although the antiquarians' consuming interests were very different from that of the political activists, the attention shown to the past and the motivation regarding the generation of historical knowledge were closely related. The nation is a political concept that implies a distinct national past, culture and identity. The fact that reference to a manufactured concept should be found in the records of an antiquarian society, as well as in the publications dealing first and foremost with the subject of archaeology or early Irish manuscripts, indicates that the idea of the nation had succeeded. In addition, reference to 'the nation' in such contexts would have helped to feed the stereotypes being created by political processes.

Involvement with archaeology could therefore easily adopt a distinct social or political function beyond that of an academic endeavour. Reverend James Todd, when speaking to the members of the Irish Archaeological Society, disclosed his motivation for the collection and publication of Irish manuscripts. He hoped it would:

> Assist in removing the prejudice, or scepticism, that has unreasonably prevailed on the subject of the ancient literature of Ireland; a prejudice which is founded chiefly, if not entirely, upon ignorance, and which cannot better be assailed than by laying before the learned public specimens of what Irish artists in the middle ages really did effect; since it must be evident, that a people, whose literary remains are adorned with such exquisite designs of penmanship could hardly be the rude and ignorant barbarians that it has hitherto been the fashion to present them.[100]

Likewise, Lord Talbot de Malahide in his Presidential Address to the Royal Irish Academy in 1866 referred to the deferring tactics of 'the bitterness of party' which was slowing down the production of an Irish language dictionary. He presented his wish that Ireland should be 'in great measure, free from those jealousies and heartburning which are so fatal to the prosperity of our land'. He appealed, 'Let us continue to present a bright example of what can be done by a cordial union and co-operation of all classes, all parties, and all creeds, to heal the wounds of our beloved country ... Let us not despair of the future of Ireland, but trust, with the blessing of God, to see it a free, happy, and united land'.[101]

Though Talbot de Malahide was preaching a message of patriotism and peace by the way of archaeology, he was also making comment on the political management of Ireland. This is also apparent in the words of another President of the Royal Irish Academy — Petrie's biographer William Stokes. Stokes claimed that the heritage of the past should be preserved as an example of good government. National distinctions, he stated, should be 'precious in the eyes of all men, and England should seek to cherish, not extinguish them'. He also said that:

> this high principle should be greatly carried out in the art of government. It is not by obliterating all national distinctions and melting them into one that unity is truly attainable; but by respecting them, and raising them to fullest life. Thus the way may be opened to self-respect in each nation individually, all that is good and great in each may be drawn forth, and thus united, form true harmony.[102]

It was in keeping with the time that Stokes should acknowledge the existence of distinct national identities, but it is also interesting that he should use the opportunity to write of the need to respect those differences. That archaeology should be justified because of its social purpose, both by politicians and antiquarians, is an important point to think of when considering the purpose of the past. The statements made by Stokes, and those by Petrie and Todd, illustrate an interest in Irish antiquity that mirrored the rhetoric of nationalism. In addition, the objects and sites regarded by the antiquarians as being of historical importance were often the same as those chosen by political figures as symbolic of the nation. For instance, Petrie's most important works were on round towers and the Hill of Tara. In addition, when Charles Graves spoke at a Parliamentary Commission that considered the running of the Academy museum, he declared the 'Tara' Brooch and the Cross of Cong as 'public objects'. William Wilde, speaking at the same enquiry, selected artefacts from the Early Christian Period — the book shrine 'The Cathach of the O'Donels', the Shrine of St Patrick, and the Bell of St Senan — as examples of the most important objects in the Royal Irish Academy collection.[103]

Also reflecting the political context, prominent antiquarians were not afraid to make references to external matters whilst pursuing their activity, such as to the educational and cultural policy of the British administration in Ireland. Regarding education, William Wilde lamented about the need for teaching Irish history. He wrote that the National Education Board would teach the history and geography of far-off places, but 'never once allude, in their system of education, to the national history of the people they are employed to teach'. He stated that the aim 'to render my country men familiar with the facts and names in Irish history — has been one of the objects I have had in view in the historic portion of this work'.[104] Such sentiment mirrored the statements made concerning education policy in Ireland by political activists such as Thomas Davis in the 1840s and, at the end of the nineteenth century, Patrick Pearse. In addition, nineteenth-century antiquarians sometimes concurred with the notion that the neglect of Irish archaeology by the English government, as evidenced by the lack of financial support, was an indication of the low esteem in which Ireland was held. For instance, Samuel Ferguson, in a letter to Lord Morpeth, remarked that twenty times more was spent on the 'advancement of learning and arts' in Great Britain than in Ireland. Giving it a more personal tone, he added: 'your lordship will allow me without arrogance, to observe, that one to twenty is not the ratio in which Irish intellect contributes to the advancement of the English name in the Republic of letters'.[105] Likewise, William Wilde referred to the British expenditure on archaeology in Ireland being a 'miserable pittance'.[106]

In a similar manner, the notion that the Irish nation held a superior position in antiquity, popular in nationalist political sources, is found endorsed in some of the works of the prominent antiquarians. For instance, Samuel Ferguson described Ireland's heritage as unique because it 'escaped this obliterating march of Roman civilisation' and therefore 'the whole country may be said to be one vast museum, still but half explored'. He continued in highly sentimental language to describe this wealth:

> Every time that the spade or the plough enters an ancient fallow — every time that the progress of agriculture requires the drainage of a bog, or the prostration of a rath or tumulus — these silent witness to antiquity are turned forth from their beds of rust and corrosion, to divulge the secrets which have now lain buried in the faithful bosom of the earth for better than two thousand years.[107]

This was also proclaimed by William Wilde who prefaced one of his works with the statement: 'it may be regarded as a boast, but nevertheless incontrovertibly true, that the greatest amount of Celtic history in the world, at present, is to be found in Ireland'.[108] Wilde presented his views to the Royal Commission of Enquiry into the

Irish science and art institutions. When asked if the Academy museum was the 'greatest Celtic museum in Europe', he replied: 'no doubt it is the largest and truest, and the least affected by external influences'.[109] In 1848 Wakeman contended that the Irish remains were 'unrivalled in Europe'.[110] All of these statements reflect those made by proponents of Irish nationalism throughout the nineteenth century. That the assertions about the importance of archaeology in both the political and antiquarian context should mirror each other closely reveals the existence of shared values towards the past.

Though the members of the Royal Irish Academy often used similar language to that of the political activists, one must consider the possibility of the Academy members using the same language with a different political meaning. Certainly their use of the language of nationalism, demonstrated by references to the past as 'national', would have been a result of the political context. However, even though the antiquarians brought political language into archaeology, it did not necessarily follow that they were separatist in their politics. For Samuel Ferguson, revival of interest in Irish archaeology had the purpose to strengthen the union rather than to end it; in other words, the past had a unionist purpose. In keeping with this, Ferguson wrote of the development of the arts and the foundation of a national museum as not only essential for Ireland but also for the Empire on the grounds that this was good government. He stated:

> It is unquestionable — all history affirms it — and the learned of every age have acknowledged it — and the wise of all ages and nations have acted on it — that, whenever a country or a city has been made the settled abode of science and literature, it has never wanted for the presence of wealth: and, where wealth has been so attracted, there we may reasonably look to find industry and peace.[111]

This apparent anomaly is evident elsewhere. Ferguson was one of the joint founders and a main contributor to the *Dublin University Magazine*,[112] which has been described as 'unionist and nationalist without contradiction'.[113] During the Parliamentary Enquiry into the Ordnance Survey, the magazine came out in support of the continuation of the memoirs, exhibiting both their cultural nationalism and their loyalty to the union. The work of the Survey was celebrated both for creating knowledge of the Irish past and as evidence of the liberality of the British government. It was argued that the continuation of the Survey in Ireland would 'raise the character of that government in the esteem of the enlightened men of the empire and of Europe, and ... ensure the gratitude of those in Ireland more particularly'. As a result it was argued that the British government should be celebrated as 'the most powerful and wealthy nation in the universe, the most illustrious for her bravery, and spirit of enterprise'.[114]

One can argue, therefore, that the Academy, although an Irish institution, wished to strengthen its place in the British context. This is demonstrated by Sir William Hamilton who, in his 1838 Presidential Address to the Academy, referred to its antiquarian interest as an 'unpolitical activity' which deliberately abstained from 'introducing polemics and politics, or whatever else might cause an angry feeling in this peaceful and happy society'. However, this was on his terms, whichwere Christian and Unionist, as he concluded: '[I] trust that I will never see [the day], when piety to God, or loyalty to the Sovereign, shall be out of fashion here'.[115]   One can also assume that Thomas Robinson in his Presidential Address to the Academy delivered in 1851 was declaring his loyalty to the crown when he declared: 'if there be any cloud that throws a shadow over our prospect, it is the dread of DISUNION, that bane of Ireland, whose poison has tainted every page of her history from the beginning to the present time'.[116] William Wilde illustrated his loyalty by closing the preface of *Beauties of the Boyne and its Tributary the Blackwater* with a welcome to the recent visit of Queen Victoria.[117] This is also evident in the letter sent to Queen Victoria by the Academy on the death of Prince Albert in 1862. It lamented the 'insuperable loss which the nation has sustained' and presented the Academy members as her most 'dutiful and loyal subjects'.[118] Loyalty to the establishment can also be seen in a lecture given by William Wilde entitled 'Ireland past and present: the landscape and the people', delivered to the Young Men's Christian Association in 1864. In his address, through the unlikely analogy of the shifting of the continents, Wilde took the opportunity to air his opinion on the contemporary political situation in Ireland. He claimed that, as a result of the shifts, 'Great Britain and Ireland came as they now are, and as they are likely to remain, geographically separated, although united in interest and government'. Wilde argued that the Irish were now 'living under the mildest Government in the World, a truly regal republic, with the Crown as the symbol of fealty and a Parliament as the palladium of liberty'. In his concluding statement, Wilde dismissed the political movements established by O'Connell and the Young Irelanders by stating that 'I for one think that there is still a good time coming, not for "Old" nor "Young", but for New Ireland'.[119]

Engagement with the Irish past did not always exhibit a philanthropic ideal, and divisive rhetoric was not absent from antiquarian writing. William Wilde, in the same address, used archaeological evidence to provide reasons for some of the catastrophic events of nineteenth-century Ireland. He spoke of the impact of the Irish Famine in the mid-nineteenth century which had a devastating effect, causing the death of at least eight hundred thousand people and the loss of a similar number through emigration.[120] According to Wilde the Famine was predetermined by antiquity. He claimed:

> From the earliest period ever recorded, until now, the Irishman has been the very worst cook in creation. He had no idea how to do anything but boil a potato, or broil a herring; in fact, he was so low in the culinary scale, that when lately his potato food failed, and he could not purchase a herring, he had difficulty in learning how to dress and eat Indian meal.

On the subject of the associated emigration, he claimed that the huge loss of population in past years to America was simply a further westward move of the 'restless Celt' and 'the cry is "westward, ho!" The manifest destiny of the Celt is being fulfilled'.[121] Though the event of this address was mentioned in Wilde's biographies, the content was not.[122] However, the newspaper of the Irish Republican Brotherhood did comment on the address. It threw scorn on it and condemned it as 'leaden antiquarianism leavened but not enlivened with bad jokes [which] apparently is quite compatible with their notions of Christianity'.[123]

The antiquarian circles in nineteenth-century Ireland, as occupied by members of the Royal Irish Academy such as George Petrie and Samuel Ferguson, were central to the creation of knowledge about the Irish past. These individuals were also intensely aware of the political context within which they were working. There is, however, no straightforward interpretation of the political intent of the antiquarians since, in an almost chameleonic manner, they can evoke what appear to be either romantic-nationalist or unionist opinions through their work. However, their research was essential for the purposes of nationalism and one can argue that the popularity of nationalism and archaeology bore some mutual influence. The language used to express how the past was valued in predominantly political and antiquarian spheres was not dissimilar. In both contexts, the past was assigned a social role and particular periods and artefacts were labelled as national. The various archaeological institutions and antiquarians significantly contributed to the revival of interest in the Irish past; their work was justified by an increased public interest and their products provided the materials for nationalism. Given the quantity of references to archaeological sites and artefacts, and individual antiquarians, one can go so far as to say that the activity of antiquarians inspired cultural nationalists, such as Thomas Davis. In addition, the use of the terminology of nationalism in the Presidential Addresses of the Royal Irish Academy indicates that the idea of 'the nation' had become so naturalised that those who were pro-union failed to question the use of the language and ideas of nationalism. One may argue, therefore, that the influence of nationalism in Ireland transcended the political context and entered into the antiquarian sphere to influence the personal agendas, including those of people who did not hold the political ideal at the core of Irish nationalism — that of independence from Britain. As a result, the idea of 'an Irish nation', rooted in antiquity, became popular aided by the endorsement of antiquarians such as George Petrie.

It is important to distinguish between cultural revivalism and cultural nationalism. The research generated by cultural revivalism fed nationalism. In addition, cultural nationalism provided a political context conducive to historical research. However, the political intentions of each are not necessarily equal. This is evident in the manner in which Academy members legitimised their interest in antiquity. They referred to it as revivalist and they believed that it contributed to the national interest, but this was not necessarily with the aim to create an independent state. Since this revivalist activity fed nationalism it brought its own political tensions. The antiquarians were aware of this, and one can argue that the conflict inherent in the political significance of culture is one that has not yet been resolved in the Irish context. Engagement with the Irish past must always be considered to have some political resonance because of the politicisation of cultural activity that became deeply rooted in the nineteenth century due to the effect of nationalism.

CHAPTER FIVE

The Establishment of a Public Museum in Ireland

THE DESIRE TO create a large public museum in Ireland came from two main sources, both of which were the product of differing ideological agendas. The interest in Ireland must be considered both in the context of Irish nationalism and of the British role in the establishment of a museum in Ireland. The latter should be regarded as part of the interest in science and art education fed by the industrial revolution and which resulted in the formation of museums in Britain. In order to understand the values held in Ireland that underpinned the establishment of a public museum, one must consider how important 'the past', and the institutions that manage the past, were to Irish nationalism. One must also think of the significance placed by Irish antiquarians on the social and political consequences of their activity. Political, antiquarian and industrial interests influenced the management and establishment of Ireland's first major public museum, the Dublin Museum of Science and Art. Its history reveals the extent to which the Dublin museum was a stage, a place where different perspectives on the political history of Ireland met and were acted out.

MUSEUMS IN NINETEENTH-CENTURY DUBLIN

An acquaintance with the character and history of the museums in nineteenth-century Dublin adds both to an understanding of the nature of the museum movement of that time and to our knowledge of how the Dublin Science and Art Museum (later known as the National Museum of Ireland) was eventually shaped. In the early nineteenth century, several prominent museums existed in Dublin, including the Trinity College Museum, the Royal Dublin Society agricultural collection, the Natural History Museum, the Museum of Economic Geology (later renamed as the Museum of Practical Geology and, later again, the Museum of Irish Industry) and the Royal Irish Academy collection.

To begin with, the Royal Dublin Society was one of the most important leaders of cultural developments in Dublin. As well as encouraging research in scientific subjects, the Society published a newsletter, established a school of art, created a library and formed botanical gardens.[1] In addition, influenced by the collections held by its members and by the existence of a museum in Trinity College Dublin,[2] the society formed a collection of agricultural implements. The purpose of the collection was the education of agricultural artisans and it was housed in the vaults of the Parliament House.[3] In 1813 the society produced a catalogue that included natural history specimens and some antiquities.[4] Both the Trinity museum and the early form of the Dublin Society collection were in the exhibition style typical of this period, that of the 'cabinet of curiosities' with an apparently miscellaneous character. This form was maintained into the early nineteenth century and is recorded in descriptions of both collections published in the *Dublin Penny Journal*. The account of the Trinity collection described six cases, five of which contained the ethnographic finds from Cook's voyages to the South Seas in the eighteenth century. The sixth contained:

> A very curious collection of Irish antiquities – various celts, chip-axes, arrow-heads, hunting spears of brass, and military spears; the war axe, golden crescents, head ornaments, fibulae; curious headstall and bitt, found in Roscommon; the Liath Meisicith, or incense box of the ancients, consulted only upon the interests of the church or election of a king. The most interesting curiosity is the Irish harp, once the property of King Brain Boroimhe.[5]

In a later account of the collection presented to the Royal Commission in 1851, the collection was described as being composed of 'two brazen bombshells used by the Sikhs in the late war', a skull of a man executed for murder, mummy crocodiles, ancient Scandinavian almanacs, pug-dogs, skull, and bricks and mortar from the Great Wall of China.[6] A contemporary etching of the collection, complete with stuffed giraffe and shark and published in the history of Trinity College by Constance Maxwell,[7] confirms the eccentric exhibition style. The *Dublin Penny Journal* also provides a room-by-room description of the Royal Dublin Society collection as it stood in the 1830s in Leinster House, the Society's building that had been purchased from the Duke of Leinster in 1815.[8] The six rooms of the museum included collections of Irish antiquities as well as geological and zoological exhibits. Of the antiquarian collection, the journal describes a 'miscellaneous assemblage of curiosities' which included a 'mummy in a very perfect state of preservation', 'four brazen lamas' and 'the armour of one of the Tiger-guards of Tippoo Sultan'.[9] The commitment to the establishment of a museum as a significant public institution is demonstrated when, in the 1850s, the Royal Dublin Society increased the status of its collection by moving it into the purpose-built 'Natural History Museum', which it established with its own funds of subscriptions and donations. The British government also made money available to the museum, but this was in lieu of another building that the Society had ceded to the School of Design. The Natural History Museum was erected, within the space of eighteen months, alongside the Society's main buildings. Important stages of this event were marked with much pageantry: the foundation stone was laid on 7 March 1856 by the Lord Lieutenant to the sound of a military band and was followed by three cheers to Queen Victoria. The opening took place in August 1857 on the occasion of the meeting of the British Association for the Advancement of Science in Dublin.[10]

Meanwhile, the antiquities collection being formed by the Royal Irish Academy was beginning to gain prominence. The Academy had always placed immense value on archaeology and the creation of an antiquarian and manuscript collection. This was made possible by the nature of the membership: 'most of the early members of the Academy were men of means, and for them there will have been an ever-present temptation to assemble a private cabinet of antiquities'.[11] As with the other collections, the Academy collection would have started out in the style of a cabinet of curiosities. However, in 1827 an Antiquities Committee was appointed to take charge of the collection, and from that date its purpose became more defined. Even greater emphasis was placed on the collection when in 1841 the Academy granted the Antiquities Committee £200 as a purchase fund, and in 1850 the Committee was given an annual expenditure of £50. This was later supplemented by an annual grant of £100 from the government for the purchase of treasure trove. The collection was to 'becom[e] a depository for everything which may illustrate the habits and history of the Celtic tribes'.[12] At this time the Minutes of the meetings of the Committee of Antiquities record a steady stream of the purchases of antiquities: 'a gold torque' acquired for £50 on 7 June 1841, 'a gold fibula' bought on 18

October 1841 for 'its weight in sovereigns' and, on 2 April 1842, the 'ancient silver seal of O'Brien' for £3.

By this stage the Academy was beginning to consider its public role; indeed, the first large collection purchased in Ireland that was associated with an idea of public ownership, rather than a sense of adding to a private cabinet, was that acquired by the Academy in 1841. This was the collection of the late Dean Dawson of St Patrick's Cathedral purchased by means of a public subscription. The powerful text of the appeal reveals the sense of value and significance attached to antiquities. In addition, with the past already being labelled as 'national' in the political sphere, the nature and language of the Dawson appeal was in keeping with the time and served to bring the work of the Academy into the public sphere. The appeal read, in part:

> [The Academy] urge upon every friend of Ireland the importance of the present opportunity of securing the extensive and interesting collection of the late lamented Dean of St Patrick's as the basis of a national museum of antiquities. The want of such a museum has been of incalculable injury to the History of Ireland, has led to the destruction of many most interesting objects of ancient Irish art, and has been the remote cause of that disgraceful apathy towards our national antiquities, which has, unhappily, characterised the gentry of this country ... It is therefore hoped that ... every friend to literature and antiquities of Ireland, will zealously contribute to prevent the dispersion of his collection, and to assure its perpetual preservation in the hands of a body best qualified to protect it ... Steps have therefore been taken to form local committees in the principal towns of Ireland, for the purpose of collecting subscriptions. Noblemen and gentlemen who are desirous of promoting this national design, are requested to send their names to the Royal Irish Academy'.[13]

The appeal was published in the Dublin paper *Saunder's Newsletter* on 4 December 1840. The language of this text reflects the language of romantic nationalism. This is evident in the description of the collection as a 'patriotic object' and of those who would contribute to its purchase as 'friends of Ireland' who would be aiding a 'public and national design'. This is an indication of the pride the Academy members had in the Irish past and their belief that this ought to be recognised. This increased interest and regard for the Irish national past is also a reflection of the socio-political context. It coincided with the rise of cultural nationalism and revivalist activity of the 1830s and 1840s. As discussed earlier, the increased publishing of penny journals brought an idea of a 'national past' to readers and the writings of those such as Thomas Davis gave this a political edge. Indeed, the text of the appeal would not be out of place in the pages of the *Nation* and used similar language as found in the writings of Davis.

In all, the mid-nineteenth century marks the beginning of a trend towards a more focused role for Dublin's museums. This is illustrated in a number of ways. In the first place the museums were clearer about their role as public institutions with a specifically national purpose. At this time, 'a feeling began to develop that private cabinets were not enough, and that Ireland, like many other countries of Europe ought to have a national collection'. Secondly, collections like those held by the Academy and the Dublin Society were moving away from the style of the miscellaneous cabinets and towards becoming specialised museums. For instance, at this point, the geological, zoological and agricultural collections of the Royal Dublin Society were taking prominence and the Society was lending the antiquarian portions of its collection to the Academy. By this time the Academy had given the Dublin Society its small geological collection and was concentrating on antiquities. Thirdly, the Academy collections were assuming a more 'national identity'. The Irish element of the Academy collection had begun to take precedence over any non-Irish material derived from the days of grand tours of members and their families and the eighteenth-century interest in curiosities. The Minutes of the Antiquities Committee state that in 1855 it was decided that 'only Irish material was to go into the museum, non-Irish was to go into the "back parlour"'.[14] This decision reveals how awareness of the 'nationality' of the past was growing amongst the members of the Academy. Reverend J. H. Jellett in his Presidential Address to the Academy in 1870 provided some interesting points in his vision for the purpose of the collection of antiquities. For him the Academy held the 'archaeological treasures, not as owners' but 'in trust for Archaeology ... for the benefit of archaeological science' rather than 'a collection of pretty curiosities to amuse an idle hour'. For him 'a thought of patriotism should mingle' through the Academy.[15] He stressed: 'let us work earnestly, bravely and faithfully, to promote the great objects for which we were instituted, yet not without thought that we are an *Irish* Academy; remembering that when we labour in the cause of Literature and Science, we labour too for the honour of our country'.[16]

Motivation towards the establishment of an antiquities collection in Dublin was linked to the increasing value of the past in the political context. The idea of the nation and the national community, as well as the importance of archaeology as a public endeavour, became naturalised in the minds of the antiquarians and was expressed in the collections. The Academy museum, therefore, emerged as a characteristically Irish and national institution and the members attempted to jealously protect this identity.

THE DEPARTMENT OF SCIENCE AND ART IN SOUTH KENSINGTON AND THE IMPERIAL INFLUENCE

In the mid-nineteenth century, the Royal Irish Academy museum was growing in size and significance and was gaining national and international recognition. This is evident from the visit from Denmark in 1847 of the pioneering archaeologist J. J. A. Worsaae. In addition, ten years later, the British Association for the Advancement of Science paid the collection the same compliment.[17] Whilst gaining this recognition the Academy was receiving an annual grant from the British Treasury. So although the Academy was a private society, the British government was free to investigate the management of the collection and did so in two enquires held in the 1860s – the first in 1864 and the second in 1868.

The interest of the British government in Dublin institutions must also be placed in the context of museum development throughout Britain. The Department of Science and Art in South Kensington London, and the museums it administered, had a three-fold function. The first function was to disseminate knowledge about manufactures, aesthetics and culture. The second was to 'naturalise' state intervention as an ideal governing tool, and the third to produce a sense of national identity.[18] It must be noted that the latter would have been a commitment to a sense of the British nation administered from London. South Kensington, in this period, can be regarded as a governmental instrument, a tool for the state to retain direction over that which generates self-education and self-regulation throughout Britain.[19] As a consequence the state, by way of the establishment of museums, spread its power throughout Britain and into Ireland. In this context, South Kensington saw itself as a 'sort of nerve centre' with 'branches [that] ramify into every part of England, Ireland, Scotland and Wales'.[20] The reports of various Parliamentary Commissions explicitly stated that provision of science and art instruction in Ireland must be considered as part of a prestigious 'Imperial system' and as forming 'part of a great system spreading over the whole kingdom'.[21] As well as arising from the policy of industrial development in Britain, the establishment of the Dublin Museum of Science and Art must be seen in the context of political and social reform in Ireland. Reform is evident in the disestablishment of the Church of Ireland in 1869, the establishment of an intermediate education system in 1878, the University Education (Ireland) Act 1879 and the passing of the Land Act in 1881 that improved tenant rights. These activities were all undertaken 'with the aim of creating a progressive educated native middle class eager to participate like the Scots and Welsh in the running of the British Empire'.[22]

British interest in the provision of services for industrial development in Ireland can first be detected in 1845 when the Lords of the Treasury and the Commissioners of Foods and Forests recommended the formation of a 'General Museum of Economic Geology' in Dublin modelled on the Museum of Practical Geology in London. This was established in Dublin in 1852 as the 'Museum of Irish Industry and Government School of Science applied to Mining and the Arts'. It was soon placed under the management of the Department of Science and Art at South Kensington. The Museum of Irish Industry ceased to exist in 1867 when its collections were amalgamated with the Natural History Museum and its responsibilities were given over to the Royal College of Science for Ireland established in the museum building.[23] The long-term significance of the Museum of Irish Industry lies in the fact that it provided the practical and instructive basis of the Dublin Science and Art Museum. In 1864 the collection of the Museum of Industry was described as being in three parts: a mineral, rock and palaeontological collection; the technological collection; and the Portlock collections of Irish fauna and flora. The technological collection later became the chief collection of the Dublin Museum of Science and Art. It comprised exhibitions of building stones and plaster, Irish marbles, cements and stuccoes, coal, iron, lead and copper ores, metallic manufactures, ceramic and glass manufactures, and collections of woody fibres.[24]

The Dublin Society was awarded a grant in 1761 by the Irish Parliament. With the Act of Union in 1800 this fund was administered from the London Parliament, which was less generous, and from then on it steadily declined. Under this new arrangement the Dublin Society and the Academy lost some of their status: '[The societies] had grown up and prospered under the patronage of the Irish Parliament [they] now had to deal with the less sympathetic supervision of the British civil service.'[25] In addition, when the Dublin financial administration ended and was replaced by that from London, the societies had to become increasingly accountable to London, something that they did not appreciate. Dissatisfaction with such an arrangement mirrored the dissent of nationalist political figures of the time.

The line of questioning pursued during the 1864 Royal Commission of Enquiry indicates that the Commissioners were most concerned about how adequately the private bodies were accomplishing their self-proclaimed public role, that of public educators. When the then President of the Academy, Reverend Charles Graves, was questioned on this issue he presented the work of the Academy as a public endeavour rather than a private pastime. He also chose to emphasise the 'national' perspective of its activity. He stated that the Academy 'was originally a private society, but I do not think it is now. It contributes both directly and indirectly to the benefit of the State.' Later on he informed the enquiry: 'I regard ourselves as being simply trustees for the national benefit.'[26] He claimed that this was demonstrated by the fact that the collection was available for public viewing. On the basis of this 'public' role, Graves went on to assert that more public money should be made available to the members to alleviate 'the necessity of continually making private subscriptions for the purpose of attaining what are really public objects'.[27] 'Public objects' is a revealing collective phrase which was applied to certain artefacts of the collection deemed significant by the members of the Academy. The Dean Dawson collection, the Tara Torcs and the Cross of Cong were given as examples of 'public objects' – the objects of nationalism. The members of the Academy based both the value of the collection and its right to exist as an independent institution upon its care of such 'public objects'. In this example, the artefacts were being assigned a special significance; they were being elevated to become tools in the struggle between the Academy and the London Department of Science and Art.

The 1864 Commissioners recommended an overhaul of the provision of science and art instruction in Ireland. They believed that it should constitute a public responsibility rather than be an occupation of the Dublin societies. On these grounds the government set up a full review of the efficiency of science and art institutions in Dublin that materialised in May 1868. The original instruction given by the Council was that a separate science and art department should be formed in Ireland, and any suggestions were only to be made on that basis. However, on the advice of the Dublin Commissioners, the Lords later amended their instruction so that the Commissioners were not tied to the idea of a separate department in Ireland. This granted them the freedom to make general proposals, as long as they had the sole purpose of 'the advancement of science and art in Ireland'.

To undertake an extensive review the Commissioners had to interview a large number of people who were connected with the pre-existing institutions or who could make recommendations from their own experience. The Commission was composed of eight prominent figures who were representative of various public spheres.[28] It was headed by the Irish peer Marquis of Kildare and included the prominent British scientist and philosopher Prof T. H. Huxley who represented the Department of Science and Art in South Kensington. Reverend C. W. Russell and Reverend Samuel Haughton represented the interests of Irish academia. Russell was the President of the Catholic seminary at Maynooth where he was Professor of Humanity and the co-editor of the pro-nationalist *Dublin Review*.[29] By contrast, Haughton was Professor of Geology at Trinity College Dublin and was President of the Royal Irish Academy. In addition to academia, politics was represented by George Alexander Hamilton, an Irish-born, English-educated, conservative politician who was MP for Dublin University during the years 1843 to 1859. The other members of the group were Colonel Laffan and Captain Donnelly, who also acted as secretary. In all, fifty people were interviewed by the Commissioners, some of them twice. The majority of the interviews took place between 17 September and 1 October 1868, although some also took place in July of the same year. Those interviewed included representatives of science and art administration in Scotland; the Director of the South Kensington Museum; members of the Royal Irish Academy and the Royal Dublin Society; the Director of the Natural History Museum in Dublin; the Lord Mayor of Dublin; members of Dublin Town Council; Members of Parliament; academics from Trinity College Dublin; the Chief Inspector of the National Board of Education in Ireland, and representatives of business and industry in Ireland, such as Belleek Pottery in County Fermanagh. The text of the report provides a valuable record of opinion about the provision of public facilities in Ireland, as well as the influence of political sentiment on management recommendations and decisions.

The general consensus of the individuals representing Irish institutions was, unsurprisingly, that Ireland should make its own arrangement for science and art instruction, independent of London. The reasons given were both practical and political. Home management, as a result of knowing its own environment and opportunities, was presented as much more useful. In addition, local management familiar with the 'nationality of the people' was presented as more appropriate. Furthermore, and most interestingly, Ireland was presented as having a *right* to its own management because, it was argued, owing to political mistrust, direction from England could not succeed. The committee interviewed the Hon. John Prendergast Vereker, secretary of a body that had already proposed such an independent institution to be known as the 'Royal Irish Institute'. Vereker stated that his 'whole object' was to recommend the foundation 'of a great national department of science and art in Ireland, managed completely under the control of Irishmen who have no object to their heart dearer than the promotion of the industry and manufactures and the progress of their own country. I think Ireland is entitled to such an institution'. Current rights and conditions were presented as a function of historic wrongs. Therefore, on the grounds of a memory of 'historic prejudices', Vereker argued: 'I don't think Irishmen would have any confidence in an institution that was dependent on South Kensington'.[30] Others also pursued this line of argument. For instance, a Dublin businessman, Mr P. P. McSwiney, claimed that the Irish would not trust London-based administration of science and art because of the suppression of Irish industry in the past, most notably the woollen industry. In his presentation to the committee, McSwiney described Ireland as a 'long misgoverned and much neglected country ... depressed and neglected by foreign rule'.[31] According to another, the Irish were presented as having 'a natural dislike to what we call the imperializing of Ireland. We don't like the spirit of centralization'.[32] This was pursued more openly by Mr Jonathan Pim who argued that 'I have the idea that the sea divides us so much from England that we do require that Dublin should be treated as the capital of Ireland, and that it does not answer so well to have a reference to London upon all matters. I take what may be called the nationalist view as regards many of the institutions of the country'.[33]

Sir Henry Cole, Director of the Department of Science and Art London, made similar references to the past treatment of Ireland, though with a different ultimate purpose in mind. He stated that Dublin should, because of this history, receive more liberal treatment in the area of arts than cities such as Edinburgh or Liverpool. He argued that 'Great Britain owes every possible compensation of Ireland for the years of tyranny and injustice to which Ireland has been subjected' and therefore the promotion of museums and the teaching of science and art would be 'justice to Ireland'. He described the 'debt' owed to Ireland:

> not only because she is part of the nation in which we are all equally interested, but more especially because she is part of the nation towards which we pursed in former times a policy that ought to make us blush. I for one will never conceal my opinion that the course of policy pursued towards Ireland during the years the penal laws were in existence, was such as ought to make England ashamed of herself.

It is interesting that Cole should consider the provision of science and art facilities, and eventually a museum in Ireland, as justified on the grounds of political compensation. However, there is a distinct difference between the opinion presented by Cole and the beliefs of Irish individuals of a nationalist persuasion. Cole's opinion was held within a distinctly pro-Union framework. He looked upon Ireland as a valued part of the British nation. With this in mind he also argued that an independent science and art museum should not be developed in Dublin. He paralleled this with the contemporary political situation: 'it is just analogous to wanting an Irish Parliament back, or anything else of that kind, or an Irish army or an Irish navy'.

Cole recognised the importance of the Irish antiquities collection held by the Academy and argued that the conditions of the collection should be improved. He showed concern about how adequately the Academy was maintaining such an important collection. He described the Academy museum as being in a serious state of neglect and claimed that it was 'the only institution that I have visited which seems not to have progressed in the last three years'. He told his audience that he found 'the floor strewed' [sic] with 'singularly beautiful and rare bronzes, surface plates ... of the most exquisite workmanship of a people, perhaps, of a thousand years ago'.

Because of this mismanagement, Cole argued that London should intervene with financial aid and establish a central institution akin to that already existing in South Kensington, but suited to Irish needs. He recommended that 'any sum of money – of public money' should be spent in making the collection of those antiquities of the Royal Irish Academy 'as useful, as intelligible, and as open as possible to the public ... I have not the least hesitation in saying that the State ought to come in and do it'. Exhibiting archaeology was not a function of the museum at South Kensington, yet Cole endorsed the idea of giving the archaeology collections prominence in the proposed institution in Dublin. In his opinion the Academy should receive 'the best frontage, the place of honour there'. He argued: 'I believe that if you established a gallery there for the archaeology of Ireland proper, and for ethnographic matters besides, you could make very splendid and fine collections'. He was passionate about the value of the Academy collection and the position it should hold in this new institution. He claimed if there were 'any wretched jealousies about putting them in proper order', he would '*vi et armis*, to take the objects away and put them into proper order for the credit of Ireland and for the benefit of the Irish people. I would do everything in the pleasantest possible way in accordance with the dictates of common sense and common justice first of all, but I should be prepared to fight for putting them in proper order if necessary.'

Cole's belief that the State should intervene in the running of the Academy collection provided a hint of what was to come for the private bodies in Dublin. The 1868 Commission concluded that 'the creation of an entirely independent Department of Science and Art for Ireland would be detrimental to the interests of Science and Art in that country'.[34] This was based on a belief in the advantage of being part of an imperial framework, which increased competition and improved the quality of work. In addition, the committee resolved that the needs of industry in Ireland had outgrown what could be provided by private societies. With regard to the Irish antiquities museum of the Royal Irish Academy the committee concluded:

> We regard the condition of the collection, which has now acquired a national character, as unsatisfactory, and we are of the opinion that in consideration of the large expenditure of public money which a suitable new building and the necessary administration will require

the Academy should be invited to place its museum under a director to be appointed by Government.[35]

It may appear paradoxical that the 'national character' of the Dublin collection should be used to justify management intervention from London. However, if one considers this in the context of Cole's earlier statement, 'national' was an expression of the importance laid on a collection that was within the British jurisdiction, part of the wider British nation. The Commissioners recommended that the services provided by the Museum of Irish Industry, the industrial collections of the Royal Dublin Society and the antiquities collection of the Royal Irish Academy should be consolidated under one institution that would materialise as the Museum of Science and Art, Dublin.

The minutes of the Council of the Royal Irish Academy record the arrival of a letter from Lord Sandon, Vice-President of the Science and Art Department in South Kensington, which announced this intention. The letter read, in part:

> It appears that the time has now arrived when the wants of the community at large have outgrown the useful action of private societies, and when a thorough rearrangement and consolidation of existing institutions have become an essential condition precedent for further progress ... with this view their Lordships propose to build ... a Science and Art Museum for Ireland, somewhat similar to that now existing in Edinburgh for Scotland.[36]

The museum would be an amalgamation of several Dublin collections: that of the Natural History Museum, the Royal Dublin Society library, the collections of the Geological Survey and the industrial collections of the Royal College of Science with the collections of the Royal Irish Academy. In addition, the collections for the new institution would consist of purchases, for which an annual grant would be allowed, and of loans from the museum at South Kensington. It would therefore be 'an entirely new institution'. Sandon recommended that the Academy should transfer its collection to this new institution, because 'declining to become a branch of the South Kensington Establishment the Academy would show a selfish inclination to stand in the way of the creation of a great Science and Art Museum in Ireland'.[37]

The reactions of the members of Academy to this matter are

interesting. All agreed that a large public museum developed in Dublin, with the aid of public money, was desirable. However, many would have preferred to have such an institution devoted solely to the archaeology of Ireland. For instance, Reverend J. H. Todd, who by 1868 had completed his term as President of the Academy, had already proposed the establishment of a 'National Museum of Irish Antiquities and Historical Monuments'. He recommended that this should be established by public grant under the control of the government but to conditions agreed by the Academy. He believed that the provision of such a museum was the 'duty of the nation' and beyond the scope of the Academy. In a document presented for consideration by the Commissioners, Todd stated:

> The members of the Academy for many years past have liberally subscribed from their own private means for the purchase of any object of remarkable interest that was offered for sale. But it cannot be expected that a national museum should in this way be acquired and supported, nor is the small grant made for the general objects of the Academy nearly sufficient for carrying into effect everything that ought to be done for the preservation and study of our national antiquities. It is clearly the duty of the nation to form such a collection, as the only mode of acquiring knowledge of the domestic life, civil and military customs and political institutions of the ancient Irish tribes.[38]

Other members objected to the aspect of Todd's proposal that included the suggestion that the London government should reign over the institution. For instance, William Wilde and Lord Talbot de Malahide were both in agreement that the Academy should maintain full control of such a museum, rather than it being placed under government direction. Talbot de Malahide described it as 'one of their most popular features' of which the members were 'justly proud' and therefore any management and changes should remain under full control of the Academy.[39] However, all the members were in agreement that the antiquities collection was worthy of its own separate institution and building, and that it should not be amalgamated with the planned institution for science and art. Wilde believed that the amalgamation of an antiquities collection of such value and importance as that of the Academy with technical and ethnographic collections, illustrative of 'foreign nations', was wholly inappropriate. He stated that his desire was 'to see this great national collection of antiquities properly housed, safely guarded, scientifically arranged and displayed as a great Celtic museum'.[40]

However, proper housing of the Academy collection was dependent on government aid, so when the new building of the Dublin Museum of Science and Art finally opened in 1890 the Academy signed over its antiquities collection. The Academy did try to influence the form the museum building would take – the amount of space allocated to its collection and even recommending the construction of a separate entrance.[41] None of these met with much success and, despite Cole's recommendations, the Academy collection took a secondary position in this new institution.

In sum, three important periods can be identified in the history of Dublin's museums. The first is that of the late eighteenth and early nineteenth centuries when the museums were largely private cabinets in the homes of the Anglo-Irish. During this period, the archaeological and other artefacts of the collections were only displayed for the enjoyment of the gentlemen members of such societies. The second was the period from the 1840s to the 1890s when the collections were considered as part of a 'public' endeavour. In this context those involved with the Academy museum, such as George Petrie and Samuel Ferguson, were very much interested in developing a characteristically Irish institution. Cultural institutions in Dublin, and their members, could not avoid the impact of the rising political interest and 'national sentiment' with regard to the value and ownership of the past. As a result the members of the Academy became interested in developing a specifically 'national' museum, which would preserve and nurture the past for themselves and the Irish public. The third important stage was that entered into in the 1890s. This was marked by the move of the Irish antiquities collection from the care of an institution of (Anglo-)Irish men in the Royal Irish Academy to representatives of the Department of Science and Art in London. This was a significant shift and an interesting development in the history of Dublin's museums.

The conflict between the interests of the British industrial ethos and the desire in Ireland to create a museum of Irish archaeology is a demonstration of a clash of interests triggered by competing definitions of the purpose of a public museum in Dublin. The move of the Irish antiquities collection of the Academy into the Science and Art Museum was, symbolically, one of placing the control of the material remains of the Irish past in the hands of a London department. Evidence that the move was interpreted in this way is found in newspapers with a nationalist inclination as well as those of political groups. It is particularly paradoxical that this shift should have come to fruition at a time when Irish culture was getting greater attention through the activity of the Gaelic League.

BUILDING THE DUBLIN MUSEUM OF SCIENCE AND ART

Though the Science and Art Museum Act was passed in 1877, it was not until 1885 that the first stone of the building to house the institution was laid. The reports of the Science and Art Department in the intervening years record both the dissatisfaction over the delay and the difficulties facing those involved with the project. Political forces played a dominant role in the establishment of the museum. It may have been under the patronage of a London department, but for some public figures in Ireland the museum was regarded as an important national institution and flagship at the end of the nineteenth century. The Department of Science and Art, on the other hand, considered the museum as part of a system developed for the mutual benefit of all members of the Union. These two images of the institution are demonstrated quite simply in how the two groups referred to it. While those in London spoke of the 'Dublin Museum of Science and Art', those in Dublin referred to the 'National Museum'. It is interesting, but not unexpected, that this institution could symbolise different things at the same time.

On the issue of the site of the Dublin museum, the government wished to sustain the 'cultural core' around Leinster House as already developed by the Royal Dublin Society. The proposed site for the Science and Art Museum fronted onto Merrion Square on a plot known as Leinster Lawn located between the Natural History Museum and the National Gallery (See Figure 10). Objections came from Lord Pembroke who owned the land – he did not wish to suffer the loss of the flowerbeds on the site. The 1878 Report of the Department of Science and Art recorded their disgust: 'we cannot but regret that it was not felt that the loss of a few flower beds would be far more compensated for by a handsome, commodious and well-lighted Science and Art Museum'.[42] As a result of objections the Department had to agree to build on a less prestigious site, one facing onto Kildare Street.[43]

The architectural competition for this location, managed by the Office of Public Works, was launched in 1881. The guidelines stated

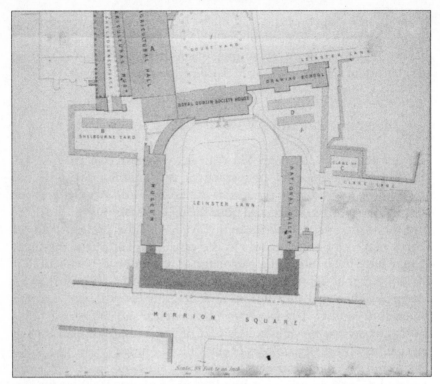

Figure 10: Aerial plan of the site of some of Dublin's main cultural institutions prior to building the museum and library (*Parl. Rep.* 1868/9.XXIV p. 667). On the lower part of the plan, to the right, is the National Gallery and, to the left, the Natural History Museum. The Science and Art Museum was built in the upper left corner of the plan with the Library facing it. This completed the set of four cultural institutions.

that the eventual building should cost £100,000 to erect, architectural sketches should be received by 15 November 1881 and entries were to be submitted anonymously with only a motto for identification. The five best designs would be chosen by an appointed committee made up of the Irish peer Lord Powerscourt; the Lord Mayor of Dublin, Dr Moyer; the President of the Dublin Institute of Architects, Mr McCurdy; Sir Robert Kane, the Director of the Museum of Irish Industry; and Sir George Hodson.[44] The five selected entrants would be each given £150 to finance the final plans to arrive by 1 May 1882, and the winning design would then be chosen.[45] Building was anticipated to start at the end of 1882.[46]

By the middle of 1882 the process of the design competition was well underway: out of sixty-seven entrants five designs had been chosen and announced. Lord Powerscourt described them as constituting a 'wealth of entries', adding that the eventual building would be a 'credit to Dublin and Ireland', a 'magnificent structure' and an 'attractive and instructive National Museum' deserving of the 'unrivalled collection' of the Royal Irish Academy.[47] Despite this progress, objections were raised about the positioning of the building on Kildare Street site and dissatisfaction was being voiced over the designs that had got through the first stage of the competition. The newspaper *Hibernia* announced to its readers: 'we regret having to announce that the new museum of Science and Art in Dublin is not to be the work of an Irishman'. The readers were told that 'a serious error detrimental to our interest as Irish men, and an unmerited reflection upon our intellectual status, has been committed by the Department of Science and Art under the very cover of doing us service'. This was interpreted as an attack on Irish ability in the area of art and design; the readers were asked 'are the English designs necessarily superior to ours?' Rather than the competition being limited to Irishmen, the newspaper claimed that, yet again, 'we see our efforts subverted by some cruel blunder such as this that takes our own work out of our own hands'.[48] Many letters on the matter were also written to the *Irish Builder.* The letters reveal a general disgust over the perceived influence of South Kensington on the choice of architect.[49] Continuing on this theme, the editor of the newspaper stated that the design of an Irish architect should be adopted only because it is Irish: 'we candidly say however we have not much faith in the good intentions of the South Kensington officials respecting Ireland or matters Irish'.[50]

The debate continued in the House of Commons where questions were raised on the positioning of the building on Kildare Street site and the nationality of the architect. Mr Sexton, MP for Sligo, asserted that 'every public journal in Dublin without the distinction of political opinion has joined in condemnation of the project'.[51] Later Sexton reported on a meeting of thirty-six of Ireland's principal architects which concluded that the site of the museum was 'cramped, inconvenient, badly lighted and deficient in ventilation'.[52] Since the position of the building had not been objected to when the competition was originally launched, the government did not believe that there were any grounds to reopen the competition.[53] The members considered that the objections raised were driven by political rather than practical issues. The Treasury Minister told the House that 'we heard nothing of any change [of support for the site] until after it was discovered that the designs of no Irish architects had obtained a place among the selected designs'.[54] These statements illustrate the value that was placed on the physical presence of the museum. It was not only important to create a museum that was a magnificent institution, but also that it should be a reflection of the brilliant ability of Irish design.

On 1 December 1882 Mr Sexton asked that the competition be reopened and, despite previous objections from the government to this, the decision to have a second competition was announced. This was presented by the government as being made on the basis of the positioning of the building, rather than the more political issue of the nationality of the architect. The Department announced that 'it is now proposed – in consequence of objections made to the site for the proposed buildings not to carry out those buildings as originally intended but to have an open competition of Architects for new designs according to the changed intentions'.[55] This necessitated the passing of an Act to give the Department powers of compulsory purchase in order to acquire additional land for the buildings.[56]

The second competition was announced in February 1883 and for the most part took the same format as the original. Differences included the decision that the design should also incorporate a library that would be on the north side of the site and the museum on the south side; the building was also to make full use of Irish materials. The design that won the second competition was from an Irish firm, T. N. Deane and Son. Interestingly the motto they used to maintain anonymity in the first stage of the competition made no secret of their nationality: it was 'Crom-a-Boo', the battlecry of the Irish family the FitzGeralds. However, even at this stage the building of the museum was plagued with difficulty. A second flurry of questions was being raised in the House of Commons over the delays in starting Deane's design. The government did not receive such comments kindly. In its opinion the delays to date were caused by objections from those on the Irish side. This particular delay, however, was a result of the realisation by the government that the cost of building the winning design would necessitate going over budget. The Irish members of the House considered this a poor excuse. Edmund Dwyer Gray, MP for Carlow County, suggested that the compound interest that the Government must have been earning on the £100,000 allocated since the project's inception would cover the increased cost of the building.[57] Charles Dawson, MP for Carlow Borough, claimed that the Government was neglecting the education of the Irish people for the sake of a few thousand pounds. He even hinted that the Government wished to abandon the chosen Irish design in favour of one by an English architect and was using the financial constraint as the excuse.[58] He later poured scorn on the fact that current work on Westminster Hall in London should be undertaken so promptly.[59] Finally, on 7 August 1884, the Chancellor of the Exchequer informed the House of Commons that the Deane design would be undertaken, even though it had been estimated that it would cost £140,000, clearly well over budget. He reported that the selection committee did consider the other entrants but calculated that their cost would in fact exceed the Deane design (see Figure 11 which is one of the unsuccessful entrants and Figure 12 which shows the winning design). The Treasury followed this by granting the Office of Public Works in Dublin, on 24 November 1884, authority to begin preparing the site and to place contracts with builders.[60] As if problems would never end, the *Irish Builder* reported a strike of seventy stoneworkers at the site of the museum over a pay issue[61] and objections were later raised because English oak was being used for the interior doors.[62]

It is interesting to note at this point that the purpose-built Royal College of Science in Dublin, the first stone of which was laid in 1904, was not the design of an Irish architect. The Royal College of Science, though not a museum, was an important public institution and the resultant building took its place as one of the finest in Dublin erected under British rule. It was the work of Sir Aston Webb who also designed the facade of Buckingham Palace and the front of the Science and Art Museum at South Kensington (by 1904 known as the Victoria and Albert Museum). Webb did have the assistance of the Deane architectural firm in Dublin, apparently granted as a token gesture, a 'sop to Irish feeling',[63] but the design was 'wholly the work of Webb'.[64] That an English architect should have been accepted for the College of Science but not for the museum is a reflection of the symbolic importance of a museum in itself. The museum is the image that a place wishes to portray of itself, both of its past and its future. Therefore it was fitting that the museum building in Dublin should have been to an Irish design; in the case of the College of Science it was not so important.

The successful design for the museum and library created a building in a neo-classical style. The front of the museum is composed of a central rotunda[65] surrounded with classical colonnade, flanked with wings of Dalkey granite and Mount Charles sandstone. On the inside this rotunda has a mosaic floor, which

Figure 11: 'Proposed Science and Art Museum. Design submitted by Mr G. P. Beater, Archt' published in the *Irish Builder*, 1 May 1885.

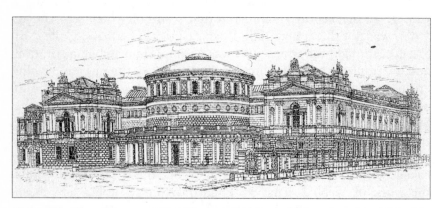

Figure 12: 'New Science and Art Museum Buildings, Kildare Street', published in the *Irish Builder*, 1 December 1887.

depicts the signs of the zodiac, and is circled with columns of Irish marble. The main feature of the exhibition hall is the wrought iron and glass dome roof in a style characteristic of Victorian exhibition halls. Around the main hall are rooms and galleries of various sizes with a large gallery at each end. A grand staircase off the central court leads to further galleries on a second level.[66]

The first stone of this winning design was laid by HRH the Prince of Wales on 10 April 1885. This was an important state occasion – a chance to celebrate the success of the British Empire and strengthen its place in Ireland. It was also an opportunity to express the hope put into words by Lord Powerscourt that 'the laying of the stone ... would mark a new era of peace and prosperity in Ireland'.[67] Accounts of the event, published in the newspapers of the day and in a pamphlet produced by the museum, recreate a sense of the atmosphere of the occasion. The ceremony began with a flourish of trumpets that announced the arrival of the Prince of Wales for whom the national anthem was played, followed by an address given by the Director of the museum and replied to by the Prince. The stone was then laid and the band played 'St Patrick's Day' and 'God Bless the Prince of Wales'. The address of Mr Valentine Ball, Director of the institution,[68] brought together the aspects that he considered important. He referred to the archaeological collections originating from the 'patriotic labours of the Royal Irish Academy'. Then he stated his belief that the science and art collections would be 'illustrative of the Art and Industry of this country at various periods of her history' and give the museum 'an unique and local character of the highest interest'. Finally, Ball celebrated the contribution of native workmanship; the buildings were 'designed by an Irish Architect and built largely of Irish materials by Irish hands'.[69] The Prince of Wales made clear his pleasure at being involved with the development of a cultural institution that would now be 'even more worthy than heretofore of the pride of the Irish nation, and the admiration of Literary and Scientific Bodies throughout the world'.

That a Royal heir should have laid the first stone is interesting consider the political context. The 1880s marked a renewed effort to achieve home rule – the Parnell–Gladstone alliance produced the failed 1886 Home Rule Bill. Also the Gaelic revival was at its height. The Gaelic League seemed to take little interest in the activity of the museum. Moreover, the newspapers of the day did not record any objections to Royal involvement with the occasion, over and above a few individuals in the crowds flying green flags.[70] What royal involvement does convey is the status of Dublin within the kingdom of Britain and Ireland and the value placed by the Department of Science and Art on the Dublin museum. Leading from this, the event was an affirmation of the links between London and Dublin.

Some dissatisfaction was evident with regard to the management of the Dublin museum. For instance, in January 1883 the *Irish Builder* told its readers, as a warning, that South Kensington was administering a negative influence over the Dublin institutions. On this occasion, the paper provided its own history of the management of cultural institutions in Dublin. It wrote of the Act of Union and stated that though the Act did not intend to prevent the two countries from having separate institutions, it had been poorly administered and, as a result, 'one after another our institutions have been centralised or managed from the sister kingdom'. According to the newspaper, this was to the detriment of the Royal Dublin Society and the Royal Irish Academy. The Society, it insisted:

> in an evil hour and by the advice of pretending friends, made dangerous avowals, and then came a surrender, without a proper safeguarding of position and condition. One false step led to a long series of vexatious devices and annoyances which seem to have been adopted for obvious purposes, and these purposes and objects were apparent to us long since. [London] was also determined to swallow up the [Academy]. Its splendid collection of antiquities, literary and art treasures, were hungered for by the rapacious maw of South Kensington manipulated by officials who will be nameless at present. Dishonourable threats were resorted to of the possibility of grants being with held if the Academy did not subscribe to the conditions of the scheme devised by the designing bureaucrats at South Kensington.

A direct link between political interests and cultural institutions seems to be evident in this extract from the *Irish Builder*. However, in the same essay the paper informed its readers that it wished to look upon the proposed museum as 'apart from politics or any sort of sectarian bias, if possible'. Instead, art and science was presented as important 'from a practical and patriotic point of view', because 'we believe in these matters the Irish people are the best judges of their own wants, and should be allowed to exercise their undoubted rights'.[71] Here the *Irish Builder* claimed to be trying to divorce the management of the museum from politics, a vain goal. The statement is clearly political. The political relevance of the management of Irish cultural institutions was also taken up by some nationalist political figures. For instance, William O'Brien made highly critical remarks about the establishment and make-up of the Dublin Museum of Science and Art. His was not an objection to the idea of a public museum in itself, but rather, in common with the *Irish Builder*, to the fact that the Academy passed its collection of Irish antiquities over to a museum which was part of a British institution. The move was damned as one of giving up the Irish past to English administration. O'Brien claimed that the Academy had, in an act which was 'languid of spirit', given up its patriotic heritage and 'surrender[ed] to a South Kensington collection of curiosities, the inestimable relics of Celtic antiquity, bequeathed to them by the pious patriotism of generations of Hudsons, Hardimans and Wildes'.[72]

THE DUBLIN MUSEUM OF SCIENCE AND ART: EARLY YEARS

The Dublin Museum of Science and Art existed for the good of Irish industry. However, the fact that the needs of Irish industry were determined within the same framework as those for other major cities in the United Kingdom gives the impression of the Department of Science and Art in London as a monolithic institution dictating the content of provincial museum services. The influence the London Department had over the Dublin museum was closely felt. In return for an annual grant, the Director of the Dublin museum had to make annual reports to the Department of Science and Art in London, gain permission from the Secretary of the Department for purchases of over £20, and negotiate with the Department for the recruitment of extra staff.[73] As well as this, the staff of the museum had to co-operate with regular Parliamentary Enquires held to investigate the running of the museum.

Instead of being any sort of force for Irish nationalism, the primary public function of the Dublin museum was industrial education. This is evident in the acquisition and display policy, the form of the exhibition catalogues and the nature of the public lectures arranged by the museum. The Dublin Museum of Science and Art was established as having three divisions: the Natural History Division, which exhibited in the buildings opened by the Royal Dublin Society; the Art and Industrial Division; and the Antiquities Division, dominated by the Royal Irish Academy collection. The annual reports made to the Department of Science and Art in London depict the Dublin museum as having an active collecting policy. Each report included lists of acquisitions and, by 1889, the Art and Industrial Division had registered some 10,372 objects.[74] The emphasis on industrial needs is evident in the first report presented to the Department by the Director of the museum. He stated that he hoped that the collection of antique lace recently purchased, which was 'mostly foreign', would be 'highly suggestive to the lace workers of Ireland'.[75] From the Director's reports one gets a sense of the dominance of the industrial collection and the international nature of the acquisitions. The list of those received in 1889 is typical, and it reads in part:

> During the past year among the principal acquisitions, by purchase, [which] may be mentioned [are]: a cross bow, early 17th century; specimens of modern wrought-iron work from Munich; a fine *kakemono* from a temple in Ooyeno, Japan, and several shrines with figures of deities in carved and gilt wood; two chairs upholstered with old French tapestry; collections of old East Indian drawings and printed stuffs. ... Among the plaster casts, added, may be mentioned the centrepiece of the porch of Amiens cathedral, and a carved wood reredos at Lübeck. The ceramic collection had been enriched by a fine vase of enamelled pottery (Delft); specimens of old Italian Majolica. Some old Persian tiles and glass, oriental weapons, Russian enamelled silver work and pottery, and modern French pewter, were secured at the Paris exhibition.[76]

These international industrial collections were also given greatest priority in the layout of the museum. The entrance was dominated by the collection of Greek and Greco-Roman sculptures and the casts of international architectural features were given prominent display in the central court of the museum. The extract below, from the 1894 report, listed the content of this area:

> A cast of an ancient cross at Kilkieran co. Kilkenny (from moulds presented by the Royal Irish Academy); ... Cast of a Buddhist Column (British Museum); Recumbent figure 'Admiral Chabot' (Louvre); Tomb of the children of Charles VIII (Tours); A font attributed to Jacopo della Quercia (Siena); Judith and Holofernes, by Donatello (Florence); Doorway from the Corso Magenta, (Milan); Niche from Pulpit (Siena); Column, octagonal from the Abbey of Souvigny,

France; Doorway from St Maclou, Rouen; Portion of Doorway in Bordeaux Cathedral.[77]

In addition, the ground floor galleries off the main court were devoted to the display of a miscellaneous range of artefacts all deemed to be useful for Irish industry, such as collections of Indian and Persian art, Egyptian and Assyrian antiquities and Greek and Roman antiquities. The galleries on the first floor included a collection of furniture, mostly loaned from the South Kensington Museum, as well as glass and ceramic exhibitions. This space was also devoted to collections of woodcarvings, arms and armour, lace, embroideries, textile fabrics and various industrial exhibits, including several working models of looms.[78] The industrial nature of the museum was also evident in the nature of the guides produced and the subject matter of the public lectures. From 1899 to 1913 the museum produced numerous guides to individual parts of the collection (see the list in Appendix 1). The subject matter of these guides spanned from Greek and Roman sculpture to Chinese porcelain and Italian furniture. The links between Dublin and the London institutions were emphasised in the catalogue to the Greek and Roman antiquities collection. The reader was informed that the display of Greek and Roman coins in the Dublin museum was an electrotype copy of a collection in the British Museum and was laid out in an identical manner. Since this was the case, the Dublin Museum catalogue was a reprint of that used in the British Museum.

At this time the Royal Irish Academy collection of Irish antiquities did not play a significant role in the museum. It was displayed in a less prominent space, in a room on the first floor. Yearly additions to the collection were much smaller than those to the industrial division, partly due to the nature of what was being collected, but also because this responsibility was, for the most part, left to the Royal Irish Academy budget. The collection also generated fewer accompanying catalogues and fewer lectures based on its content (see Appendix 2). The evening lectures that dominated were those on natural history themes and those developed for people involved in local industry, dealing with relevant subjects such as lacemaking and silver work.

To place the Dublin developments in the context of science and art development in Britain, one may consider the experience of institutions in Scotland. The history of the Edinburgh institutions reads in a similar fashion to that in Dublin. Indeed, in the 1860s the London administration presented the success of the Scottish case to support the recommendation for changes in Ireland. The Society of Antiquaries of Scotland was formed in the early eighteenth century and given a Royal Charter in 1783.[79] It considered itself having a status equal to the Society of Antiquaries in London.[80] It was suggested that the antiquarian activity of the Society, namely the preservation the objects of 'national importance', might raise emotions that would be a threat to the Union. A member of the Society observed that though 'we are cordially united to England, not in government only, but in loyalty and affection to a common Sovereign, it was not perhaps altogether consistent with political wisdom to call the attention of the Scots to the ancient honours and constitution of their independent monarchy'.[81] As in the Irish case, the interest in the formation of these establishments in the eighteenth century was the result of local initiative. However, the funding of the societies was largely dependent on and answerable to the treasury in London. Also in common with experiences in Ireland, inadequate financial provision from the treasury was interpreted as having ulterior motives. In 1844 a petition was sent from the Scottish Society of Antiquaries to the Queen and the Prime Minister stating that the lack of funds for the Society and its museum 'so closely connected with their past history and most patriotic feelings' was a 'slight' to Scotland. Later, in 1851, because of financial burdens the Society moved its collection to rent-free accommodation in the Royal Institution building in which the collection came under financial control of the government. Revealing competing priorities, the collection was recognised simultaneously as the 'National Museum of the Antiquaries of Scotland' by the Society and 'The Museum of Antiquities, Royal Institution' by the British government. In the 1860s the proposal that the Antiquaries collection should be incorporated into the Edinburgh Science and Art Museum, which had been established in 1855, met with much disapproval. The scheme 'to incorporate the National Collection in the section of general antiquities in another institution' was described by the Society as being one 'calculated to destroy both its scientific value and its public utility, by depriving it of its distinctively national character'. The Society was able to resist the move, only for it to be again mooted in the 1880s. The space that the collection was occupying in the Royal Institute was in demand for other purposes. As a result the Society was obliged, in the early

1880s, to move its antiquities collection to the Science and Art Museum. Objections were aired about the lack of space allocated to the collection in the new premises and interest in a separate entrance was put forward. In reference to the lack of space, the members of the Society wrote that 'the proposal, to store the priceless National Collection of Antiquities in two small upper floors of a building in which these floors probably represent about one-fifth part, would be in a national sense discreditable'.[82]

The Dublin museum would, therefore, have had the outward appearance and priorities of the other public museums developed in Britain from the same source with the result that the other museums of Science and Art in England and Scotland shared a similar relationship with the London Department of Science and Art in London. This very point was made by a contemporary observer, Dr A. B. Meyer, Director to the Royal Zoological, Anthropological and Ethnographical Museum in Dresden, who toured the science and art institutions of America and Europe at the turn of the century and published his findings in 1905. He remarked that the science and art institutions in Edinburgh, Dublin, Liverpool and Glasgow had much in common, not only in management structure but also in the layout and subject of the collections. Of the Museum of Science and Art in Dublin he remarked that 'this museum, like the one of the same name in Edinburgh, is copied more or less after the South Kensington Museum, with the addition of a natural science collection'. Meyer concluded 'this uniformity of the museums in the Island Kingdom corresponds to the uniformity of life there'.[83]

The Department of Science and Art at South Kensington may be interpreted as a symbol of a 'British nation' which attempted to standardise and take control of science and art instruction throughout the whole kingdom, being prepared to take collections or services from the smaller antiquarian societies in its progress. Again, the control of the societies and their collections is an indication of the broader political aspirations. In this context the management of museums was an expression of the 'power relationships' between the establishment and the members of the societies and the people they claimed to represent. The Dublin museum at this point in its history therefore demonstrates the power of the London administration in Ireland.

Two important points have emerged. The museum that developed in Dublin was a stage – a place where different perspectives on the political history of Ireland met and were acted out. The history of the Dublin museum is, in its own particular way, a microcosm of the history of Ireland in the last quarter of the nineteenth century. For instance, the continual debate concerning a local management board to be responsible for museums in Ireland reflects what was going on in the political sphere. The 1868 Commission of Enquiry was held against the background of increased Fenian activity and the political atmosphere in which Isaac Butt founded the Home Rule movement in 1870. An enquiry into the museum in 1898, which is discussed in the following chapter, was held in the wake of the failure of the second Home Rule Bill, which was rejected by the House of Lords in 1894. The issue of representative management of the Dublin museum was, therefore, particularly pertinent and reflected political discussion elsewhere. In addition, the debate about the design and management of the museum, in all its details, may also be interpreted as an alternative setting in which the larger political question of the government of Ireland was aired.

The second point is the radical change in collecting practice, both in structure and purpose, through the nineteenth century. What had originally been private, and often eccentric, philanthropic cabinets had become rationalised public institutions, with a distinct industrial and public purpose. The history of this period provides an interesting demonstration of the political nature of museums. The Dublin museum, not only as an institution but also as a building and a collection of artefacts, was a reflection of particular values arising from definitions of 'the public' – how they should be represented, what their needs were and how best to meet them. It was important that the museum in Dublin should be a symbol, and what it should symbolise became a matter of conflict between competing interests. Those involved in Irish industry wished to see an institution managed by a local board of representatives. The Royal Irish Academy wanted a separate museum worthy of its rich collection of Irish antiquities. Both bodies stressed the importance of the eventual institution being seen as a 'national museum'. The conflict around the architect of the museum indicates the importance of the museum building for the creation of a sense of place and as an expression of identity. That objects in museums, their classification and the museological context are all demonstrations of a larger master narrative is easily demonstrated by the Irish case. The contested nature of these narratives is the theme of the following chapter which discusses how the Dublin Museum of Science and Art was gradually redefined.

CHAPTER SIX

From the Dublin Museum of Science and Art to the National Museum of Ireland

THE NEED for the establishment of institutions that would nurture the emerging nation was acknowledged by a century of cultural nationalists in Ireland. Despite these aspirations, the public museum that materialised in the 1870s and 1880s was an imperial institution established to further the joint industrial development of Britain and Ireland. It was, however, also a Dublin institution and as such was not immune to the influence of the heightened aspirations for independence that characterised the decades at the turn of the century.

A BATTLE OF TWO NATIONS: THE CASE OF THE BROIGHTER HOARD

At the turn of the nineteenth century the most controversial and political issue to be faced by the patrons of the Dublin museum was concerned with the ownership of a collection of Irish antiquities exhibited in the British Museum known as the Broighter Hoard. The case raised questions about the implementation of treasure trove and the legal and moral ownership of antiquities, and it remained a political problem until the return of the collection to Dublin in 1906. The various responses to the issues it raised demonstrate the political importance and sensitivity of the ownership of antiquities. Stemming from this, the matter represents a particularly interesting example of the tensions that can exist between cultural institutions as a result of competing definitions of the nation, and therefore the area of the nation that they administer. It also symbolises the tensions raised between Britain and Ireland throughout the nineteenth century with regard to cultural affairs.

The hoard comprised a collection of gold ornaments that included a decorated tubular gold collar, two rod-twisted bracelets, two woven-chain necklaces, a gold boat complete with oars and a small gold bowl.[1] The hoard was found in land being ploughed in Broighter townland, County Londonderry in 1896. The landowner, Joseph Gibson, sold the collection to a Mr Day in Cork, a well-known antiquarian and collector. Day had the collection mended by a Dublin jeweller and subsequently exhibited it at the Society of Antiquaries in London. The Trustees of the British Museum then purchased it in 1897. At this point, the Royal Irish Academy became aware of the collection and objected to it being in the possession of the British Museum rather than the Academy, under the normal conditions of treasure trove. John Redmond MP brought the case to the attention of Westminster and introduced a Bill 'to enable the transfer of Irish Antiquities from the British Museum to the National Museum in Dublin'. The Bill failed but, as a result of the increased interest, a Royal Commission was set up in 1898 to advise on the circumstances of the case and the relations between the British Museum and the museums of Edinburgh and Dublin regarding the acquisition and retention of antiquities. The Commission recommended that the British Museum should place the objects in the Dublin museum on long-term loan, but the British Museum refused to co-operate. As a result the Crown (represented by the Attorney-General) brought the British Museum to court. The membership of the Counsel of the Crown included Sir Edward Carson, the Irish Solicitor-General and later leader of the Ulster Unionists. In court Justice Farwell declared the collection to be treasure trove. This meant that it should have been, by Royal prerogative, in the possession of the Royal Irish Academy and that the British Museum was holding the artefacts illegally. The Academy was successful; Edward VII subsequently ordered the return of the hoard to Dublin.[2]

The text of the 1898 Royal Commission report recorded the opinions held by those invited to contribute to the case. They included representatives from London institutions, such as the British Museum and the Society of Antiquaries, as well as members of the Royal Irish Academy and representatives of the Dublin Museum of Science and Art. The British Museum representatives gave a number of reasons why they would reject Redmond's Bill. They made it clear that by law the British Museum was unable to part with artefacts in its collection and that the broad use of terms in the Bill could result in the museum losing a significant part of its collection. In addition, as evident in the words of the Director of the British Museum, Sir Edmond Thompson, the staff recognised the worth of the Broighter collection: 'we consider these ornaments very valuable for the British Museum'. The most interesting reason given for their retention in Dublin was, however, the contention that the British Museum was an institution qualified to hold collections for the entire nation and empire. Obviously putting forward a definition of 'the nation' that included Ireland in its scope. The British Museum, Thompson argued, 'represents the Empire. It is not a London Museum, it is not an English Museum, it is a "British Museum" and as such we naturally have to look after its interests, and make our collection as perfect as possible, to represent every portion of the British Empire'.[3] Viscount Dillon, a former Trustee of the British Museum and President of the Society of Antiquaries, argued along similar lines. He then presented an even more contentious claim: that the British Museum should be granted first refusal for all artefacts found in Britain and Ireland. He stated: 'I think London, as the capital of the United Kingdom, is the best focus for objects to come to ... I look at the people of England, Scotland and Ireland as being all members of one nation.' When questioned on the relevance of 'national feeling' in Ireland which desired their return, he stated 'it is not a national calamity ... particularly as, after all, Ireland is part of England. If these things had gone abroad to some foreign country I could understand it being regarded as a national calamity'.[4] In the same polemical vein, Sir John Robinson, Fellow of the Society of Antiquaries in London, stated: 'I think the sentiment of the Empire at large is as important as the sentiment of Scotland or Ireland ... I take an Imperial view of this Museum. I regard the British Museum as the Central Imperial Museum.'[5]

In reply the Council of the Royal Irish Academy stated that the Dublin Museum both qualified as a national museum and was treated as such. The Council argued that this was evident from the wide-scale recognition of the importance of its collection, as well as the fact that the institution was entrusted with the care of treasure trove found in Ireland with large sums of public money being granted for this purpose.[6] Likewise, Colonel Plunkett, the Director of the Dublin museum, stated that 'the museum in Dublin is recognised and is a national museum, quite as much as the British Museum. It was founded in order to supply the want of a national museum in Ireland'. In this context the Broighter artefacts 'are of infinitely more value to archaeologists and antiquarians in Dublin than they could possibly be in any other city'. Plunkett also made it clear that the Broighter controversy was attracting public attention in Dublin. He told the enquiry that 'it has created a very strong feeling indeed among all who are interested in archaeology and ancient art in Ireland, and beyond that there is great popular feeling; every newspaper in Dublin, I think without exception, has taken the matter up warmly'.[7]

Some of what Plunkett referred to can be found in the Dublin newspapers of the time. The newspapers interpreted the events in a number of ways. For instance, not only was the Broighter Hoard taken to illustrate what was so special about Ireland, but also, in its superior craftsmanship, taken as a reflection of qualities which Ireland possessed but which the rest of the world, and Britain in particular, could not match. Evidently, Britain was trying to claim title to some of this glory. The readers of the *Evening Herald* were informed:

> By the destiny of history we are in Ireland the natural custodians and the sympathetic spokesmen for the relics and the repute of a great part of the Human Race whose name and fame have in other lands been obliterated by the all devouring uniformity that the Roman world stamped upon the regions it subdued. It is our duty as well as our privilege to jealously assert and zealously discharge our responsibilities in this regard.[8]

These comments must also be considered in the context of a century of writing about the importance of archaeology and antiquities for defining the Irish nation. Similar cultural arguments were rehearsed and used as justification for returning the Broighter Hoard. As with achieving home rule, the care of this heritage was represented as not only a necessity, but also an Irish right. It was deemed impossible for the British authorities to appreciate the historic nature of such a claim. Referring to the Broighter objects, the *Evening Herald* continued by saying that 'their retention by an English Museum would be a flagrant violation of one of the few national rights of Ireland that has been allowed to us'. Furthermore it believed with 'every confidence' that the Government will 'at once take action to set the matter right. For it must be obvious that the entire body of Irish Members in Parliament will be unanimous in insisting that our National right to have custody of all such objects shall be recognised and inforced [*sic*] in this and in all like cases'.⁹ A similar theme was put forward in the *Irish Times*, a strongly Unionist paper. Redmond's Bill received the support of the editor, who believed that Redmond 'spoke for all people of Ireland when he demanded that these rare objects of ancient art should be restored to us'. In a patriotic tone, the paper continued with the notion of ownership and national rights. The artefacts, it continued, 'belong to us. It is our right to possess them ... these gold relics belong to Ireland and it is unfair and unjust that they should be housed in London. In the British Museum they are out of place. Amongst us they are at home'.¹⁰

An interesting debate about the definition of the 'national interest' was played out in a letter published in the *Irish Times*. The letter was written by Sir Thomas Esmonde of Gorey, in reply to an earlier one written by Mr Stanley Leighton. Leighton believed that such artefacts had an important place in a British Museum. In his reply Esmonde raised a number of issues which were central to the debate: that of the links between national interest and a sense of place in Ireland, the contribution of the artefacts to a sense of Irish national identity and the links between the nation and ownership as symbolised by the collection. He wrote:

> They are not of national interest anywhere, or to anyone in Great Britain, and least of all in that vast Cosmopolitan aggregation of artistic and antiquarian treasure known as the British Museum. They are of national interest only in their rightful resting place, the National Museum in Dublin ... Ireland has an indefeasible right to the possession of these Celtic ornaments. It is a case of the right of the nation of Ireland against the power and influence of the British Museum. ... As to your correspondent's 'nation' being the 'loser' by the doing of justice to Ireland in this particular, may I suggest that your correspondent's 'nation' has already possessed itself of much of Ireland's national property that we have some reason for refusing to acquiesce in its carrying off such scattered fragments of our archaeological inheritance as yet remain to us ... With us Irish, what is left of our national treasures is so little that we hold what we have saved in all the greater reverence. Your correspondent's 'nation' ... is so rich in spoils gathered together from the ends of the earth, that what is priceless to us is but a drop in the ocean of its accumulations.¹¹

The editor of the *Irish Times* wrote in support of Esmonde. He summarised the right of the Irish nation: '[it] is not represented by the British Museum Trustees, but by the Irish people ... it is granted that the ancient Irish ornaments are of "immense national interest" but they are not of national interest anywhere outside Ireland'.[12]

Two points were raised by this controversy, which emerge clearly both from the enquiry and the newspapers. The first point is that Britain was a very powerful nation, keen to exert that power through the ownership of treasures from all around the world and, secondly, that many Irish people wished to portray Ireland as a separate nation within the United Kingdom with its own right to its national treasures. This controversy over the ownership of antiquities draws on and mimics the wider political issue concerning the right to national self-determination in Ireland that was rehearsed throughout the nineteenth century. The Broighter Hoard became a trigger that raised complex emotions regarding Irish national rights, patriotism and identity. The hoard became a carrier, a medium through which political and ideological aspirations were expressed. The very public nature of this enquiry, and the court case connected with it, made it pivotal in shaping popular values towards archaeology, antiquities and the Dublin museum. More than a collection of artefacts, the hoard became symbolic of the Irish nation and the struggle of that nation with her more powerful neighbour. On its return the hoard may have become, for some, a war trophy representing a victory over Britain.

THE BEGINNING OF CHANGE FOR THE DUBLIN MUSEUM OF SCIENCE AND ART

By way of the Broighter Hoard case, the members of the Royal Irish Academy and those involved with the Dublin Science and Art Museum asserted the national status of the Dublin collection. The Dublin museum opened the doors of its new building at the height of the Gaelic Revival in the 1890s. At first glance it does not appear to have been quite so obviously embroiled in the cultural disputes which seemed to dominate other institutions in Dublin at a similar time, such as that surrounding the Irish Literary Theatre. However, through the Broighter Hoard case, and some of the objections to the identity that the Dublin museum was assuming, dissent is evident. The previous chapter noted the debate over the nationality of the architect of the building and noted some of the objections to the move of the Academy antiquities collection to the Science and Art Museum. These debates were based on similar ideological grounds to those triggered by activity at the theatre; in both cases they were centred on contested definitions of the national role that cultural institutions should assume in Ireland.

Dissatisfaction regarding the character of industrial education and arts facilities in Ireland, as evident in some of the Parliamentary Commissions of the nineteenth century, was also to be seen in the positive action of individuals in Dublin. Of great significance for the Dublin Museum was the interest shown by Horace Plunkett which resulted in the management of the museum finally being transferred to a Dublin-based department. In 1895 Plunkett wrote a letter to the *Irish Times* stating that it would be 'good policy and good patriotism' if politicians from all parties, as well as 'practical Irishmen', formed an industrial committee for 'the material and social advancement of Ireland'. This committee, known as the Recess Committee, successfully brought about the conditions for a Bill to be introduced in Parliament to establish a Dublin-based Department of Agriculture and Technical Instruction. When established in 1899 the Department was responsible for the organisation of agriculture, the prevention of animal and plant disease and the supervision of the Dublin Museum of Science and Art, the National Library and the Botanic Gardens.[13]

At a similar time to Plunkett's appeal, the Department of Science and Art in London commissioned two reviews of the museums under its jurisdiction, one in 1897 and the other in 1898. As with earlier enquiries, these investigations illustrate the continual relevance of political values to the management of the museum. These two are all the more interesting considering the change of administration that was to come. The Director of the Dublin museum, Colonel Plunkett was the only person to be interviewed at the 1897 enquiry. However, the following year the committee interviewed both the Director and a representative of Irish industry, Mr Arnold Graves. Plunkett and Graves each provided conflicting reports on the success of the museum in positively influencing local industry and the usefulness of its links with South Kensington.

Arnold Graves was involved in various aspects of the development of Irish industry. He was secretary of the Irish Charity Commissioners, Honorary Secretary of the Technical Educational Association of Ireland and Honorary Secretary of the City of Dublin

Technical Schools. Graves asserted that the Dublin museum was an excellent museum, but he also argued that it was failing in its role as a public educator in the area of technical instruction in art and industry for Ireland. He condemned the displays, which, in his opinion, did not recognise the character of Irish industry, and he felt that the facilities were in need of expansion and technical displays in need of modernisation. Furthermore, he asserted that the current financial relationship between South Kensington and the Dublin museum was not to the advantage of the people of Ireland. He claimed, for example, that *per capita* much less was invested by the London Treasury in museums in Ireland than in England. Graves also made it clear that he would prefer an Irish managerial board, which he believed would be more in touch with the needs of the local people. This was, in the spirit of the time, a blatantly political viewpoint. Indeed, a member of the committee presented him with the question: 'whatever your opinions are as far as management of the Dublin Science and Art Museum are concerned, you are a Home Ruler?' To this Graves replied that he was 'in favour of local self-government' and, with regard to the museum, 'the general opinion in Ireland is in favour of the local control of the Dublin Museum: it would be decidedly wise and a popular measure of reform in the way of local self government'. Graves was prepared to be controversial – he suggested that because 'Ireland has suffered ... by the policy of England towards Ireland in the past century' England 'owes it to Ireland to be exceedingly generous to her in every matter'.[14]

The opinions of the Director of the Dublin museum, Colonel Plunkett, were somewhat different. He replied to Graves' assertions about the lack of a public role by claiming they were unfounded and his recommendations for change as inappropriate. Plunkett believed that the links between the museum and South Kensington should be maintained. At the 1897 enquiry he stated that the museum 'would lose a great deal if [it] were independent; I get the most valuable assistance from the officers [in London] ... they are ready to give me their time most liberally'.[15] He brought this point up again at the 1898 enquiry when he argued: 'I think that separation would be a mistake ... I think that a local board which must in the end cut us off from the great advantages we get here in South Kensington would be unfortunate.'[16] Colonel Plunkett's sentiment is interesting because it is a record of the positive relationship that had been formed between London and Dublin. However, despite Colonel Plunkett's support for the museum remaining under the Department of Science and Art in London, its management passed to the Department of Agriculture and Technical Instruction in 1899.

Transfer of responsibility for the museum to an Irish-based managerial board was a significant change. In his first report as Vice-President of the Department of Agriculture and Technical Instruction, Horace Plunkett asserted the purpose as being to develop the institutions that were its responsibility in such a way that would provide 'inspiration' for the Irish people. Indeed, his ambitions were suggestive of ongoing political aspirations. He continued to state that the Department would set about 'encouraging local freedom, aiming at distinctive national qualities [and] having at its hand, as part of its inspiration, the beautiful and suggestive objects in the Museum'.[17]

Under this new arrangement the museum still had its own Director. In 1907, on the retirement of Colonel Plunkett, a new Director was appointed: George Noble, Count Plunkett. He was an interesting choice, as at that time he was known as both a cultural and a political figure. In 1892 he unsuccessfully contested a seat as a Parnellite Nationalist, repeating his attempts in 1895 and 1898,[18] and he was founding editor of the nationalist paper *Hibernia*.[19] Count Plunkett was a member of the Gaelic League Industrial Committee and, as well as being a member of the council of the Royal Irish Academy and its Vice-President (1908–9 and 1911–14), he was President of the Royal Society of Antiquaries of Ireland.[20] Plunkett was not alone in his political sympathies within the museum; the archaeologist George Coffey who was appointed as superintendent of Irish Antiquities in 1890 also addressed public meetings in support of Home Rule.[21]

With Count Plunkett's appointment the identity of the museum began to shift. One of the changes that must, to an extent, be associated with his arrival is the renaming of the museum. The title of the museum had always been mildly contentious. Some referred to it as the 'National Museum' rather than by its official title 'The Dublin Museum of Science and Art', so betraying political preferences.[22] Significantly, a year after Plunkett's arrival to the Directorship the museum was renamed. His report of 1908 reads that it was decided that the Museum should henceforth be styled 'the National Museum of Science and Art, Dublin'. This title was, according to Plunkett, 'more appropriate for the institution having regard to its representative position in the capital as the Museum of

Ireland and the treasury of Celtic antiquities'.[23]

In keeping with the affirmation of this national status, Count Plunkett also set about redefining the purpose of the museum and rearranging its collections. In his new layout the Irish antiquities collection gained greater prominence, a shift made complete on independence. Count Plunkett justified this change as being more suited to local needs. He argued that those visiting the national museum would 'hold in less consideration the foreign objects that the museum contains than the great historical series of Irish antiquities and the general illustration of Irish arts and industries. Hence our work inclines largely towards the collection of things distinctively Irish, both ancient and modern.'[24]

Within, therefore, the first decade of the twentieth century the museum was already beginning to shift focus. Count Plunkett was able to give further justification for his changes at a meeting of the Museums Association in Dublin in 1912. Plunkett informed those gathered that a museum must be seen as an essential part of the nation and an expression of the 'national life',[25] thus repeating much of the cultural nationalist sentiment of the previous decades. When nationalism reached its height, four years later, Plunkett and the museum was affected by the political upheaval. In the wake of the 1916 Rising, Count Plunkett lost his position as Director of the museum because of the involvement of his son Joseph in the Rising and the inherent danger in having a republican sympathiser in a high civil service position.[26] On his son's execution, Count Plunkett became politically active and in the by-election in February 1917 he stood and won a Sinn Féin position.[27] However, for some the museum Director did not appear an obvious political figure. The *Irish Nation*, a republican paper, objected to him standing, fearing that his political views would not be radical enough. The paper described him as a 'very estimable old gentleman of a very innocuous type', whose only claim to the position was the loss of his son in the 1916 Rising.[28]

The operation of the Royal Irish Academy was also affected by the events of 1916. In June of that year the Council of the Academy expelled Eoin MacNeill after his conviction by court martial for his compliance with the 1916 Rising. Though there was no immediate reaction from the Academicians, by 1919 MacNeill's membership had not been reinstated. Consequently there was discontent amongst the nationalist members who began a campaign to restore his position. This discontent was made public through a furious attack on the Academy in the *Irish Nation* criticising the very basis of the society. Despite its vast contribution to learning, it was described as the 'most high Royal and Imperial un-Irish Academy'. MacNeill's expulsion was described as 'absolutely unwarranted'. The paper provided a warning that 'we intend in the near future to investigate the conditions of this wretched body. It is one of the cancerous spots of political and religious prejudice existing in the very midst of us. It must be rooted out.'[29]

MacNeill's expulsion was not overturned until June 1921. Since some of the members found this wait offensive, they decided to challenge the authority and legitimacy of the Academy by preparing to found a rival 'National Institute or Academy' which aimed to 'secure the Irish language, its literature and history'.[30] This initiative was led by a number of professors in University College Dublin, and Eoin MacNeill was included amongst the original members. A further 105 people joined the body at the foundation meeting of the National Academy in March 1922, amongst whom were Count Plunkett and many members of the Royal Irish Academy.[31] Plunkett was delighted at the chance to challenge the Royal Irish Academy and wrote that the new academy would aim to secure manuscript treasures in the care of men 'true to the nation's honour'.[32] In the end, however, this rival body did not represent a realistic challenge. MacNeill joined Robert Macalister in 1922 to form a committee to oversee the Royal Irish Academy antiquities collection. The first annual general meeting of the rival Irish Academy, which was planned for November 1923, was not held and nothing more was heard of it.[33]

PARTITION AND MUSEUM PROVISION

In reaction to continuing dissatisfaction and unrest in Ireland after the 1916 Rising, the British government introduced the Government of Ireland Act (1920) in an attempt to reconcile the differences. The Act provided for parliaments in Dublin and Belfast, which would have executive powers; allowed Westminster to maintain power on various issues of imperial concern (such as defence and foreign affairs); and established a 'Council of Ireland', which would oversee certain public services that could not be easily divided. Politicians in the south rejected the idea of a Dublin parliament in favour of the *Dáil* and the Council of Ireland was rejected by unionists who saw it as a step towards all-Ireland Home Rule. The Act, however, can be described as the blueprint for partition. Partition, put in place by the Anglo-Irish Treaty of 1921, divided Ireland, for the first time in its history, into two separate states. This had an obvious impact for the management of the archaeological and cultural record.

During the negotiations over the Government of Ireland Bill, the management of the National Gallery the National Library and the National Museum were amongst the services designated as the responsibility of the Council of Ireland. It was also briefly suggested that these three particular services would be better managed from Westminster as they were 'obviously unitary' but this suggestion was dropped and their management under the Council of Ireland was retained, in theory. The administration of the Public Record Office in Dublin passed to Westminster. This was a popular choice for Ulster Unionists who were against the proposed Council of Ireland. The Act, however, allowed the northern and southern assemblies to establish their own repositories for records pertaining to their own areas of administration. On partition, the Public Records Act (NI) of 1923 established a record office in Northern Ireland and this resulted in the division of the Irish archive.[34]

During the negotiations the Prime Minister of the northern parliament, Sir James Craig, was advised to claim those heritage items that were connected with the six counties. Sir Ernest Clark, assistant under-secretary in Belfast, informed Craig that 'the north should claim a share of the pictures and contents of museums in Dublin ... of these things the north ought to have its fair share, and although the matter is not immediate, it might be well to prepare the way for a claim'.[35] However, when partition was made legally complete with the passing of the Government of Ireland Act (1920), the collections of the National Gallery and the National Museum were not divided as those of the Public Record Office were. It has been suggested that the original intention was to move parts of the collection to the Belfast Museum, namely the artefacts and collections pertaining to the six counties that had been gained by the Dublin museum as treasure trove and which were Crown property. However, the Northern Ireland government did not pursue that option, and may have accepted money in exchange.[36] It is interesting that the northern authorities should have given up the opportunity to care for the antiquities of the six counties (which would have included the Broighter Hoard). If money was accepted instead it would appear that at this time greater importance was attached to the financial compensation than to securing the artefacts. Indeed, cultural policies do not seem to have taken a high priority in the early decades of Northern Ireland. The authorities had more pressing concerns, as summarised by Estyn Evans: 'monies set aside for building cultural centres in the North were diverted to the more urgent needs of civil defence, and police stations were erected instead of museums and galleries'.[37] As a result the Belfast museum was not upgraded to its current position of Ulster Museum[38] until the Museum Act of 1961.[39] With the role of political factors in mind, it is also possible that many of the items of treasure trove, being symbols of Irish nationalism, were considered by the unionist authorities as not being of significant worth because they were not part of the identity that they hoped to nurture for the six counties. If this was the case, this exclusivist policy denied Northern Ireland of some of its material heritage. On the other hand, one must also consider that some may appreciate the value of keeping such a collection together in one institution, and not imposing the political geography of twentieth-century Ireland on the material remains of antiquity.

THE *LITHBERG REPORT* AND THE REDEFINITION OF THE NATIONAL MUSEUM

The establishment of the Irish Free State in 1922 carried with it the suggestion that the National Museum of Science and Art could then be formally heralded as the 'National Museum of Ireland'. To have a museum that would be recognised as 'national' had eluded those involved with the institution since its foundation. Under the administration of the new state, the Dublin museum would become the national institution which had been demanded by nineteenth-century antiquarians and political activists alike. How the museum emerged from the ashes of the 1916 Rising and nineteenth-century nationalism to take its place in the new state provides for an interesting study. The transition brought about a change in identity, but it was not as dramatic as some would have wished. It is interesting, therefore, to consider how the rhetoric of nationalist politicians concerning the importance of museums became a reality.

In the early years the new State set about defining its own distinct identity. It instigated various enquires, such as that into the Irish language and education, in order to establish a new purpose for its public services.[40] Five years after the formation of the Irish Free State the government sanctioned an enquiry to examine the direction the museum should take under the new arrangements. The terms of reference were:

> To enquire and report to the Minister of Education upon the main purposes that should be served by the National Museum; the needs of the Museum, if it fulfil these purposes effectively; and the reorganisation, if any, which may be necessary in order to enable it to supply those needs.

It seems that the government was interested in having the purpose of the museum clearly and professionally defined. Gone were the romantic sentiments of the pre-independence era and more practical concerns were addressed. Two issues in particular were evidently considered important. The first was the definition of the 'proper use' of the collections and managing their future development 'without undue strain on the finances of the country'. The second concerned how the museum should mould itself – for instance 'whether the Museum should be such a one as to be as suitable to any other country as to Ireland, or should it have its Irish character strongly emphasised'.[41]

Five experts were appointed to consider these questions. The Irish members were representatives of archaeology and the arts in Dublin. They were Charles McNeill, an expert on archaeology; Thomas Bodkin, representing the interests of art and industry; Dermod O'Brien of the Board of Visitors of the National Museum: and Dr P. A. Murphy who represented Natural Science (later replaced by Mr Adams of the Department of Lands and Agriculture).[42] Significantly, the committee was headed by a foreign expert, Professor Nils Lithberg, Director of the Northern Museum in Stockholm. It is interesting that a Swede should have been chosen. This appointment could be regarded as another way of breaking links with Britain simply because Lithberg was not English. However, Scandinavia had a long history of influencing cultural developments in neighbouring European countries. Sweden, since the mid-nineteenth century, had led the interest in folk culture and, by its own example, had inspired the establishment of open-air museums in northern and eastern Europe in the early twentieth century.[43] Interest in folk heritage was also in keeping with the style of Irish nationalism of the period that romanticised the rural way of life of the West of Ireland.[44]

In December 1927 the museum committee produced a document that was popularly known as the *Lithberg Report*. It comprised two parts: a general report made by the committee and an individual contribution made by Professor Lithberg. The former was a largely practical report with over thirty specific recommendations spanning the whole museum infrastructure, while the latter was a personal offering. The general report provided the National Museum with a definition of purpose and a multitude of recommendations on the internal management structure and its public duties. For instance, it advised on the public facilities provided within the existing natural history division, the geological collection was commented on and recommendations were made towards the improvement of current display practices. The committee also advised that a topographical survey with excavations, as well as intervention on the protection of monuments, should be administered from the museum. The report included further recommendations on the establishment of temporary exhibitions and evening opening, the provision of a students' room, a lecture hall and a library, the formation of an artefact registration index, and the development of workshops for in-house maintenance of the galleries.

These were all highly practical rather than ideological concerns, but the latter were to be found in Professor Lithberg's report. Lithberg's personal contribution contained three essays: one on the structure of museums in Stockholm, a second containing his views on the duties of an Irish historical museum, and a third on his vision for the National Museum in Dublin. His essays provide an interesting insight into the purpose of a national museum as defined by a Director of a prominent museum in the early twentieth century. With respect to the definition of purpose, Lithberg stated that the idea of a national museum 'should be to give consecutive representations of the native civilisation of the country from the time when human mind first showed its creative power until the present day, and it should embrace all classes which have been or still are components of its society'. He also laid down a structure that he considered as the ideal. He claimed that a national museum should be divided into three categories: antiquities, folklore and applied art, each with its own archives. Within this framework the museum should investigate two main areas: past civilisation and present-day culture. The latter was specifically defined as 'folk culture', that being 'the principal characteristics of the native race'. Lithberg regarded this as particularly important because it was likely to be a reflection of the past: 'the peasant culture imparts, therefore, a wider perspective of social manifestations – these have roots in earlier social institutions'.[45]

It is instructive to note which of the ideas the Dublin authorities were prepared to act on and which they disregarded. Of their many recommendations, three principal points were adopted by the Department of Education: the definition of the purpose of the National Museum, the recommendation to remove the non-Irish casts to the school of art and the idea to transfer the Museum's collection of artwork to the National Gallery. These were approved on 3 July 1928.[46] Regarding the first point, the committee resolved that the main purposes of the National Museum of Ireland should be to 'accumulate, preserve, study and display such objects as may serve to increase and diffuse the knowledge of Irish civilisation, of the natural history of Ireland and of the relations of Ireland in these respects with other countries'.[47] The chief practical recommendation of the report was the rearrangement of exhibits and the removal of certain objects from display. The report argued that although the historical development of Ireland was 'excellently illustrated', this was not immediately apparent because of the existing arrangement where, despite the alterations of earlier years, the industrial collections still had priority.[48] It therefore recommended that the Irish archaeological collection 'which in several respects is pre-eminent among the collections of the world, should receive the most prominent position in the Museum, so that the visitor at his first entrance should at once recognise its national character'.[49]

These recommendations were, in essence, the restoration of the main objectives that drove the Royal Irish Academy to form an antiquities collection in the 1840s. Following on the recommendations of the Lithberg committee the ground floor of the museum, which until the 1930s predominantly displayed casts of statuary from all over Europe, was devoted to the archaeological collections that had been formerly displayed on the first floor. The shift in the identity of the institution is clearly illustrated by a simple comparison of the room-by-room descriptions of the layout and displays given in the Director's Report for 1890 with those in the *Short General Guide to the National Collections* published in 1932. In addition, the comparison of acquisition lists published from the foundation of the museum with the National Museum's Director's Annual Reports is revealing. Before independence, the number of acquisitions in the Art and Industrial Division of the museum far exceeded that for the Irish Antiquities Division. In the early years the museum bought very few Irish antiquities, leaving that responsibility to the Royal Irish Academy, which deposited its acquisitions with the museum. In contrast the Art and Industrial Division would yearly acquire over a hundred additions.[50] In the post-independence decade, on the other hand, the Director's Report proudly boasted about the scale of archaeological purchases in addition to the Royal Irish Academy deposits. The 1929 report, for instance, recorded the addition of 598 single or groups of Irish antiquities, plus 898 lithics; in the 1931 report the accession of 730 items or small collections is recorded; and the 1932 report noted the addition of 1,292 artefacts, plus 8,700 lithics.[51] Additions to the Art and Industrial Department were much fewer and what was acquired was mostly Irish silverware and glassware rather than international examples.[52]

In short, one can say that the museum, like the country, was reinventing itself. In politics, a Gaelic and Catholic character was being nurtured for the state[53] and, in keeping with this, the Eucharistic Congress was held in Dublin in June 1932. In his report of that year, the Director of the National Museum declared Ireland as an ideal venue because, in his mind, it was 'a country which has a monument heritage dating back to the Early Christian Period' and 'a considerable contribution to offer in museum matters towards providing a fitting reception for such an assemblage of Church dignitaries'.[54] This was highly symbolic, and with this event the transfer of identity was made complete. No longer in need of endorsement from the British Association for the Advancement of Science, or indeed the British-based Museums Association, the collection was now getting support from the Catholic Church. This is not to suggest, though, that the museum totally cut itself off from British influence. The Director's Reports for the 1920s and 1930s acknowledge the help provided by British museums in training staff and providing services. The 1931 Director's Report noted co-operation with the British Museum laboratory in the form of research on bog butter and the restoration of finds from Lambay Island.[55] The Director's Reports for 1932 and 1933 both acknowledged National Museum of Ireland staff-training provided by the British Museum as well as by museums in Cardiff, Bristol and Cambridge.[56]

The transformation within the museum in the early decades of the Irish Free State was not complete enough for some. Though some of the principles of the *Lithberg Report* were adopted, the government considered the full extent of the suggestions made to be 'uncomfortably forthright'. Therefore, of the many and detailed recommendations made in the report, only the three just discussed were put forward to the Cabinet for approval, and the remainder were 'quietly shelved'.[57] A prominent figure in Dublin's cultural activity, Thomas Bodkin, aired his disappointment that the government did not act more extensively. Bodkin was, at the time of his position on the Committee of Enquiry, the Director of the National Gallery and in a lecture delivered in Trinity College Dublin several years later he reflected on that time. He commented on the long period of creative stagnation which Ireland had suffered as a result of 'oppression, turmoil, dissension and economic disability' at the hands of British rule. He described the past neglect of the fine arts that 'troubled thoughtful men and women for generations'. Many people, he claimed, hoped that with the establishment of the Irish Free State in 1922, 'enlightened action would soon be taken by our own government to help us to make up the leeway which sundered us from other civilised states of Europe'. For Bodkin, however, a native government had not yet done enough to nurture Irish arts and was not fulfilling the aspirations of cultural nationalism. He regretted that a Minister for the Arts had not been established. He recommended that such a position should have direct responsibility for the administration of the cultural institutions in Dublin, namely 'the National Gallery, the National Museum, a National College of Arts, a National Academy of Painting, a National Academy of Music and, possibly, a general benevolent supervision of the affairs of the Royal Irish Academy and the Abbey Theatre'. On the subject of the management of the National Museum he condemned bad staffing decisions, poor use of funds that had been made available for the purchase of artefacts, the cramped display method and the lack of an education service provided for the public. Though he recognised the contributions of the individuals concerned, he stated that 'it is little short of a national disgrace that the Directorship of our National Museum and our Department of National Antiquities should have been occupied in recent years by a German and now by an Austrian', Dr Adolf Mahr. Furthermore, Bodkin was sure that Mahr would have been the first to agree that his post 'for the honour of our country, should be occupied by a native of Ireland'. In a still more critical vein, he added:

> Lack of sufficient official interest in the Museum has resulted in late years in the loss of a great number of objects of real

national importance. I would weary you with a list of these. When I go to the ceramic department of the Victoria and Albert Museum and am shown specimens of beautiful delft produced in Dublin in the eighteenth century, acquired recently for that collection, I felt, as you would a sense of almost intolerable grievance.[58]

Under British rule references to the 'ancient Irish nation' were used to endorse nationalist aspirations; furthermore, statements about the importance of the collections exhibited in the Dublin museum dominated the writing of cultural nationalists. However, in the early years of the Free State, management of the museum did not seem to have a high priority. Under the new administration government interests were transferred to economic and social needs.[59] This is another reminder of the nature of the relationship between nationalism and museums. In the case of the Dublin museum, it was important only to have it reorganised into a useful national symbol and certain artefacts prominently displayed. With that achieved, not as much political support was given for the provision of less appealing museum services.

The National Museum in Dublin was, at each stage, a symbol of power. At some points the history of the museum is a demonstration of the capacity of the British administration in Ireland. Later, when the collection was altered on independence, it was indicative of the ability of the Irish Free State to reinvent itself. This transformation, within the museum premises, clearly illustrates that the museum itself is a place for exerting and reflecting ideological and political concerns. The Irish antiquities collection had its own social life. Its metamorphosis, in the century between the 1830s and the 1930s, was a function of the impact of differing political agendas. Regarded first as the 'national' collection within the Royal Irish Academy, it went on to hold a secondary position in the Museum of Science and Art in Dublin, later to return to its enhanced status on independence in the redefined National Museum of Ireland. The museum was both a social space where political agendas were acted out, and a contested space where competing identities wrestled for prominence.

CHAPTER SEVEN

Museums, Archaeology and Politics: Links and Legacy

Let us continue to [use archaeology to] present a bright example of what can be done by a cordial union and co-operation of all classes, all parties, all creeds, to heal the wounds of our beloved community.

Talbot de Malahide 1866[1]

Museums have an important role to play in developing cross-community contact in neutral settings.

Alistair Wilson 1995[2]

ARCHAEOLOGY AND collecting were invariably ascribed a social and political purpose in nineteenth-century and early twentieth-century Ireland. The legacy of these associations continues today with the result that the sentiment of Talbot de Malahide cited at the head of this chapter is still to be found, reworked and relatively unchallenged, in contemporary statements and views on the importance of museums in Ireland. This is evident by the way in which expressions of 'heritage', both inside and outside museums, and political agendas are still integrated. In 1998, for instance, Mary McAleese, President of Ireland, spoke at the Gulbenkian Foundation and Heritage Council Museum of the Year Awards in Dublin. In her address she claimed that the memorabilia and artefacts held in museum collections were an important starting point in the process of discovering identities and, in this role, played an essential part in reconciliation.[3] With such value judgements being voiced by public figures, those working in archaeology and museums must develop an awareness of, and be prepared to take some of the responsibility for, this political legacy. As noted by John Collis, 'unless we accept the political nature of our subject and face it head on, others will usurp it and use it in ways we might find unacceptable'.[4] It is therefore not enough to recognise the evidence of connections made in the last century, but it is also necessary to acknowledge the continuing effect of the potency of this inheritance.

LINKS BETWEEN THE CENTURIES

Current and past events around Europe have revealed the potentially negative impact of nationalism. Because of this, claiming a 'national identity' may be regarded as divisive and threatening.[5] Hroch argued that these links should not always be considered as 'nationalist misuse' but rather had some forms of investigation into the archaeology of the national past are 'potentially "neutral"'.[6] Indeed, in the Irish case, one can argue that nationalism has had some positive influence. It not only raised the profile of archaeology, justified the preservation of monuments and the creation of collections as a national or state duty, it also fuelled archaeological research. This should not necessarily be labelled as 'misuse'. However, to deny the political roots of this interest in archaeology, and the employment of the past to legitimise political campaigns, would be to overlook an association that has the potential to be damaging. In addition, archaeological theory, which recognises how the past has been appropriated for political ends, must also come to terms with the point that archaeologists, and those who manage the care of the material remains of the past, are also influenced by political ideals. In this sense, the political significance and role of archaeology comes as much from within the discipline as it is imposed from the outside. Recognition of this places archaeology and the museum profession in stronger positions because it is now possible to engage more fully with the social implications of practising archaeology and the relationship between archaeology, museums and the public.

Three linked concepts have emerged throughout this book as important in any attempt in preserving the past and representing events: ownership, and leading from this, time and memory. Ownership dominated nationalist rhetoric both in the material and the theoretical sense. It is important, for instance, to be able to define a political identity by laying claim to the artefact, the collection, the museum display and the museum building. In addition, having a sense of owning the past and the creation of knowledge of the past in the theoretical sense (in other words without necessarily ever coming into contact with archaeology) forms a part of the freedom to create the imagined space of the nation. We have seen that ownership is a concept that was continually contested in Ireland, because being able to lay claim to the past, and the security which this brought, aided definition and brought authenticity to the nation. Possession of the material remains of the past and knowledge of antiquity gave Irish nationalism its substance. The idea of intellectual and material ownership of the past persists in Ireland as both a unifying force and an agent for conflict. Ownership, and the sense of identity brought with it, are key elements which provided political justification for interest in history, prehistory, collecting and preserving the material remains in the nineteenth century, and it is just as potent in present-day Ireland.

Throughout the period considered in this study, claiming ownership of the past was necessary to create a sense of place and to symbolise power: Protestant revivalists used the past to strengthen their position in Ireland and nationalists to legitimise their campaign for home government. Taking control of the material remains was a method of controlling time, both in the form of the memory of past events and the aspirations that would mould the future. Both resulted in similar material expression. The members of the Royal Irish Academy, who were instrumental in creating an Irish antiquities collection, believed that 'noblemen and gentlemen' appropriately led this interest[7] and, as such, they were taking their rightful position as 'hereditary counsellors of crown and nation'.[8] This activity resulted, in their minds, in the creation of a collection of antiquities thought to be 'the most perfect national museum'.[9] On the other hand, for nationalist Ireland the artefacts in the collection were 'relics of the heroic time'[10] and, more directly, an exemplar of what Ireland would care for if it were 'governed by Irishmen, instead of being occupied by an enemy's garrison'.[11] These two spheres, the antiquarian and the more directly political, operated in close tandem. Their cultural politics shared many characteristics. In the first place, similar arguments were employed by politicians and archaeologists to justify public expenditure on archaeology. Secondly, the interpretation of antiquity popularised by antiquarians, such as George Petrie, was used to bolster political arguments. Thirdly, the products of antiquarian research, materialising in the creation of an antiquities collection, provided the subjects for nationalist iconography. This had important consequences for how archaeology was valued and managed. The result would have been a narrowing of the appreciation of antiquity and an unrealistic understanding of the material remains. This was observed by the archaeologist T. S. J. Westropp who wrote in 1916 that when 'hapless persons' who went to see Tara Hill 'and found only grassy mounds and a couple of small pillars came away saying in their haste that all Irish antiquarians were liars'.[12]

Political activists expressed their understanding of ownership by reference to archaeology as belonging to the 'public' and as being an expression of the 'nation'. Nationalism has been likened to a new religion for a disjointed society; within this, archaeology became the religious icon. In Ireland, nationalist rhetoric used quasi-religious language to express a commitment to archaeology. Douglas Hyde, for instance, spoke of collections being 'enshrined' in a temple raised to the 'godhead of Irish nationhood'.[13] William O'Brien referred to the Irish landscape and its history as being 'invested with something of the mysterious sanctity of religion'.[14] He, and many others, spoke of majestic shrines, ecclesiastical sites and the importance of Ireland's early saints. In this context, the Early Christian Period became inspiration for the new Ireland.

Raising the status of the ancient past was a method of shortening the distance between the present and the 'ancient nation', in the hope that the time taken to recreate the independent nation of the future would also be lessened. Archaeology was, therefore, a medium by which to resurrect the nation and became associated with ideas of what was sacred, venerable and hallowed. Repeated reference was only made to a handful of artefacts, most frequently the 'Tara' Brooch, the Ardagh Chalice and manuscripts such as the Book of Kells. Because of this, these objects became part of the 'public mind',[15] and they were presented as 'national' and part of the 'heritage'.[16] Eoin MacNeill made it clear that the value of Irish manuscripts increased once they were made a part of the 'national record'.[17] Similar comments about Irish manuscripts were made in the *United Irishman*[18] and various political figures called for the development of national collections. Individual artefacts and collections emerged as national symbols best held in the public sphere. The 'Tara' Brooch, for instance, has assumed iconic status as a symbol of the achievements of the Christian Period, the Golden Age of Irish nationalism. Having this in the public domain was preferable to it being held in private hands. Neither context would alter the historical importance of the object, but its worth as a political symbol would be altered. It is, therefore, the shared nature of the ownership of public collections that aids the political claims of the nation. However, it is interesting to raise the example of the Book of Kells again. In an address delivered to the Royal Society of Antiquaries of Ireland, the archaeologist Robert Macalister reported on a friend who quipped that 'the Irish base their claim to Home Rule on the beauty of the Book of Kells!'[19] Throughout the nineteenth century, and currently, the Book of Kells was in the private possession of Trinity College Dublin, a detail which, given the importance of the book for Irish nationalism, was conveniently disregarded.

Archaeology played a very particular role in the memory of the nation. Separated from the present by centuries it was elevated to a privileged and revered status. For some cultural revivalists interest in archaeology was considered a non-partisan pastime: Horace Plunkett made the point that prehistory was a time prior to division.[20] The Young Irelander Charles Gavin Duffy described 'ancient history and native art' as a neutral interest and an activity through which 'Unionist and nationalist could meet without alarm'.[21] Due to this temporal distance prehistory was idealised as a perfect state, one that was above the discord dominating the contemporary age. However, others used it used to legitimise division. The comparison of the appropriation of the Hill of Tara and the Ráth of Mullaghmast into nationalist politics (discussed in Chapter Three) is a demonstration of the effect of time on how history and prehistory can be appropriated into the nationalist narrative. Major historical events are still, even a century or more later, very active in popular memory because of being handed down through generations of families by storytelling. History may therefore hold negative connotations and become a tangle of fact and fiction. Archaeology, however, has greater potential for exaggeration, the creation of myths and increasing self-respect.

The development of archaeology in Ireland as a discipline and the progress of nationalism are interwoven. Archaeology was justified as a national duty, and independence was considered as deserved because of the ancient character of the Irish nation. This mutual service shaped the development of antiquities collections and, as shown, its effect persists. In each context the relationship with material remains of the past became symbolic of other aspirations. In each case archaeology provided material antecedents that provided legitimisation and an improved sense of stability. This is a fluid process; the interpretation of archaeology and the presentation of the past in museums, and as 'heritage', is continually reworked with every generation in order to reconstitute and represent the country anew. The museum acts as the voice allowing the administration to proclaim and justify its existence and, as a result, museums and the artefacts preserved in them have their own social life. Similarly, political ideals become institutionalised into the framework of preservation and care of the material remains of the past. The creation, management and display of collections must be seen as a pedagogic space where definitions of authority, the state and the people are voiced.

The advantage of the historical perspective is that it reflects the changing nature of what archaeological collections signify. For example, the Dawson Collection and similar antiquities purchased as by the Academy antiquarians in the 1840s were symbols of their interest in the cultivation of an appreciation of the achievements of Irish antiquity, and this did not contradict their interest to maintaining the Union with Britain. George Petrie used the objects of the collection as an educational tool in order to popularise his social agenda. Simultaneously for Irish nationalism, such objects were an indication of the Golden Age to be recaptured by the creation of a political state. When this collection received secondary status in the Dublin Museum of Science and Art, the Department at South Kensington was exercising its power over museum provision in Dublin and the individuals connected with it. In the decades between the opening of the new Science and Art Museum buildings and the *Lithberg Report* of 1927, objects and collections were moved about according to who was in control and what they wished the public to see. In the 1890s Greek and Greco-Roman casts and sculptures dominated. In the 1930s, however, the main galleries displayed Ireland's Golden Age. Then, ideal for the purposes of nationalism, Bronze Age lunulae, the Broighter Hoard, the 'Tara' Brooch and the reliquaries and shrines, were set off to their best advantage, openly styled as the 'Golden Age'. Significantly, the subject matter of the Irish collections ended with the 'Last Period of National Independence: 1014–1170'.[22] By the rearrangement of the collections in the Dublin museum, and its renaming in the early decades of the last century, a particular order of things was put in place. The museum, and the Irish nation, was reinventing itself. Each period in the history of the collection and its display was a mirror of thoughts.[23]

When these findings are considered alongside the perspective on museum development provided by Tony Bennett,[24] which established public museums as government tools used to facilitate the definition of new social management, they become more revealing. In Ireland the British cultural policy regarding museums, and the development of the Dublin Museum of Science and Art as a branch of the London institution, became a further method to draw the management and development of Ireland into the British structure. The history of the establishment of the Dublin museum can also be used as evidence of the tensions that existed between Britain and Ireland in the nineteenth century. Well-voiced discontent is seen at the administration of British museum and industrial policy in Ireland. This was felt not only by Irish antiquarians regarding the provision of funds for the creation of antiquities collections, but also by members of the Royal Irish Academy dependent on the generosity of the London government to house and develop their collection, and in the tensions felt by those interested in the establishment and building of the Dublin Museum of Science and Art. Although similar discontent was felt in the antiquarian institutions in Edinburgh, in the Irish case the feelings were of greater consequence as they were used to fuel a successful independence campaign. In the nineteenth century gaining control of the presentation in museums was useful for two competing social agendas: British industrial policy and the Irish nationalist ideal. Flora Kaplan has argued that national museums, and the collections within them, are 'purveyors of ideology and a downward spread of knowledge to the public'.[25] This is true of the Dublin museum, both before and after achieving independence from Britain. However, regarding the spread of nationalism, prior to independence, this ideology came from below when it diffused into the museum through political campaigning. Only after independence did the ideals of the Irish nation become expressed in the museum as a downward spread.

One can argue, therefore, that the definition of the national past, preserved in national collections and museums, will become a focal point and a window on state aspirations. In this sense, the national museum may be seen both as a form of memorial and monument. As a memorial a national museum is a place where history is made and remade, memories are formed and emotions triggered.[26] The management of archaeology is, in its different forms, a display of alternative expressions of political power and social relationships. To understand the role of the past one must create a 'philosophy of the present'.[27] With this being the case, a museum can be described as 'a staging ground for symbolic action' wherein the objects become symbols that can speak with many meanings in many combinations.[28] What is emphasised through the history of the Dublin museum is the cultural life of the collection, the meaning of which changed as it passed through time. Drawing from this, a national museum and its collection as a monument is an exhibition of aspirations. The status of a 'national' history will be raised and be dominant in the display. Other elements will be excluded, made invisible, so that a particular image is manufactured and portrayed. Since the employment of the past for political ends continues to prevail, it is the responsibility of archaeologists to create an awareness of the manufactured nature of political identity, to be clear that the interpretation and presentation of the past must be seen as a cultural stage where, either openly or in a more clandestine manner, cultural and political agendas are expressed. It can then be seen that 'the past' is an active symbol in a process of identity building within which the past is not static, but continually replayed according to the needs of the contemporary age.

LEGACY: CAN WE LEARN FROM THE PAST?

The complexity of Irish history and politics is found in the range of attitudes to the Irish past, which are revealed in the management and ownership of the material remains of antiquity. In addition, the belief in the social and political role of archaeology and museum collections, which is grounded in the nineteenth century, is equally prevalent in contemporary Ireland. It is clear, therefore, that the interpretation and presentation of the past in today's museums is underpinned by a sense of perceived social or political function, which is linked to the nineteenth-century origins of a public archaeology. These links between culture, museums and politics are now firmly embedded in the consciousness of Irish society with the result that ideas which dominated the evaluation of archaeology in the nineteenth century are still expressed today, and even taken for granted. How this legacy is enshrined in the management of archaeology and the presentation of the past in museums can be understood by looking at heritage management practices both in the Republic of Ireland and in Northern Ireland. In Northern Ireland, where the issues of identity and representation are still unresolved political issues, the potency of the links between politics and heritage are intensely felt, and an analysis of the political dimension of heritage management practices in Northern Ireland has the potential to make a revealing study. This section looks at one particular aspect – it links the role of heritage today with concepts rooted in the nineteenth century.

The predominant theme is the reinterpretation of the past for political or social agendas, which then becomes legitimised through links with archaeology and museum collections. The past has become a form of memorial that is shaped and sculpted by various groups until it becomes representative of how those groups want past events to be remembered and preserved. This process can still be identified in Ireland in four key ways: in the first place, by the presentation of a certain form of the past in museums as 'heritage' and providing it with a political identity; secondly by the continual act of using the past to support a social agenda; thirdly by the interest in presenting archaeology as a political monument, and finally by the continual reinterpretation of the past according to its political potential for the present.

To deal with the first proposition, a certain definition of 'heritage' is still being created and presented to support political aspirations. Interest in Protestant heritage is now cultivated in Northern Ireland by unionist interests and used to provide cultural justification for the position of Northern Ireland as separate from the Republic of Ireland. Unionism has its own myths of history that are used to promote its political message,[29] including a distinct version of history that is used to prove cultural links with Scotland.[30] Employing a methodology usually associated with nationalism, extreme Protestantism has appropriated historical symbols to provide its claims with authenticity. In some cases, established nationalist motifs have been appropriated by unionism. For instance, the Book of Kells, perhaps compiled on Iona, has been claimed as part of a Scots-Irish heritage. Similarly, Cuchulainn, the Irish hero who inspired republicanism, particularly Patrick Pearse, has been appropriated as a loyalist motif. This is illustrated, for example, in a Belfast mural that named Cuchulainn as the 'ancient defender of Ulster from Irish attacks over 2000 years ago'. Ironically, Cuchulainn has been used in identical poses in both loyalist and republican political murals.[31] Another nationalist icon has also been reinterpreted: the Hill of Tara has long been considered by the British Israelites to be the burial ground of the Ark of the Covenant and this claim is being used to add historical superiority to the British connection by claiming descent from the ancient Israelites. In a sinister development, a loyalist paramilitary group has made use of this claim and named itself 'Tara'.[32]

In addition, museums have opened in contemporary Northern Ireland dealing with new subject matters which draw on elements of Ulster's history, elements that traditionally have been seen as predominantly Protestant and loyal to the Crown. Examples of this would be the Irish Linen Centre opened at Lisburn Museum[33] and the Somme Heritage Centre.[34] Similarly, Ulster-Scots language is being promoted and revived, and some of those involved believe that it should be accorded a similar status to the Irish language.[35] This is not to suggest that forms of Irish nationalism are not also showing their effect on heritage management in Northern Ireland. The landscape of Derry city, a walled city used as a symbol of Protestant power in Ulster, is undergoing transformation. Pre-plantation Derry was the site of the O'Doherty clan; to revive this association, a pastiche medieval tower called 'The O'Doherty Tower' was recently built and now houses a heritage centre.[36] In these recent cases, history is being reinterpreted and traditions are invented. This cyclical action, in which history is constantly recreated by every new generation, suggests that the crises of identity, which dominated nineteenth-century nationalists and Protestant patriots, continue to exert their influence and are particularly felt in Northern Ireland.

A further political issue which influences attempts to engage with history in Northern Ireland is the act of dividing past history into 'Protestant' and 'Catholic' heritage. Again, this is a consequence of nationalism and its role in defining the people and history of the nation. The role museums and preservation plays in either challenging or endorsing such divisions led Anthony Buckley to ask the question: 'Collecting Ulster's Culture: are there *really* Two Traditions?'[37] Buckley's main thesis was that, rather than having two distinct traditions, the people of the region share a general cultural uniformity, difference being more a result of geography and class rather than of any deep ethnic diversity. He suggested that the continual assertion of a dichotomy of difference was one of political rhetoric. Buckley emphasised that people within regions of Northern Ireland share traditions and dialects that are peculiar to their areas, and he cited evidence of a shared tradition of marching, murals and music expressed in a similar manner by both political groups. He would recommend that museums and collecting should avoid such stereotyping and embrace the variations that exist within Northern Ireland.[38]

To take the second proposition, a social agenda underpinned collecting for some nineteenth-century antiquarians, particularly George Petrie. Today Northern Ireland's museums have assumed a social and political role in society evident by their use as a backdrop for the various schemes established for reconciliation. For instance, according to a former Director of the Ulster Folk and Transport Museum, Northern Ireland's museums are used to 'enhance mutual respect for varying cultural traditions' and to provide a 'neutral' space for such visits, where social discovery is 'safe'.[39] The museums are seen as 'oases of calm' and 'a vision around which people of all persuasions could unite'.[40] The paradox inherent in such 'neutral' presentations is emphasised by the Ulster poet, the late John Hewitt, in a poem titled 'Cultra Manor: The Ulster Folk Museum'. On visiting the museum, Hewitt wrote about looking at the photographs of 'obsolete rural crafts, the bearded man winnowing, the women in long skirts at their embroidery'. He then recorded his companions' statement made as they walked through the cottages on the recreated landscape: 'What they need now, somewhere about here is a field for the faction fights'.[41]

Instead, the issue of faction fighting is avoided in the majority of Northern Ireland's museums and one may argue that this has good reason. Derry City Museum hit the front page of a Belfast newspaper with the headline 'Museum war over IRA gun'.[42] In this case the object carried too much emotion; it had not become memory and it was still too soon to face it in an exhibition context. Instead culture is used being used for reconciliation in a way that is, for many, less controversial. Frequently, for instance, Protestant and Catholic school groups go on joint excursions, funded by the government sponsored scheme 'Education for Mutual Understanding', to museums or other heritage sites.[43] Since they tend to avoid the divisive elements of history, Northern Ireland's museums are considered as potential sites for 'conflict-resolution' where different religions can meet and share the past. Similarly, the work of the Cultural Traditions Group, developed by the government's Central Community Relations Council, was established with the aim to enable the people of Northern Ireland to meet and discuss their history for positive ends. Since then it has hosted conferences, exhibitions, public lectures and discussion groups, as well as funding research, for instance that by McCartney and Bryson into the use of flags, anthems and other national symbols in Northern Ireland.[44] Another initiative led by the Group was the *Symbols* exhibition that toured museums and public halls in Northern Ireland in 1994.[45] Some of the hurt evoked by stark political images in Northern Ireland, such as the balaclava, the sash, the British flag and murals, was removed by presenting them alongside similar less threatening symbols, such as the European Union flag. In this context, the items were sanitised, made into aesthetic objects, and thus became art. The implication of the hurt generated by the use of the symbols outside the exhibition context was not addressed. A question remains: is this avoidance of reality, or is it a positive reinterpretation of the past?

Thirdly, the archaeological object is continually drawn into the public act of remembrance as a 'political-monument'. Early Christian Period artefacts, such as the Broighter Hoard, which gained most reverence in nationalist writing, still dominate as symbols of the Irish nation. For instance, from the onset of the Irish Free State and to this day, Irish archaeology has been memorialised on stamps. This ensures that the association of the people of Ireland with the idea of a rich archaeological heritage remains. The stamps of the first definitive series (1922–68) included an image of the Cross of Cong. The design of the second series (1968–82) was based on motifs from early Celtic art. The third series (1982–90) celebrated Irish architecture 'down the Ages'. The present series depicts antiquities amongst the National Museum collection, in ascending cash value: the Silver Kite Brooch, the Dunamase Food Vessel, the Derrinboy Armlets, a gold dress fastener, the Lismore Crozier, an enamelled latchet brooch, the Broighter collar, the Gleninsheen Collar, a silver thistle brooch, the Broighter Boat, the Ardagh Chalice, the 'Tara' Brooch and the St Patrick's Bell Shrine.[46] Irish archaeology has also inherited further characteristics that can be associated with nineteenth-century nationalism. The name of Tara has been linked with the 'Tara' Brooch since it was found in 1850, despite the fact that the brooch was not found near the Hill of Tara.[47] It is unlikely that this link, generated one may assume from popular romantic sentiment prevalent at the time, could ever be broken.

Archaeology as 'political monument' is also demonstrably linked to an approach to Irish history that aims to be inclusive, which seeks, for instance, to remember the Irish regiments that participated in the First Word War. Thirty-five thousand Irishmen from north and south of Ireland, unionist and nationalist, fell whilst fighting together.[48] In post-independence Ireland, the politics and virtue of those Irish prepared to fight in a British war was frequently questioned, and the issue of creating and preserving memorials thought inappropriate.[49] In 1998, in a spirit of reinterpretation, a round tower was erected near Mesen in Belgium, in memory of the Irish who died in the war (see Figure 13). The tower has been presented as the 'Irish Peace Tower' since it was the product of the activity of a cross-border charitable trust in Ireland. In the words of a journalist, the tower was 'as much about present-day reconciliation as about the events of 1917'.[50] For Mary McAleese, publicly accepting this Irish

Figure 13: The 'Peace Tower' Mesen, Belgium. Source, A journey of Reconciliation Trust. A round tower is firmly established as a symbol of Ireland. This image can be compared to O'Connell's tower and the depiction of a tower in other figures.

contribution to the First World War was part of the 'maturation process' current in Ireland. Speaking at the opening ceremony she described the tower and the 'peace park' in which it was erected as an opportunity to invite the Irish 'not to forget the past but to remember it differently', a chance to change 'the landscape of our memory'.[51] For those involved in erecting the monument a round tower appeared fitting. It was chosen as a 'most appropriate symbol that transcends Ireland's present divisions and problems. It is slender and looks fragile but is anything but - it gives a wonderful sense of stability and continuity'.[52]

This event demonstrates the enduring appeal and political-symbolic role of archaeology and forms an important part of Irish identity.[53] The round tower in Belgium, as well as remembering the dead of the First World War, subtly encapsulated the progress of the Northern Ireland 'peace talks'. This is a method of 'monu-mentalising discourse'.[54] There is something both poignant and paradoxical in the fact that a round tower should have been used both as a memorial to Daniel O'Connell in 1868 and again in 1998 for First World War dead. In the earlier period, the tower, as a symbol of nineteenth-century Irish nationalism, was ultimately divisive; recently the tower was used in an attempt to draw Irish nationalism and unionism together. That a tower can be thought a useful representation of two opposing agendas is a reflection of the ease with which symbols can be manipulated in order to alter their meaning according to the context.

Finally, it is also possible to see how the past is still being reinterpreted according to its political potential in the present. History is continually being manipulated to suit the needs of the contemporary age, and in Ireland today a less divisive history is thought necessary and is increasingly being adopted. The different ways in which the 1798 Rising, a rebellion led by the United Irishman inspired by revolutionary France and America, was memorialised in 1898 and 1998, is one example. In 1898, the Rising was interpreted as a Catholic and Gaelic event and the commemorations were a platform to launch the independence movement of the early twentieth century.[55] In 1998 a more pluralistic approach was adopted: the Protestant 'dissenters', mostly Presbyterians, who were involved are now being acclaimed as 'The Lost Leaders' of 1798.[56] This recent approach brought Protestants and Catholics of Ireland together and provided a historical point of unity. Museums have also engaged in this process – both the Ulster

Museum and the National Museum of Ireland hosted major commemorative exhibitions and a 'National 1798 Centre' was opened in Enniscorthy, Co. Wexford.[57] In Belfast the exhibition became a venue for 'two communities desperate to reach out to one another', and 'some 60 Catholics and 40 Presbyterians from the village of Crumlin, outside Belfast, boarded a couple of buses paid for them by the borough council and headed for the Ulster Museum'.[58] The outing was described as 'something we could do together, something that would compromise no-one's principles – theological or otherwise – something that would offer us a shared history'.[59]

Different approaches are being adopted for the preservation of built heritage in the Republic of Ireland. In some aspects, the Irish example provides both a parallel and a contrast to the demolition of Japanese colonial architecture in Korea, specifically the building used to house the Korean National Museum. In Ireland the initial response to the architectural remains of the previous administration was similar to that in Korea. In post-independence Ireland most imperial statuary on the streets of Dublin was either removed or destroyed: the statue of Queen Victoria was removed from outside the National Museum, and statues of King William III and George II were blown up. On the fiftieth anniversary of the 1916 Rising, Nelson's pillar was demolished, most probably by a Republican group.[60] By contrast, the architectural and monumental remains of eighteenth-century Ireland are now being embraced as 'heritage'. Erasing the material remains of 'unwanted' history is no longer thought useful. Kilmainham Gaol, for instance, where the leaders of the 1916 Rising were imprisoned and later shot, has been a museum since 1988, and in 1996 specially redesigned exhibitions and visitor facilities were opened to the public.[61] Similarly, the Royal Barracks built for British military in 1700 and capable of accommodating 3,000 men and 1,000 horses was, on the creation of the Irish Free State, used as a base for the Irish army.[62] It was also renamed Collins Barracks, after the political leader Michael Collins. In 1994 the buildings were secured as an extension of the National Museum of Ireland,[63] and this was opened in 1997.[64] The history of Irish archaeology in the twentieth-century also reveals shifts in interpretation that reflect wider changes in political thinking. For instance, as Gaelic, and sometimes Anglophobic, nationalism of the early twentieth century evolved, the importance placed on the archaeology of post seventeenth-century Ireland has gradually increased.[65] In addition, urban sites formerly considered as the result of foreign influence are increasingly being accepted as Irish, to the extent that sites once symbolic of the Golden Age of Irish nationalism, such as the ecclesiastical settlement at Clonmacnoise, are even being interpreted as proto-urban.[66] The architecture of Georgian Dublin, once regarded as symbolic of the negative influence of the English in Ireland, is now being regarded as Irish heritage.[67]

In a place where the past is a political issue, the methods of remembering, creating and preserving history are of fundamental and serious consequence. As asked by Lowenthal, 'if the role of a museum is to remember the past, what kind of past should it remember? Should it remember everything? Are some memories best forgotten?'[68] The mature Irish nation is now finding it more useful to remember aspects of its history that it previously neglected. However, in Northern Ireland the paucity of exhibitions which consider the political tensions in Irish society give way to the prevalence of displays in which there is no hint of the most dominant issue in the province's history. Museum professionals in Northern Ireland rarely publicly engage with the issue of the political role of the past and the question of whose tradition is being collected. It seems that more time is needed before 'the troubles' can be faced in the local museums. Time and memory are linked and the objectification of a nation's history in memorials involves a certain amount of forgetting, as well as remembering.[69] Time must pass and people need to be allowed to forget before memories can be symbolised. It is therefore necessary for those who do attempt to challenge the presentation of the past in museums to consider the emotions associated with remembering and to be prepared for the consequences which will follow.

Notes

NOTES TO INTRODUCTION

1 See the *Museums Journal* (February 1912), p. 34.
2 *Irish Times*, 10 July 1912; similar in the *Freeman's Journal*, 10 July 1912.
3 For instance, John A. Atkinson, Iain Banks and Jerry O'Sullivan (ed.), *Nationalism and Archaeology* (Glasgow, Cruithne Press 1996); Margarita Díaz-Andreu and Timothy Champion (ed.), *Nationalism and Archaeology in Europe* (London, Routledge 1996); Paul Graves-Brown, Sian Jones and Clive Gamble (eds), *Cultural Identity and Archaeology* (London, Routledge 1996) and Philip L. Kohl and Clare Fawcett, *Nationalism, Politics and the Practice of Archaeology* (Cambridge, Cambridge University Press 1995).
4 *Museums Journal* February 1995.
5 Of the former I would suggest Don D. Fowler 'Uses of the past', *American Antiquity*, 52(2) (1987); Bruce G. Trigger, 'Alternative Archaeologies: Nationalist, Colonialist, Imperialist', *Man*, 19 (1984), and for the latter Díaz-Andreu and Champion, *Nationalism*.
6 These two articles by Geoffrey Lewis are published in the *Manual of Curatorship* (London Butterworths 1994 2nd edn). The *Manual* has been core reading for those in the museum field since it was first published in 1984.
7 Such as Oliver Impey and Arthur MacGregor, *The Origins of Museums* (Oxford, Clarendon 1985).
8 A.S. Bell, *The Scottish Antiquarian Tradition* (Edinburgh, 1981).
9 Geoffrey Lewis, *For Instruction and Recreation, A Centenary of the Museums Association* (London, Quiller Press 1989).
10 Such as John Elsner and Roger Cardinal, *The Cultures of Collecting* (London, Reaktion Books 1994); Peter Gathercole and David Lowenthal, *The Politics of the Past* (London, Unwin Hyman 1990); Eilean Hooper-Greenhill, *Museums and the Shaping of Knowledge* (London, Routledge 1992); Ivan Karp and Steven D. Lavine, (eds), *Exhibiting Cultures* (London, Smithsonian Institution Press 1991); Gaynor Kavanagh (ed), *Making Histories in Museums* (Leicester, Leicester University Press 1996); Sharon MacDonald, *The Politics of Display* (London, Routledge 1998); Sharon MacDonald and Gordon Fyfe (eds), *Theorising Museums* (Oxford, Blackwell 1996), and Daniel J. Sherman and Irit Rogoff, *Museum Culture* (London, Routledge 1994).
11 Gabriel Cooney, 'A Sense of Place in Irish Prehistory', *Antiquity*, 67 (1993); see also Gabriel Cooney, 'Theory and Practice in Archaeology', in P. J. Ucko, (ed) *Theory in Archaeology* (London, Routledge 1995) and Peter C. Woodman, 'Irish Archaeology Today', *Irish Review*, 12 (1992).
12 Cooney, 1995 *ibid.*, p. 266
13 T. Ó Raifeartaigh, *The Royal Irish Academy* (Dublin, The Royal Irish Academy 1985).
14 P. Harbison, *The Archaeology of Ireland* (The Bodley Head Archaeologies 1976) or M. Herity and George Eogan, *Ireland in Prehistory* (London, Routledge 1977).
15 H. B. White, 'History of the Science and Art Institutions', *Museum Bulletin* (1911 and 1912).
16 Patrick Wallace, *The Dublin Museum of Science and Art* (National Museum of Ireland 1977).
17 A. T. Lucas, 'The Role of the National Museum' in the study of Irish Social History, *Museums Journal* (February 1965) and *The National Museum* (Dublin 1969).
18 Noel Nesbitt, *A Museum in Belfast* (Belfast 1979).
19 Some of the history of the museum can be found in Alan Gailey, 'Creating Ulster's Folk Museum', *Ulster Folklife*, 32 (1986); and *The Use of the Past* (Belfast, Ulster Folk and Transport Museum 1988).
20 Myles Dillion, 'George Petrie', *Studies* LVI (1967).

21 Michael Dolley, Aloys Fleischmann, David Greene and J. Raftery published in the *Proceedings of the Royal Irish Academy* 1972; see also Liam de Paor's introduction to the republished edition of Petrie *Rounds Towers* (Irish University Press 1970).

22 Petra Coffey, 'A Victorian Exploration of the Irish Landscape', *Archaeology Ireland* (1996); Jean Archer, 'Geological Artistry' and Maire de Paor, 'Irish Antiquarian Artists', both published in Adele M. Dalsimer, *Visualising Ireland* (London, Faber and Faber 1993); M. Bourke, 'Frederic Wm. Burton 1816–1900: Painter and Antiquarian', *Eire-Ireland*, xxviii (3) (1993).

23 Such as Robert Hewson, *The Heritage Industry* (London, Methuen 1987); David Lowenthal, *The Past is a Foreign Country* (Cambridge, Cambridge University Press 1985); David L. Uzzell (ed), *Heritage Interpretation* (London 1989); Patrick Walsh, *The Representation of the Past* (London, Belhaven Press 1992).

24 David Brett, *The Construction of Heritage* (Cork, Cork University Press 1994) and 'The Representation of Culture' in Ullrich Kockel, *Culture, Tourism and Development: the Case for Ireland* (Liverpool, Liverpool University Press 1996).

25 See Cooney's article 'Theory and Practice in Irish Archaeology' in P. J. Ucko (ed), *Theory in Archaeology* pp. 263–77 as well as Cooney, 'Building the Future on the Past' in Diaz Andreu and Champion (eds), *Nationalism and Archaeology* (London, Routledge).

26 An example of interesting discussion of how the archaeology of Early Medieval Period has been written is provided by Michael Tierney in 'Theory and Politics in Early Medieval Archaeology' published in Monk and Sheehan, *Early Medieval Munster* (Cork, Cork University Press 1996). Peter Woodman also provides interesting reading in 'Who possesses Tara?' in P. J. Ucko (ed), *Theory in Archaeology*. For other writing which explains some of the links between politics and Irish archaeology see: Dorcas Boreland, 'Anglophobes and Anglophiles' in John A. Atkinson *et al.* (ed), *Nationalism and Archaeology* (London, Routledge 1996); Diarmait Mac Giolla Chriost, 'Northern Ireland: culture clash and archaeology' in Atkinson, *Nationalism and Archaeology*; John O'Sullivan, 'Nationalists, Archaeologists and the Myth of the Golden Age', in Monk and Sheehan, *Early Medieval Munster* (Cork, Cork University Press 1998); Matthew Stout, 'Emyr Estyn Evans and Northern Ireland' in Atkinson, *Nationalism and Archaeology*.

27 Brian J. Graham 'Heritage Conservation and Revisionist Nationalism in Ireland' in G.J. Ashworth and P. Larkham, *Building a New Heritage* (London, Routledge 1994).

28 Brian Graham (ed), *In Search of Ireland* (London, Routledge 1997).

29 Brian Graham, 'The Search for a Common Ground: Estyn Evans's Ireland', *Transactions of the Institute of British Geographers* 19 (1994) p. 184.

30 Cooney, *Theory and Practice*, p. 272.

31 Brian Graham, 'The Search for a Common Ground', p. 184.

32 Such as in Virgina Crossman and Dympna McLoughlin, 'A Peculiar Eclipse: E. Estyn Evans and Irish Studies', *Irish Review*, 15 (1994); Graham, *Common Ground*; Stout, *Evans and Northern Ireland*.

33 Stout, *Evans and Northern Ireland*.

34 Gwyneth Evans, 'Emyr Estyn Evans', *Ulster Journal of Archaeology*, 58 (1999) pp. 134–42.

35 See the articles in Ciaran Brady (ed), *Interpreting Irish History* (Dublin, Irish Academic Press 1994).

NOTES TO CHAPTER ONE

1 Karel Sklenár, *Archaeology in Central Europe* (Leicester, Leicester University Press 1983) p.80.

2 Cited in Osswoldo Chinchallo Mazariegos, 'Archaeology and Nationalism in Guatemala', *Antiquity*, 72 (1998) p. 380.

3 See both Richard Clogg, *Sense of the Past in Pre-Independence Greece*, in Roland Sussex and T. C. Eade *Culture and Nationalism* (Columbas, Australian National University 1985) pp. 10–30 and Maria Avgouli, 'The First Greek Museums', in Flora

Kaplan, *Museums and the Making of Ourselves* (Leicester, Leicester University Press 1994).

4 G. Ruiz Zapatero, 'Celts and Ibernians', in Paul Graves-Brown *et al.* (eds), *Cultural Identity and Archaeology* (London, Routledge 1996); see also Margarita Díaz Andreu, 'Archaeology and Nationalism in Spain', in Philip L. Kohl and Clare Fawcett, *Nationalism, Politics and the Practice of Archaeology* (Cambridge, Cambridge University Press 1995).

5 Margarita Díaz Andreu, 'Nationalism, Ethnicity and Archaeology', *Journal of Mediterranean Studies*, 7(2) (1997).

6 Marie Louise Stig Sørensen, 'The Fall of a Nation, the Birth of a Subject', in Margarita Díaz Andreu and Timothy Champion, *Nationalism and Archaeology in Europe* (London, Routledge 1996).

7 Michael Dietler, 'Our Ancestors the Gauls' Archaeology and Ethnic Nationalism, and the Manipulation of Celtic Identity', *American Anthropologist*, 96 (1994).

8 W .J. MacCann, '"Volk and Germanentum": the Presentation of the Past in Nazi Germany', in Peter Gathercole and David Lowenthal, *The Politics of the Past* (London, Unwin Hyman 1990).

9 Robert Perks, 'Ukraine's Forbidden History: Memory and Nationalism', *Oral History*, Spring (1993).

10 For discussion of this see Monika Ginzkey Puloy, 'High Art and National Socialism', *Journal of the History of Collections*, 8(2) (1996).

11 Philip Wright, 'Germany', *Museums Journal*, 3 (1996); also see Detlef Hoffman, 'The German Art Museum and the History of the Nation', in Daniel J. Sherman and Irit Rogoff, *Museum Cultures* (London, Routledge 1994).

12 Philip Wright has claimed: 'within twentieth-century Europe the museum in Germany has held a uniquely high-profile socio-political role, which continues to haunt it today', in Wright, *Germany*, p. 20.

13 Barbara Heuser, 'Museums, Identity and Warring Historians', *The Historical Journal*, 33(2) (1990) pp. 419, 422.

14 Stuart Piggott, 'Foreword', in Karel Sklenár, *Archaeology in Central Europe the First 500 Years* (Leicester, Leicester University Press 1983) p. v.

15 See Susan M. Pearce (ed) *Objects of Knowledge: New Research in Museum Studies* (London, Athlone 1990).

16 Susan M. Pearce, *Objects as Meaning or Narrating the Past*, in Susan M. Pearce, *ibid.* (1990) p. 127.

17 Chris Tilley, 'Interpreting Material Culture', in Ian Hodder (ed), *The Meaning of Things* (London, HarperCollins 1991) p. 192.

18 Michael Shanks, *Experiencing the Past: On the Character of Archaeology* (London, Routledge 1992) p. 29.

19 M. Jones, 'From Haggis to Home Rule', *Museums Journal*, 2 (1995).

20 Edel Bhreathnach, 'Cultural Identity and Tara from Lebor Gabala Erenn to George Petrie', *Discovery Programme Report*, 4 (Dublin, 1997).

21 Auslan Ramb, 'Scotland's Touchstone Fulfils its Destiny', *Daily Telegraph*, 4 July 1996.

22 Robert Hardman and George Jones, 'The Stone of Scone Goes Home', *Daily Telegraph*, 4 July 1996.

23 Editorial, *Daily Telegraph*, 4 July 1996.

24 Jette Sandahl, 'Emotional Objects', *Museum Ireland*, 6 (1996) p. 19.

25 David Lowenthal, '"Trojan Forebears", "Peerless Relics": The Rhetoric of Heritage Claims', in Ian Hodder *et al.*, *Interpreting Archaeology*, p. 129.

26 Ian Hodder, 'The Contextual Analysis of Symbolic Meanings', in Susan M. Pearce, *Objects as Meaning*.

27 See Tony Bennett, *The Birth of the Museum. History, Theory, Politics* (London, Routledge 1995) and 'Speaking to the Eye', in Sharon MacDonald (ed), *The Politics of Display* (London, Routledge 1998).

28 Tony Bennett, *The Birth of the Museum*, pp. 17–30, 80–1; see also Peter J. Bowler, *The Invention of Progress. The Victorians and the Past* (Oxford, Blackwell 1989).

29 A. A. Shelton, 'In the Lair of the Monkey, Notes Towards a Post Modernist Museography', in Susan M. Pearce, *Objects as Meaning*, p. 98.

30 Flora E.S. Kaplan, *Museums and the Making of Ourselves* (Leicester, Leicester

University Press 1994) p. 9.

31 Kevin Whelan used this analogy in referring to Irish regionalism, see Whelan, 'The Basis of Regionalism in Proinsias O Drisceoil', *Regions: Identity and Power* (Belfast, Institute of Irish Studies, Queens University Belfast 1993) p. 5.

32 David L. Uzzell, 'Creating a Place Identity Through Heritage Interpretation', *International Journal of Heritage Studies*, 1(4) (1996).

33 Michel M. Ames, 'Cannibal Tours, Glass Boxes and the Politics of Interpretation', in Pearce (ed), *Objects as Meaning*, p. 102.

34 Kenneth Hudson, *Museums of Influence* (Cambridge, Cambridge University Press 1987) p. 25.

35 B. McKillop, 'Soeul Searches for a New Image', *Museums Journal*, 2 (1995) p. 27.

36 Hongham Kim, 'Removing the Legacy of the Korean Past', *Curator*, 41(3) (1998) p. 181.

NOTES TO CHAPTER TWO

1 My emphasis, *Nation*, 9 September 1843 p. 760.

2 Miroslav Hroch, *Social preconditions of National Revival in Europe* (Cambridge, Cambridge University Press 1985) pp. 178–88, 180, 22–3. It is also interesting to consider Hroch's model in the context of Czech nationalism and the rise of archaeology and the establishment of museums. Karel Sklenár discusses this point in his book *Archaeology in Central* Europe (Leicester, Leicester University Press 1983).

3 Such as Benedict Anderson, *Imagined Communities* (London, Verso 1983); Ernest Gellner, *Nations and Nationalism* (London, Blackwell 1983); E. J. Hobsbawm, *Nations and Nationalism* (Cambridge, Cambridge University Press 1990); Anthony D. Smith, *Theories of Nationalism* (London, Duckworth, 1983 2nd edn).

4 Gellner, *Nations and Nationalism*. See also Gellner, *Culture Identity and Politics* (Cambridge, Cambridge University Press 1987).

5 Anthony D. Smith, *Theories*; 'National Identity and Myths of Ethnic Descent', *Research in Social Movements, Conflict and Change*, 7 (1984a) pp. 95–130; 'Ethnic Myths and Ethnic Revivals', *European Journal of Sociology*, 15, pp. 283–305 (1984b); 'State-Making and Nation-Building', in J. Hall (ed), *States in History*, pp. 228–63 (London, Blackwell 1986); 'The Myth of the "Modern Nation" and the Myths of Nations', *Ethnic and Racial Studies*, 11 (1) (1988) 1–26; *National Identity* (London, Penguin 1991).

6 Hobsbawm, *Nations*; see also E. J. Hobsbawm and Terence Ranger, *The Invention of Tradition* (Cambridge, Cambridge University Press 1983).

7 Smith, *Theories*, p. 21.

8 *Ibid.*, pp. 65–7, 14.

9 Gellner, *Nations*.

10 D. George Boyce, *Nationalism in Ireland*, pp. 17–23 (London, Routledge 1991 2nd edn).

11 Gellner, *Nations*, p. 94.

12 Anderson, *Imagined Communities*.

13 Hobsbawm, *Nations*, pp. 46–79.

14 Gellner, *Nations*, pp. 48–9, 56.

15 Walker Connor, 'A Nation is a Nation, is a State, is an Ethnic Group, is a ... ', *Ethnic and Racial Studies*, 1 (4) (1978) p. 37.

16 Hroch, *Social Conditions*, p. 12.

17 Kevin Whelan, 'The Basis of Regionalism', in Proinsias O Drisceoil, *Regions: Identity and Power*, pp. 26–31 (Belfast, Institute of Irish Studies Queens University Belfast 1993).

18 Jonathan Bell, 'Intelligent Revivalism: The First Feis na nGleann', in Alan Gailey, *Use of the Past* (Belfast, Ulster Folk and Transport Museum 1988) pp. 8–9.

19 Gabriel Cooney, 'Building the Future on the Past', in Margarita Diaz Andreu and Timothy Champion (eds), *Archaeology and Nationalism* (London, Routledge 1996).

20 Tom Garvin, *The Evolution of Irish Nationalist Politics* (Dublin, Gill and Macmillan 1987) p. 5.

21 Peter Alter, 'Symbols of Irish Nationalism', *Studia Hibernica*, 14 (1974).
22 L. M. Cullen, 'The Cultural Basis of Modern Irish Nationalism', in Rosalind
    Mitchison (ed), *The Roots of Nationalism* (Edinburgh, Donald 1980); Maurice
    Goldering, *Pleasant the Scholars Life* (London, Serif 1993); John Hutchinson, *The
    Dynamics of Cultural Nationalism* (London, Allen and Unwin 1987); F. S. L. Lyons,
    Culture and Anarchy in Ireland (Oxford, Oxford University Press 1982 2nd edn);
    Oliver MacDonagh *et al.* (eds), *Irish Culture and Nationalism* (Dublin, Macmillan
    Press 1983); Margaret O'Callaghan, 'Language, Nationality and Cultural Identity',
    Irish Historical Studies, 94 (1984); Brian Ó Cuív, 'The Gaelic Cultural Movements
    and the New Nationalism', in K. Nowlan (ed) *The Making of 1916*, (Dublin, Dublin
    Stationery Office 1969). See also the papers in Tadhg Foley and Sean Ryder (ed),
    Ideology and Ireland in the Nineteenth Century, (Dublin, Four Courts Press 1998).
23 D. George Boyce, '"One Last Burial": Culture, Counter Revolution and Revolution
    in Ireland', in Boyce (ed), *Revolution in Ireland 1879–1923* (1988) p. 116.
24 Boyce, *ibid.*; John Hutchinson, *Dynamics of Cultural Nationalism*, pp. 154–68.
25 Hutchinson, *The Dynamics of Cultural Nationalism*.
26 Original emphasis, Hutchinson, *Dynamics*, pp. 13, 16.
27 Hutchinson, *ibid.*, pp. 49–50, 115–16.
28 'Hyde 1905', in Brendan Ó Conaire, *Douglas Hyde*, pp. 178–9.
29 Boyce, 'One Last Burial'; Robert O'Driscoll, 'Ferguson and the Idea of an Irish
    National Literature', *Éire-Ireland*, vi (1), (1971).
30 Boyce op. cit. p. 129.
31 George Russell, 'Nationality and Imperialism', in Alice Gregory (ed), *Ideals in Ireland*
    (London 1901) p. 16.
32 Boyce, *Nationalism*, pp. 244–50. See also the references to this in F. S. L. Lyons,
    Culture and Anarchy in Ireland (Oxford, Oxford University Press 1982) p. 68; and
    Lyons, 'The Watershed 1903–7', in William Vaughan (ed), *A New History of Ireland*
    (Oxford, Clarendon 1996) pp. 119–21.
33 D. P. Moran, 'The Battle of Two Civilisations', in Gregory (ed), *Ideals*, p. 39.
34 Hutchinson, *Dynamics*, pp. 168–9.
35 Foster, *Ireland*, pp. 475–6.
36 Pearse in *An Claidheamh Soluis*, 19 November 1904, cited in Ruth Dudley Edwards,
    Patrick Pearse. The Triumph of Failure (London, Faber and Faber 1979) p. 72.
37 Original emphasis, Pearse in *An Claidheamh Soluis*, 27 August 1904 cited in
    Edwards, *Patrick Pearse*, p. 70.
38 Redmond Preface to Gwynn, *The Case for Home Rule* (Dublin, Maunsel and Co.
    1912 3rd edn) p. vii.
39 Hutchinson, *Dynamics*, p. 1.
40 *Nation*, 1 April 1843, p. 394.
41 Alter, *Symbols*.
42 O'Driscoll, *Ferguson*, p. 83.
43 Boyce, 'One Last Burial', p. 120.
44 Boyce, *Nationalism*, p. 230.
45 Jonathan Bell, 'Intelligent Revivalism'.
46 Plunkett, cited in Bell, *Ibid.*, p. 8.
47 Boyce, 'One Last Burial', p. 120.

NOTES TO CHAPTER THREE

 1 See E. J. Hobsbawm, *Nations and Nationalism* (Cambridge, Cambridge University
    Press 1990). Hobsbawm opens Chapter Two with a reference to Benedict Anderson's
    imagined community, which is formed by the bond created by national symbols such
    as language. See Anderson, *Imagined Communities* (London, Verso 1983).
 2 John Hutchinson, *The Dynamics of Cultural Nationalism*, pp. 123–7 (London, Allen
    and Unwin, 1987).
 3 Clare O'Halloran, 'Irish Recreations of the Gaelic Past', *Past and Present*, 124 (1989)
    p. 78.

4 Gabriel Cooney, 'Building a Future on the Past', in Margarita Díaz Andreu and Timothy Champion, *Nationalism and Archaeology* (London, Routledge 1996).

5 William O'Brien, *The Irish National Idea* (Cork, Young Ireland Society 1886). O'Brien later republished this address in *Irish Ideas* (London, Longmans 1893).

6 William O'Brien, *National Idea*, p. 7.

7 *Hibernia* February 1883, p. 14.

8 Sean P. Ó Ríordáin, *Antiquities of the Irish Countryside* (London, Methuen 1964 3rd edn) p. 15.

9 See Elizabeth Malcolm, 'Popular Recreation in Nineteenth-Century Ireland' in Oliver MacDonagh *et al., Irish Culture and Nationalism* (Dublin, Macmillan Press 1983).

10 Gary Owens, 'Hedge Schools of Politics', *History Ireland*, 2(1), (1994).

11 Daniel O'Connell 1843, cited in the *Nation*, 19 August 1843, p. 706.

12 *Nation*, 19 August 1843, p. 712.

13 *Ibid.*, p. 706.

14 Edel Breathnach, 'Cultural Identity and Tara from Lebor Gabala Erenn to George Petrie', *Discovery Programme Report*, 4 (1997).

15 *Irish Builder*, 15 March 1893 p. 88.

16 *Irish Nation*, 22 September 1917, p. 2.

17 *Gaelic Journal*, June 1883, p. 271.

18 See W. Fitz Gerald, 'Mullaghmast: Its History and Traditions', *Journal of the Kildare Archaeological Society*, 1 (1891/5) for an account of the significance of Mullaghmast.

19 D. George Boyce, *Nationalism*, p. 145.

20 Original capitals, *Nation*, 9 September 1843, p. 776.

21 This is a reference to the antiquarian George Petrie. The social and political significance of his work is discussed in Chapter Four.

22 Original capitals, *Gaelic Journal* (May 1892), p. 157.

23 'Thomas Davis c1840', in O'Donoghue, *Essays Literary and Historical by Thomas Davis* (Dundalk, Dundalgan Press) pp. 164–6.

24 Illustration in Barbara Hayley, 'A Reading and Thinking Nation', in Hayley and Enda McKay (eds), *Three Hundred Years of Irish Periodicals* (Dublin, 1987) p. 43.

25 For an explanation of this link see Rhys Jones, 'British Aborginal's Land Claim to Stonehenge', in Christopher Chippendale *et al.* (eds), *Who Owns Stonehenge?* (London, Batsford 1990) pp. 69–70.

26 Chris Corlett, 'Interpretation of Round Towers', *Archaeology Ireland*, 12 (2), (1998).

27 See the discussion in Timothy Champion, 'The Power of the Picture', in B. L. Molyneaux (ed), *The Cultural Life of Images. Visual Representation in Archaeology* (London, Routledge 1997).

28 'Thomas Davis c1840', in O'Donoghue, *Essays*, p. 167.

29 William O'Brien, *Ideas*, p. 157.

30 'Davis' c1840', in O'Donoghue *Essays*, p. 117.

31 *Nation*, 15 April 1843 p. 426.

32 Original capitals, Thomas Davis c1840 in O'Donoghue, *Essays*, p. 200.

33 *United Irishman*, 19 February 1848, p. 26.

34 *Nation*, 26 November 1842, p. 105.

35 *Nation*, 10 December 1842, p. 137.

36 *Irish Nation*, 26 January 1918, p. 3.

37 Arthur Griffith, *The Resurrection of Hungry* (Dublin, Duffy and Co .1918 3rd edn) p. 73.

38 *Ibid.*, p. 170.

39 *Gaelic Journal* (April 1909), p. 364.

40 'Douglas Hyde 1905', in Brendan Ó Conaire, *Hyde Douglas, Language Lore and Lyrics* (Dublin, Irish Academic Press 1986) p. 184.

41 Such as in Janet Egleson Dunleavy and Gareth W. Dunleavy, *Douglas Hyde: A Maker of Modern Ireland* (Berkley Oxford, University of California Press 1991).

42 In making this point I have paraphrased Prof. Denis Donoghue who was speaking about Yeats and nationhood in his Parnell Lecture delivered in Magdalene College Cambridge 1997.

43 *Irish Builder*, 15 March 1883, p.88.

44 Chris Tilley, 'Interpreting Material Culture', in Ian Hodder *et al.* (ed), *The Meaning of Things* (London, HarperCollins 1991) p. 192.
45 D. George Boyce, *Nationalism*, p. 164.
46 John O'Connell (ed), *Life and Speeches of Daniel O'Connell* (Dublin, 1846).
47 'Thomas Davis c1840', in O'Donoghue, *Thomas Davis.*
48 T. W. Moody, 'Irish History and Irish Mythology', *Hermathena*, 124 (1978) p. 17; S. J. Connolly, 'Culture, Identity and Tradition: Changing Definitions of Irishness', in Brian Graham (ed), *In Search of Ireland* (London, Routledge 1997) p. 56.
49 Thomas Davis, cited in Moody, *History and Mythology*, p. 17.
50 D. George Boyce, *Nationalism*, p. 118.
51 'Davis c1840', in O'Donoghue, *Thomas Davis*, p. 118.
52 *Nation*, 15 October 1842 p. 10.
53 'Davis c1840', *passim* in O'Donoghue, *Thomas Davis.*
54 Original emphasis, *Nation*, 25 February 1843 p. 314.
55 D. George Boyce, *Nationalism*, p. 173.
56 *United Irishman*, 19 February 1848 p. 26.
57 Tom Garvin, *The Evolution of Irish Nationalist Politics* (Dublin, Gill and Macmillan 1987) p. 5.
58 *Irish People*, 19 December 1863 p. 56.
59 D. George Boyce, *Nationalism*, p. 177.
60 *Irish People*, 23 January 1864, p. 137.
61 Roy F. Foster, *Modern Ireland* (London, Penguin 1988) p. 446.
62 Standish O'Grady 1899, autobiographical extract in E. A. Boyd, *Standish O'Grady, Selected Essays and Passages* (Dublin, The Talbot Press 1917).
63 Boyd, *O'Grady*, p. 118.
64 Standish O'Grady, *History of Ireland, Critical and Philosophical* (Dublin, 1881) pp. 46–7.
65 Foster, *Ireland*, p. 447.
66 D. Thomson, *The Aims of History, Values of the historical attitude* (London, Thames and Hudson, 1969). p. 12.
67 Boyd, *O'Grady*, p. 2.
68 Standish O'Grady under the pseudonym of Arthur Clive, Irish Archaeology, *Dublin University Magazine* (1876) p. 650.
69 O'Grady 1899, in Boyd, *O'Grady*, pp. 3–4.
70 *Irish Nation*, 25 August 1917 p. 1; similar references can also be found in the paper published on 3 March 1917, p. 1.
71 *Irish Nation*, 3 March 1917, p. 7.
72 Robert Macalister, *The Present and Future of Archaeology in Ireland* (Dublin, Falconer 1925), pp. 11–12.
73 Bruce G. Trigger, 'Alternative Archaeologies, Nationalist, Colonialist, Imperialist', *Man*, 19 (1984) p. 360.
74 These articles were published on 15 July 1916, 22 July 1916, 29 July 1916, 5 August 1916, 12 August 1916, 19 August 1916 and 26 August 1916.
75 20 October 1917, 13 October 1917 and 8 December 1917
76 These were by J. E. McKenna, *Irish Art* (Catholic Truth Society of Ireland 1909), de Blácam, *What Sinn Féin Stands For* (c1921) and S. Gwynn, *The Case for Home Rule* (Dublin, Maunsel and Co. 1912).
77 D. George Boyce, *Nationalism*, p. 247.
78 Richard Kearney, *Postnationalist Ireland, Politics, Culture, Philosophy* (London, Routledge 1997) p.189.
79 *The Indestructible Nation* (O'Hegarty 1918) and, published in post-independence Ireland, *The Story of the Irish Nation* (Hackett 1924), *And so Began the Irish Nation* (Seamus MacCall 1931) and *Ireland a Nation* (Robert Lynd 1936).
80 Boylan, *A Dictionary of Irish Biography* (Dublin 1998 3rd edn.) p. 231.
81 Bulmer Hobson, 'Saorstat Éireann' (Dublin 1932).
82 R. B. McDowell, *Alice Stopford Green* (Dublin, 1967) p. 3.
83 Boylan, *Biography*, p. 134.
84 Roy F. Foster, *Paddy and Mr Punch* (London, Allen Lane 1993) p. 14.
85 Alice Stopford Green, *Irish Nationality* (London 1911) pp. 9, 74, 12.

86 This point about Coffey was made by E. C. R. Armstrong in his volume *Catalogue of Irish Gold Ornaments* (Dublin 1920) p. 3.
87 Green, *A History of the Irish State* (London 1925) p. 1.
88 Green, *Nationality* (London 1911) pp. 14–15.
89 Such as Francis Joseph Bigger, 'The Ruins of Ireland', in J. Dunn *et al.* (eds), *The Glories of Ireland* (Washington, 1914); Robert Lynd, *Ireland a Nation* (London, Grant Richards 1936); J. E. McKenna, *Irish Art* (Catholic Truth Society of Ireland 1909).
90 McKenna, *Art*, pp. 51–5, 21.
91 The authors of these essays are as follows: 'The Islands of Saints and Scholars' by D'Alton; 'Irish Metal Work' by Coffey; Irish Manuscripts' by O'Carroll; 'Irish Nationality' by Ashbourne; 'The Sorrows of Ireland' by Rooney; and 'Irish Wit and Humor' by Graves.
92 Bigger, *Ruins*, pp. 89, 94.
93 Lynd, *Ireland*, pp. 21–4.
94 *Irish Nation*, 5 August 1916 p. 7.
95 Robert A. S. Macalister, *The Archaeology of Ireland* (London, Methuen 1949 3rd edn) pp. xii, x, xiii.

NOTES TO CHAPTER FOUR

1 E. J. Hobsbawm, *Nations and Nationalism* (Cambridge, Cambridge University Press 1990) pp. 14–20.
2 Philippa Levine, *The Amateur and the Professional* (Cambridge, Cambridge University Press 1986) p. 4; Timothy Champion, 'Three Nations or One?' in Margarita Díaz Andreu and Timothy Champion, *Nationalism and Archaeology* (London, Routledge 1996).
3 Joep Leerssen, *Remembrance and Imagination* (Cork, Cork University Press 1996) p. 157.
4 R. B. McDowell, The main narrative in T. Ó Raifeartaigh, *The Royal Irish Academy* (Dublin, The Royal Irish Academy 1985) p. 1; Philippa Levine, *Amateur and Professional*, pp. 7–13.
5 McDowell, *Narrative*, p. 2.
6 James Meenan and Desmond Clark, *RDS the Royal Dublin Society* (Dublin, Gill and Macmillan 1981) pp. vii–1.
7 McDowell, *Narrative*, pp. 6–9.
8 Leerssen, *Remembrance*, p. 15.
9 Burrowes 1787, cited in McDowell, *Narrative*, p. 13.
10 See references later in this chapter.
11 John Hutchinson, *The Dynamics of Cultural Nationalism* (London, Allen and Unwin 1987) p. 90.
12 Sir William Rowan Hamilton, Presidential Address to the Royal Irish Academy, *Proceedings of the Royal Irish Academy*, 1 (1838) p. 120.
13 Samuel Ferguson, Presidential Address to the Royal Irish Academy, *PRIA*, 2 (1882) p. 197.
14 F. S. L. Lyons, *Culture and Anarchy in Ireland* (Oxford, Oxford University Press 1982) p. 18.
15 L. M. Cullen, 'The Cultural Basis of Modern Irish Nationalism' in Rosalind Mitchison, *The Roots of Nationalism* (Edinburgh, Donald 1980) p. 101.
16 D. George Boyce, *Nationalism in Ireland* (London, Routledge 1991 2nd edn) p. 39.
17 Leerssen, *Remembrance*, p. 12.
18 Charles O'Conor, 'Origins of the Royal Irish Academy', *Studies* 1949 p. 325.
19 McDowell, *Narrative*, p. 45.
20 *Report of the First Annual General Meeting of the Irish Archaeological Society* (1841).
21 Rev. Patrick M. MacSweeney, *A Group of Nation-Builders* (Dublin, Catholic Truth Society 1913) p. 22.
22 *Report of the Irish Archaeological and Celtic Society* (1857).
23 See Barbara Hayley, 'A Reading and Thinking Nation', in Barbara Hayley and Enda

McKay (eds), *Three Hundred Years of Irish Periodicals* (Dublin 1987) pp. 31–5.

24 Leerssen, *Remembrance*, p. 114.
25 *Dublin Penny Journal*, 1 July 1832, preface.
26 Hayley, *Reading and Thinking Nation*, p. 38.
27 *Dublin Penny Journal*, 1 July 1832: preface.
28 Original capitals, *Dublin Penny Journal* 1 July 1832, preface.
29 *Dublin Penny Journal*, 7 July 1832, pp. 9–10.
30 *Dublin Penny Journal*, 1 July 1832, preface.
31 J. H. Andrews, *A Paper Landscape: The Ordnance Survey in Nineteenth Century Ireland* (Oxford 1975).
32 Angèle Smith, 'Landscapes of Power in Nineteenth Century Ireland', *Archaeological Dialogues*, 5(1) (1998), p. 80.
33 G. F. Mitchell, 'Antiquities', in T. Ó Raifeartaigh, *The Royal Irish Academy* pp. 101–2.
34 Cited in Andrews, *A Paper Landscape*, pp. 160, 167.
35 *Report of the Commissioners Appointed to Inquire into the Facts Relating to the Ordnance Survey Memoir of Ireland. Together with the Reports, Minutes of Evidence, Appendix.* 1844.XXX.
36 *Ibid.*
37 *Nation*, 15 October 1842 p. 10.
38 *Dublin Penny Journal* (1844) p. 494. Leerssen (1996 p. 294) believes that this was written by Ferguson.
39 *Dublin University Magazine* (1844) p. 500.
40 Cited in William Stokes, *The Life of George Petrie* (London, 1868) p. 97.
41 William Irwin Thompson, *The Imagination of an Insurrection* (Dublin, Wolfhound Press 1982) p. 13.
42 For a reference to such attitudes see J. H. Andrews, *Paper Landscape*, p. 174.
43 Cited in Thompson, *Insurrection*, p. 12.
44 Cited in William Stokes, *George Petrie*, p. 96.
45 William Stokes, *George Petrie*, p. 86.
46 Jeanne Sheehy, *The Rediscovery of Ireland's Past* (London, Thames and Hudson 1980) p. 20.
47 Original emphasis, Thompson, *Insurrection*, p. 12.
48 C. Barrett and Jeanne Sheehy, 'Visual Arts and Society', in William Vaughan (ed), *A New History of Ireland* (Oxford, Clarendon Press 1996) pp. 441–2.
49 A. C. Davies, 'Ireland's Crystal Palace', in J. M. Goldstrom and L. A. Clarkson, *Irish Population, Economy and Society* (Oxford 1981); see the original exhibition catalogue by J. Sproule published in 1854.
50 *The Times*, 3 September 1853, cited in Davies, *Crystal Palace*, p. 266.
51 Davies, *Crystal Palace*, p. 266.
52 Mitchell, *Antiquities*, p. 115.
53 Parl. Rep. 1868/9. XXIV p. xxii.
54 MacSweeney, *Nation-builders*, see p. 36 and foreword.
55 Roy F. Foster, *Paddy and Mr Punch* (London, Allen Lane 1993) p. 6.
56 There is a list in William Stokes, *George Petrie*, pp. 438–45.
57 J. Raftery, 'Aspects of George Petrie', *Proceedings of the Royal Irish Academy*, 72 (1972) p. 155.
58 T. S. J. Westropp, 'The Progress of Irish Archaeology', *Journal of the Royal Society of Antiquaries of Ireland* (1916) p. 23.
59 See the articles by Dolley, Fleischmann and Greene all published in *PRIA*, 72 (1972).
60 George Petrie, cited in William Stokes, *George Petrie*, pp. 112–316.
61 Myles Dillon, George Petrie, *Studies*, LVI (1967).
62 Michael Herity and George Eogan, *Ireland in Prehistory* (London, Routledge and Kegan Paul 1977) p. 8.
63 William Stokes, *George Petrie*, p. 142.
64 Herity and Eogan, *Ireland*, p. 9.
65 Chris Corlett, 'Interpretation of Round Towers', *Archaeology Ireland*, 12(2), (1998).

66 Jeanne Sheehy, *Rediscovery*, p. 20.
67 Charles Graves, 'Address Delivered to the Royal Irish Academy on the Death of George Petrie', *PRIA* (1866) pp. 331, 325–6.
68 MacSweeney, *Nation-Builders*, pp. 99, 36.
69 John Hutchinson, *The Dynamics of Cultural Nationalism* (London, Allen and Unwin 1987) p. 80.
70 Mitchell, *Antiquities*, p. 96.
71 William Stokes, *George Petrie*, p. 211.
72 Clare O'Halloran, 'Irish Recreations of the Gaelic Past', *Past and Present*, 124 (1989) p.72.
73 T. S. J. Westropp, 'The Progress of Irish Archaeology', *Journal of the Royal Society of Antiquaries of Ireland*, 46 (1916) p. 7.
74 Clare O'Halloran, *Irish Recreations*; and also *Golden Ages and Barbarous Nations* (PhD Cambridge, 1991).
75 O'Halloran, *Irish Recreations*, pp. 72, 73.
76 George Petrie in *The Dublin Penny Journal*, 8 September 1832 pp. 83, 227, 229, 84.
77 *Freeman's Journal*, 11 December 1850, p. 1.
78 For a list see Niamh Whitfield, 'The Finding of the Tara Brooch', *Journal of the Royal Society of Antiquaries of Ireland*, 104 (1974) p. 139.
79 In Dillion's words: 'Petrie lived at a time when Ireland was in the gloom that followed the Union. He remembered seeing Sarah Curran weep as she looked at a portrait of Emmet painted by his father. He saw the rise of O'Connell, he was a friend of Mangan and Ferguson, he must have known Thomas Davis. He lived through the Great Famine and saw the collapse of the Young Irelanders. The Fenian rebellion took place the year after his death. He was not active in these affairs, though he read *The Nation*' (See Dillion 1967 p. 75).
80 *Dublin University Magazine*, December 1839.
81 'Thomas Davis c1840', in D. J. O'Donoghue, *Thomas Davis Essays Literary and Historical* (Dundalk, Dundalgan Press 1914) pp. 312–27.
82 Published in Brendan Ó Conaire, *Hyde Douglas* (Dublin 1986) p. 75.
83 *Hibernia* (February 1883) p. 1.
84 Shane O'Shea, *Glasnevin Cemetery* (Dublin, Dublin Cemetery Committee 1997) p. 6.
85 George Petrie, cited in Stokes, *George Petrie*, pp. 433–7.
86 Myles Dillon, *George Petrie*, p. 276.
87 Hutchinson, *Dynamics*, p. 90.
88 Part One on 16 January 1830 pp. 33–5.
89 George Petrie, *Dublin Penny Journal* (1832) p. 83.
90 William Stokes, *George Petrie*, pp. 1, 394.
91 Sir William Rowan Hamilton, Presidential Address, *PRIA*, 1 (1838) p. 117.
92 Reverend Humphrey Lloyd, Presidential Address, *PRIA*, 3 (1846) p. 212.
93 Reverend Thomas Robinson, Presidential Address, *PRIA*, 5 (1851) p. 109.
94 Reverend James Henthorn Todd, Presidential Address, *PRIA*, 6 (1856) p. 334.
95 R. McAdam, 'The Archaeology of Ulster', *Ulster Journal of Archaeology*, 1 (1853).
96 Samuel Ferguson, in a letter to Lord Morpeth 1847.
97 William Wilde also produced other Academy catalogues in 1861 and 1862; Mitchell, *Antiquities*, pp. 118–21.
98 William Wilde, *The Beauties of the Boyne and its Tributary the Blackwater* (Dublin, McGlashan 1850 2nd edn) p. ix.
99 William Wakeman, *Handbook of Irish Antiquities* (Dublin 1848) pp. 1, v, 100.
100 *Irish Archaeological Society* 1841.
101 Talbot de Malahide, Presidential Address, *PRIA*, (1866), p. 395.
102 Stokes, *George Petrie*, pp. 326–7.
103 Parl. Rep. 1864.XIII p. 296.
104 Wilde, *Beauties*, p. vi.
105 Letter by Samuel Ferguon to James McCullagh 1840.
106 Wilde, *Beauties*, p. x.
107 1840 in Ferguson 1847.

108 Wilde, *Beauties* p. v.
109 William Wilde Parl. Rep. 1864.XIII p. 298.
110 William Wakeman 1948 p. 2.
111 Ferguson to MacCullagh.
112 Hayley, *Reading and Thinking*, p. 35.
113 Roy F. Foster, *Modern Ireland* (London, Penguin 1988) p. 315.
114 *Dublin University Magazine* (1844) p. 499.
115 Hamilton, Presidential Address, *PRIA*, 1 (1838) p. 120.
116 Original capitals. Thomas Robinson, Presidential Address, *PRIA*, 5 (1851) p. 111.
117 Wilde, *Beauties*, p. xii.
118 *Proceedings of the Royal Irish Academy* (1862) p. 81.
119 William Wilde, *Ireland, Past, Present, the Land and the People* (Dublin, 1864) pp. 5, 50.
120 Joseph Lee, *The Modernisation of Irish Society* (Dublin, Gill and Macmillan 3rd edn 1992) p. 1.
121 Wilde, *Ireland, Past, Present*, pp. 24, 37.
122 T. G. Wilson, *Victorian Doctor. Being a Life of Sir William Wilde* (London, Methuen 1942) and another by Terence de Vere White, *The Parents of Oscar Wilde* (London, Hodder and Stoughton 1967).
123 *Irish People*, 7 May 1864 p. 377.

NOTES TO CHAPTER FIVE

1 James Meenan and Desmond Clark, *RDS: The Royal Dublin Society* (Dublin, Gill and Macmillan 1981); John Turpin, 'The Dublin Society', *Éire Ireland*, 24 (1989).
2 G. F. Mitchell, *Antiquities*, in T. Ó. Raifeartaigh (ed), *The Royal Irish Academy* (Dublin, Royal Irish Academy 1985) p. 106.
3 Meenan and Clark, *RDS* p. 11.
4 B. O'Reilly, *A Catalogue of the Subjects of Natural History in the Museum of the Dublin Society* (1813) p. 1.
5 *Dublin Penny Journal*, 10 October 1835, p. 115.
6 R. B. McDowell and D. A. Webb, *Trinity College Dublin* (Cambridge, Cambridge University Press 1982) p. 197.
7 Constance Maxwell, *Trinity College Dublin* (Dublin, Dublin University Press 1946) p. 241.
8 Meenan and Clark, *RDS*.
9 *Dublin Penny Journal*, 31 October 1835, pp. 138–9.
10 C. E. O'Riordan, *The Natural History Museum* (Dublin, The National Museum of Ireland 1986) pp. 17–21.
11 Mitchell, *Antiquities*, p. 160.
12 Cited in R. B. McDowell, the main narrative, in T. Ó Raifeartaigh (ed), *The Royal Irish Academy*, pp. 38–9, 37.
13 Minutes of the Committee of Antiquities, 2 December 1840.
14 Mitchell, *Antiquities*, pp. 111, 160, 122, 118.
15 J. H. Jellett, Presidential Address to the Royal Irish Academy, *PRIA*, 11 (1870) p. 66.
16 Original emphasis, *ibid.*, p.67.
17 Mitchell, *Antiquities*, pp. 114, 119.
18 Mark Goodwin, 'Objects, Belief and Power', in Susan M. Pearce, *Objects of Knowledge* (London, Athlone 1990).
19 Tony Bennett, *The Birth of the Museum* (London, Routledge 1995).
20 Remark made in 1893 by a Science and Art Department trained teacher, cited in Sophie Forgan and Graeme Gooday, 'Constructing South Kensington', *The British Journal for the Advancement of Science* (1996), 103 (4) p. 46.
21 *Annual Report to the Department of Science and Art* 1883.XXVII p. xxx.
22 John Hutchinson, *The Dynamics of Cultural Nationalism* (London 1987) p. 115.
23 C. E. O'Riordan, *Natural History Museum*, pp. 14–15.
24 *Report from the Select Committee appointed to inquire into the condition of the scientific institutions of Dublin which are assisted by government aid; together with*

the proceedings of the committee, minutes of evidence, appendix and index. 1864.XIII p. xvii.
25 Meehan and Clarke, *RDS*, 1981 pp. 30, 33.
26 Charles Graves, 'Condition of the Scientific Institutions of Dublin' *Parl. Rep.* 1864.XIII pp. 273, 294.
27 *Ibid.*, p. 274.
28 *Reports from Commission on the Science and Art Department in Ireland together with the Minutes of Evidence, Appendix and Index.* 1868/9.XXIV pp. ii, i.
29 J. S. Crone, *A Concise Dictionary of National Biography* (Dublin, Talbot Press 1937) p. 223.
30 Vereker, *Parl. Rep. on the Sci. and Art Dept.* 1868/9.XXIV p. 56.
31 McSwiney, *Parl. Parl. Rep. on the Sci. and Art Dept.* 1868/9.XXIV p. 79.
32 Parkinson, *Parl. Rep. on the Sci. and Art Dept.* 1868/9.XXIV p. 96.
33 Pim, *Parl. Rep. on the Sci. and Art Dept.* 1868/9.XXIV p. 206.
34 Cole, *Parl. Rep. on the Sci. and Art Dept.* 1868/9.XXIV pp. 206, 119–20, 137–8, 118, 125, ii–iii.
35 *Parl. Rep.* 1868/9.XXIV p. xiv.
36 Minutes of the Royal Irish Academy Council 14 February 1876.
37 Sandon, Minutes of the Royal Irish Academy Council 14 February 1876.
38 Todd, *Parl. Rep. on the Sci. and Art Dept.* 1868/9.XXI p. 337.
39 Talbot de Malahide, *Parl. Rep. on the Sci. and Art Dept.* 1868/9.XXIV p. 338.
40 Wilde, *Parl. Rep. on the Sci. and Art Dept.* 1868/9.XXIV p. 461.
41 *An. Rep. Dept. Sci. and Art* 1882.XXVI, 1884.XXVIII.
42 *Rep. Dept. Sci. and Art* 1878.XXXVI.
43 *Rep. Dept. Sci. and Art* 1881.XXXVII p. xxii.
44 *Hans.*1882, p. 763.
45 OPW MSS 11585/83.
46 Rep. Dept. Sci. and Art 1882.XXVI p. 591.
47 *Irish Builder*, 1 April 1882, p. 108.
48 *Hibernia*, 2 January 1882, p. 2.
49 *Irish Builder*, 1 January 1882, p. 2; 1 November 1882, p. 312.
50 *Irish Builder* 15 November 1882 p. 326.
51 *Hans.* 23 November 1882, p. 1924.
52 *Hans.* 1 December 1882, p. 470.
53 *Hans.* 3 November 1882 p. 763.
54 *Hans.* 23 November 1882, p. 1925.
55 OPW Box 6839/83 43211-83.
56 The Dublin Museum of Science and Art Act, 1883.
57 *Hans.*17 July 1884, p. 139.
58 *Hans.* 24 July 1884, pp. 330–1.
59 *Hans.* 31 July 1884, p. 1181.
60 *Hans.* 13 November 1884, p. 1574.
61 *Irish Builder* 1 June 1885, p. 168.
62 *Irish Builder* 1 October 1887, p. 279.
63 Barrett and Sheehy, 'Visual Arts and Society', p. 496.
64 *Irish Builder*, 1904, cited in Barrett and Sheehy, p. 496.
65 This feature was inspired by Schinkel Altes Museum in Berlin. See the reference to this in Jacqueline O'Brien and Desmond Guinness, *Dublin, A Grand Tour*, p. 232.
66 *Irish Builder,* 15 April 1884, p.110; O'Brien and Guinness, *Dublin*, p. 235.
67 *Irish Builder,* 15 April 1885, p. 115.
68 The first 'Director of the Science and Art Institutions' was William Edward Steele M.D. (1878–83). He was succeeded by Valentine Ball LLD CB (1883–95) and later Colonel J. T. Plunkett CB (1895–1907). In 1907 Count George Noble Plunkett became Director of the National Museum of Science and Art (H. B. White 1911 History of the Science and Art Institutions, *Museum Bulletin*).
69 National Museum of Science and Art 1885.
70 *Freeman's Journal,* 10 and 11 April 1885; *Irish Times*, 10 and 11 April 1885.
71 *Irish Builder*, 15 January 1883 p. 17.
72 O'Brien *Gaelic Journal* July 1892, p. 164.

73 *Parl. Rep.* 1897.XII pp. 209, 218.
74 *Rep. Dept. Sci. and Art* 1889.XXXIII p. 284.
75 *Rep. Dept. Sci. and Art* 1878/9.XXVI p. 648.
76 *Rep. Dept. Sci. and Art* 1890.XXXII p. 315.
77 *Rep. Dept. Sci. and Art* 1894.XXXII pp. 301–2.
78 *Rep. Dept. Sci. and Art* 1890/1.XXXI p. 369; Valentine Ball 1892.
79 R. G. Cant, Davis Steuart Erskine, '11th Earl of Buchan: Founder of the Society of Antiquaries of Scotland', in A. S. Bell (ed), *The Scottish Antiquarian Tradition* (Edinburgh, John Donald 1981).
80 D. V. Clarke, 'Scottish Archaeology in the Second Half of the Nineteenth Century', in Bell, *Scottish Antiquarian Tradition*.
81 Cited in Cant, *Erskine*, p. 10.
82 Cited in Stevenson, *Museum*, pp. 76, 143, 156, 165.
83 A. B. Meyer, *Studies of the Museums of the United States and Europe* (Washington, Government Printing Office, 1905).

NOTES ON CHAPTER SIX

1 For a description of the hoard see Richard Warner, 'The Broighter Hoard' in B. G. Scott, *Studies in Early Ireland* (Association of Young Irish Archaeologists 1982) p. 29.
2 For more information see Warner (1999).
3 *Report of a Committee appointed by the Lords Commissioners of Her Majesty's Treasury to inquire into the circumstances under which certain Celtic Ornaments found in Ireland were recently offered for Sale to the British Museum, and to consider the relation between the British Museum and the Museums of Edinburgh and Dublin with regard to the acquisition and retention of objects of Antiquarian and Historic Interest,* 1899.LXXVII p. 4.
4 Dillon, *Parl. Rep. Celtic Ornaments*, pp. 24, 27.
5 Robinson, *Parl. Rep. Celtic Ornaments*, p. 29.
6 RIA Memo, *Parl. Rep. Celtic Ornaments*, pp. 40–1.
7 Plunkett, *Parl. Rep. Celtic Ornaments*, p. 35.
8 *Evening Herald*, 8 December 1897.
9 *Ibid.*
10 *Irish Times*, 16 June 1900.
11 Esmonde, *Irish Times*, 25 June 1900.
12 *Irish Times*, 25 June 1900.
13 R. B. McDowell, 'Administration and the Public Services', W. Vaughan (ed), *A New History of Ireland Under the Union* (Oxford, Clarendon Press 1996) pp. 588–9.
14 Arthur Graves, *Museums of the Science and Art Department. Minute by the Right Honourable the Lords of the Committee of the Privy Council on Education on the 2nd Report from the Select Committee (1898) on the Museums of the Science and Art* 1898.XI pp. 111–7, 120, 221–8.
15 Plunkett, *Reports from the Committees of Museums of the Science & Art Department. Report of the Select Committee Appointed to Enquire into and Report upon the Administration and Cost of the Museums of the Science and Art Department.* 1897.XII p. 221.
16 Plunkett, *Museums of the Science and Art Department Minute*, p. 136.
17 *Report of the Department of Agriculture and Technical Instruction* 1902.XX p. 541.
18 M. Stention and S. Lees, *A Who's Who of the British Members of Parliament* (Brighton, Harvester Press 1979) p. 284.
19 Roy F. Foster, *Ireland* (London, Penguin 1988) p. 488.
20 R. B. McDowell, 'The Main Narrative', in T. Ó. Raifeartaigh, *The Royal Irish Academy* (Dublin: The Royal Irish Academy 1985) p.63; Brian P. Kennedy, *Dreams and Responsibilities* (Dublin, The Arts Council 1990) p. 5.
21 G. F. Mitchell, 'Antiquties' in T. Ó. Raifeartaigh, *Royal Irish Academy* pp. 135, 147.
22 The title 'Dublin Museum of Science and Art' reflects the museum's origins with the Department of Science and Art in London and its closeness with other museums

founded by the Department such as the Science and Art Museum in Edinburgh. The title 'National Museum' would have been preferred by those who wished to emphasise its local character.

23 *Rep. Dept. Agric. and Tech. Inst.* 1908.XXII p. 14.
24 *Rep. Dept. Agric. and Tech. Inst.* 1910.VIII p. 426.
25 George Noble Plunkett, Presidential Address, *Museums Journal* (1912).
26 Mitchell, *Antiquities*, p. 154.
27 Brian Murphy, 'The first Dail Éireann', *History Ireland* 1994.
28 *Irish Nation*, 27 January 1917, p. 5.
29 *Irish Nation*, 1 July 1916, p. 8.
30 Cited in McDowell, *The Main Narrative*, p. 82.
31 R. B. McDowell, *Narrative*, pp. 80–3; Thomas Bourke, 'Nationalism and the Royal Irish Academy', *Studies* LXXV (1986).
32 Cited in McDowell, *Narrative*, p. 83.
33 Bourke, *Nationalism*, p. 206; McDowell, *ibid.* p. 84.
34 John McColgan, *British Policy and the Irish Administration* (London, Allen and Unwin 1983) pp. 35–49.
35 Clark, 21 February 1921, cited in John McColgan, *Policy*, p. 55.
36 This point was made to Richard Warner, Curator of Archaeology in the Ulster Museum, though he has not come across any official documentation to support this interpretation of events (Richard Warner pers. comm. May 1998).
37 Estyn E. Evans, 'Archaeology in Ulster Since 1920', *Ulster Journal of Archaeology*, 31, (1968) p. 4.
38 The language used in the title of the museum is interesting. The term 'Ulster' suggests a nine county remit (rather than the six counties of Northern Ireland). In 1999 the Ulster Museum amalgamated with the Ulster Folk and Transport Museum and the Ulster-American Folk Park to form the 'National Museums and Galleries of Northern Ireland'. Its use of the term 'National' gives the museums an increased sense of status and is in keeping with the organisation of museums in the UK (such as the National Museums and Galleries of Merseyside).
39 Evans, *Archaeology in Ulster* (1968) p. 3; Peter Woodman, 'Irish Archaeology Today', *Irish Review*, 12 (1995) p. 293.
40 For some useful discussions of these enquiries see Margaret O'Callaghan, 'Language, Nationality and Cultural Identity', *Irish Historical Studies*, 94, (1984); Brian Kennedy, *Dreams and Responsibilities. The State and the Arts in Ireland*. (Dublin, The Arts Council 1990) pp. 17–19; Nuala Johnson, 'Building a Nation', *Journal of Historical Geography*, 19 (1993); Johnson, 'Making Space: Gaeltacht Policy and the Politics of Identity', Brian Graham (ed.), *In Search of Ireland* (London, Routledge 1997).
41 Report of Committee of Enquiry 1927.
42 Kennedy, *Dreams* pp. 19, 228.
43 Trefor M. Owen, 'The Role of a Folk Museum', in Alan Gailey (ed.), *The Use of the Past* (Belfast, Ulster Folk and Transport Museum 1988) pp. 75–6; Jonathan Bell, 'Intelligent Revivalism', in Gailey, *ibid.*, pp. 33–4.
44 Patrick J. Duffy, 'Writing Ireland: Literature and Art in the Representation of Irish Place', in Graham, *Search*, pp. 66–9.
45 *Lithberg Report* 1927 pp. 6–8.
46 Records regarding the National Museum are in the National Archives in box S.5392.
47 *Committee of Enquiry Report* 1927.
48 Documents relating to the *Lithberg Report* 1927.
49 *Committee of Enquiry Report* 1927.
50 The Dublin Museum of Science and Art Directors Reports 1878–99. These are a useful resource. They include accounts of the activities of the museum staff during the year, number of visitors and lists of objects acquired by the different divisions of the museum.
51 *NMI Director's Reports*, 1929, 1931, 1932.
52 *NMI Director's Report*, 1927/8.
53 Roy F. Foster, *Ireland*, p. 518.
54 *NMI Director's Report*, 1932 p. 3.

55 *NMI Director's Report*, 1931 p.7.
56 *NMI Director's Report*, 1932 p. 3; 1933 p. 3.
57 Kennedy, *Dreams*, p. 20.
58 Bodkin, *The Importance of Art to Ireland* (Dublin, 1935) pp. 1, 14, 17–8.
59 Brian Kennedy, 'The failure of the Cultural Republic', *Studies*, 81(321) (1992); Kennedy, *Dreams*, pp. 1, 7, 22.

NOTES TO CHAPTER SEVEN

1 Lord Talbot de Malahide, Presidential Address, *Proceedings of the Royal Irish Academy*, 1866 p. 395.
2 Alistair Wilson, 'A Time for Change. A Review of Major Museums in Northern Ireland' (Bangor Department of Education Nothern Ireland 1995) p. 49.
3 Mary McAleese in the statement *Remarks by President Mary McAleese at the Presentation of the Gulbenkian Foundation and Heritage Council Awards at Dublin Castle* (1998).
4 John Collis, Celts and Politics, in Paul Graves Brown *et al.*, *Cultural Identity and Archaeology* (London, Routledge, 1996) p. 171.
5 Colin Renfrew, 'Prehistory and the Identity of Europe', in Paul Graves-Brown *et al.*, *Cultural Identity* (1996) p. 127.
6 Miroslav Hroch, *Social Conditions of National Revival in Europe* (Cambridge, Cambridge University Press 1985) p. 297.
7 Minutes of the Committee of Antiquities, Royal Irish Academy archives 2 December 1840.
8 Sir William Rowan Hamilton, Presidential Address to the Royal Irish Academy, *PRIA*, 1 (1838) p. 20.
9 William Wilde Parl. Rep. 1868/9.XXIV p. 460.
10 Alice Stoppford Green, *Irish Nationality* (London 1911) p. 17.
11 *United Irishman*, 19 February 1848, p. 26.
12 T. S. J. Westropp, 'The Progress of Irish Archaeology', *Journal of the Royal Society of Antiquaries of Ireland*, 46 (1916) p. 18.
13 Douglas Hyde 1905, in Brendan Ó Conaire, *Hyde Douglas, Language, Lore and Lyrics* (Dublin 1986) p. 184.
14 William O'Brien, *Irish Ideas* (Longmans, Green and co 1893) p. 3.
15 Daniel O'Connell, cited in the *Nation*, 19 August 1843, p. 706.
16 William O'Brien, *The Irish National Idea* (Cork Young Ireland Society 1886) p. 7.
17 *Gaelic Journal* (April 1902) p. 58.
18 *United Irishman* 19 February 1848 p. 26.
19 Robert Macalister, *The Present and Future of Archaeology in Ireland*, (Dublin, Falconer 1925) p.14.
20 Cited in Jonathan Bell, 'Intelligent Revivalism', in Alan Gailey (ed), *The Use of the Past* (Ulster Folk and Transport Museum 1988) p. 8.
21 Cited in Roy F. Foster, *Paddy and Mr Punch* (London, Allen Lane 1993) p. 5.
22 *Short General Guide to the National Collections*, National Museum of Ireland 1932 p. 4.
23 John Elsner and Roger Cardinal, *The Cultures of Collecting* (London, Reaktion Books 1994) pp. 1–3.
24 Tony Bennett, *The Birth of the Museum* (London, Routledge 1995).
25 Flora Kaplan (ed), *Museums and the Shaping of Ourselves* (Leicester, Leicester University Press 1994) p. 3.
26 Gaynor Kavanagh (ed), *Making Histories in Museums* (Leicester, Leicester University Press, 1996).
27 Mead 1959, cited in John Urry, 'How Societies Remember the Past', in Sharon MacDonald and Gordon Fyfe (eds), *Theorizing Museums* (Oxford, Blackwell 1996) p. 46.
28 Sheldon Annis, 'The Museum as a Staging Ground for Symbolic Action', *Museum*

38(3) (1986) p. 168.

29 Alvin Jackson, 'Unionist Myths', *Past and Present*, 136 (1992); *Irish Unionism* (1996); Brian Walker, *Dancing to History's Tune* (Institute of Irish Studies, Queen's University Belfast 1996) pp. 1–14.

30 Anthony Buckley, '"We're Trying to Find our Identity": Uses of History Among Ulster Protestants', in Elizabeth Tonkin *et al.*, *History and Ethnicity* (London, Routledge 1989).

31 Some of these are illustrated in Anthony Buckley and Rhonda Paisley, *Symbols* (Belfast, Cultural Traditions Group 1994) p. 16.

32 Buckley, *Identity*, pp. 191–4.

33 W.H. Crawford, 'Irish Linen Centre: "Flax to Fabric" Exhibition', *Museum Ireland*, 5 (1995).

34 D. Officer, 'Re-presenting War. The Somme Heritage Centre', *History Ireland*, 3(1) (1995).

35 Kevin McCafferty, 'Frae "Wile Norn Aksints" tae oor ain national?' *Causeway*, 3(1&2) (1996).

36 Diarmait Mac Giolla Chriost, 'Northern Ireland: Culture Clash and Archaeology', John A. Atkinson *et al. Nationalism and Archaeology* (Edinburgh, Cruithne Press 1996).

37 Anthony Buckley, 'Collecting Ulster's Cultures: are there *really* Two Traditions', in Alan Gailey (ed), *Use of the Past* (Belfast, Ulster Folk and Transport Museum 1988).

38 See also Anthony Buckley, 'Presenting a Divisive Culture: Two Exhibitions at the Ulster Folk and Transport Museum', Susan M. Pearce (ed), *Museums and the Appropriation of Culture* (London, Athlone Press 1994).

39 Alan Gailey, 'Conflict Resolution in Northern Ireland: the Role of the Folk Museum', *Museum* 44(3) (1992) pp. 166, 168.

40 Anthony Buckley and Mary Kenny, 'Cultural Heritage in an Oasis of Calm: Divided Identities in a Museum in Ulster', in Ullrich Kockel *Culture, Tourism and Development* (Liverpool, Liverpool University Press 1994) p. 135.

41 Published, in full, in Maurna Crozier, *Cultural Traditions in Northern Ireland* (Belfast, Institute of Irish Studies 1989) p. 34.

42 *News Letter*, 28 December 1996.

43 Buckley, *Presenting a Divisive Culture*, pp. 88–90.

44 Lucy Bryson and Clem McCartney, *Clashing Symbols* (Belfast, Institute of Irish Studies 1994).

45 Buckley and Paisley, *Symbols*.

46 An Post 1992, pp. 22–30.

47 Niamh Whitfield, 'The Finding of the Tara Brooch', *Journal of the Royal Society of Antiquaries of Ireland*, 104 (1974).

48 Tom Bartlett and Keith Jeffrey (eds), *Military History of Ireland* (Cambridge, Cambridge University Press 1996) p. 312.

49 Jane Leonard, 'Lest we Forget', in David Fitzpatrick (ed), *Ireland and the First World War* (Dublin, Trinity History Workshop 1986).

50 Hamilton, *The Times*, 12 November 1998.

51 Mary McAleese, *Irish Times*, 12 November 1998.

52 Sayer [construction engineer], cited by Pollak, *Irish Times*, 13 November 1998.

53 This is also demonstrated by the Strangford Stone. Erected in June 1999, to mark the millennium, the stone is 40 foot high and stands in Delamont Country Park, Strangford, County Down. The stone resembles a megalithic monument and was erected by 1,000 young people, without mechanical assistance, as a cross-community project. The erection of such a monument symbolises people in Northern Ireland pulling together for a common goal.

54 Michael Rowlands, 'Memory, Sacrifice and the Nation', *Cultural Memory*, 30 (1996).

55 Kevin Whelan, *Fellowship of Freedom* (Cork, Cork University Press 1998) p. 121.

56 Comerford, *Irish Times*, 10 January 1998.

57 Elizabeth Crooke, 'Exhibiting 1798. Three Recent Exhibitions', *History Ireland*, 6(4) (1998).

58 Sheridan, *Irish Times*, 13 June 1998.

59 Rev. Kennaway, cited in *Irish Times*, 13 June 1998.

60 Ó Riain, 'Nelson's Pillar a Controversy that Ran and Ran', *History Ireland,* 6(4) (1998).
61 Colleen Dube, 'Kilmainham Gaol a potent blend of fact and fiction', *Museum Ireland* (1996).
62 Jacqueline O'Brien and Desmond Guinness, *Dublin. A Grand Tour* (London, Weidenfeld and Nicolson 1994) p. 33.
63 Brian Lacey, 'The National Museum of Ireland at Collins Barracks', *Museum Ireland,* 7 (1997).
64 *Irish Times,* 19 September 1997.
65 Peter Woodman, 'Who Possesses Tara? Politics in Archaeology in Ireland', in Peter J. Ucko, *Theory in Archaeology: a World Perspective* (London, Routledge 1995) p. 286.
66 Brian J. Graham, 'Heritage Conservation and Revisionist Nationalism in Ireland', in G. J. Ashworth and P. Larkham *Building a New Heritage* (London, Routledge 1994) p. 148.
67 Graham attributed some of this to its tourist potential.
68 David Lowenthal, 'Remembering to Forget', *Museums Journal,* 93(2) (1993) p. 20.
69 The ideas of memory and history are explored in Michael Rowlands, 'The Politics of Identity in Archaeology', in G. C. Bond and A. Gilliam (eds), *Social Construction of the Past* (London, Routledge 1996); see also John Urry, 'How Societies Remember the Past', in Sharon MacDonald and Gordon Fyfe (eds), *Theorizing Museums* (Oxford, Blackwell Publishers 1996).

Appendices

In most cases the chapters of each of these guides were sold separately as catalogues to individual parts of the collection where this is not the case is indicated. The author of each chapter, the year that it was first produced and the selling price are provided below.

Science and Art Museum, Dublin. Guide to the Collection of Irish Antiquities

Chapter 1: *The Stone Age* by L-C. G. T. Plunkett 1907. (1p)
Chapter 2: (Missing)
Chapter 3: (Missing)
Chapter 4: *The Christian Period* by T. S. J. Westropp 1906. (2p)
Chapter 5: *Irish Ethnographical Collection* by T. S. J. Westropp 1911. (1p)

National Museum of Science and Art, Dublin. Guide to the Collection of Irish Antiquities.
Anglo Irish Coins by G. Coffey 1911. (3p)

Science and Art Museum, Dublin. Guide to the Natural History Department

Vertebrate Animals Part 1 – Mammals and Birds by A. G. More 1887. (4½p)
Invertebrate Animals Part 1 – Recent Invertebrates by A. C. Haddon 1887. (3p)
Guide to the Collections of Rocks and Fossils by A. McHenry and W. W. Watts 1898. (8p)
A List of Irish Birds by R. J. Ussher 1908. (4p)
Hand List of Flowering Irish Plants and Ferns by T. Johnson 1910. (3p)

Science and Art Museum, Dublin. General Guide to the Art Collections

Part I Greek and Roman Antiquities
Chapter 1: *Greek and Roman Sculpture* by C. Clutch. 1908. (1p)
Chapter 2: *Greek and Roman Pottery* by C. Clutch. 1908. (2p)
Chapter 3: *Greek and Roman Coins* by H. Barclay. 1899. (1p)
Chapter 4: *Greek and Roman Metalwork. Wall Paintings at Pompeii* by C. Clutch. 1906. (1p)

Part II Medieval and Renaissance Sculpture and decoration
        One volume 1904 (1p)
Chapter 1: *Early Christian Byzantine, Gothic* by L-C. G.T. Plunkett.
Chapter 2: *Italian Renaissance and After* by L-C. G.T. Plunkett.
Chapter 3: *French Renaissance and After* by L-C. G.T. Plunkett.

Part III Egyptian Antiquities
        One volume 1902 (3p)
Chapter 1: *Sculpture, Inscriptions, Ostraka, Egyptian Writing* by M.A Murray and F.S.A. Scot.
Chapter 2: *Mummies* by M.A Murray and F.S.A. Scot.
Chapter 3: *Pottery, Faience, Metal and small objects* by M.A Murray and F. S. A. Scot.

Part IV Lace and Embroidery
One volume by A. S. Cole 1899 (1p)

Part V
Enamels by L-C. G. T. Plunkett 1902 (1p)

Part VI Metalwork
Chapter 1: *Bronze and Brass* by L-C. G. T. Plunkett and M. S. D. Westropp. 1903. (1p)
Chapter 2: *Gold and Silver, Foreign* by L-C. G. T. Plunkett and M. S. D. Westropp. 1903. (1p)
Chapter 3: *Gold and Silver, British* by L-C. G. T. Plunkett and M. S. D. Westropp. 1903. (1p)
Chapter 4: *Sheffield Plate – Pewter* by L-C. G. T. Plunkett and M. S. D. Westropp. 1904. (1p)
Chapter 5: *Iron* by L-C. G. T. Plunkett and M.S.D. Westropp. 1904. (2p)

Part VII Pottery and porcelain
Chapter 1: *British Pottery* by A. J. Toppin. 1904. (1p)
Chapter 2: *British Porcelain* by A. J. Toppin. 1905. (1p)
Chapter 3: *French Pottery* by J. J. Buckley. 1910. (1p)
Chapter 4: *French Porcelain* by Westropp. 1905. (1p)
Chapter 5: *Spanish Pottery and Porcelain* by M. S. D. Westropp. 1906. (1p)
Chapter 6: *Dutch Pottery and Porcelain* by Col. J. Day. 1905. (1p)
Chapter 7: *Flemish and German Stoneware* by Col. J. Day. 1906. (1p)
Chapter 8: *Porcelain, Northern, Central and Eastern Europe* by Col. J. Day. 1906. (1p)
Chapter 9: *Italian Pottery and Porcelain* by M. S. D. Westropp. 1907. (1p)
Chapter 10: *Chinese Porcelain* by Col. J. Day. 1905. (1p)

Chapter 11: *Persian Pottery*
Chapter 12: *Japanese Pottery and Porcelain* by M. S. D Westropp. 1907. (1p)

Part VIII Furniture
Chapter 1: *Italian Furniture* by L-C. G. T. Plunkett. 1899. (1p)
Chapter 2: *French and Other Continental* by L-C. G. T. Plunkett. 1900. (1p)
Chapter 3: *English Furniture* by L-C. G. T. Plunkett. 1900. (1p)

Part IX Glass
Chapter 1: *Glass* by Col. J. Day. 1906. (1p)
Chapter 2: *Irish Glass* by M.S.D. Westropp. 1913. (1p).

Part X Japanese Art
Chapter 1: *Lacquer* by E. P. Alabaster. 1905. (1p)

Part X Arms and Armour (European)
Chapter 1: *Armour* by M. S. D. Westropp. 1906. (1p)
Chapter 2: *Arms* by M. S. D. Westropp. 1906. (1p)

Part XV Ivories. 1899. (1p)

APPENDIX TWO
PUBLIC LECTURES PROVIDED BY THE DUBLIN MUSEUM
1902–3 (*REP. DEPT SCI. AND ART 1904.XVI*)

Lecturer	Subject	Attendance
Colonel Plunkett	Changes to the Museum	40
Dr Scharf	Cave Animals	27
Mr Coffey	Dates in the Bronze Age	34
Mr Nicols	Deep Sea Animals	30
Mr Coffey	The Early Iron Age	24
Mr Nichols	Useful Marine Products	15
Colonel Plunkett	The loan collections	18
Mr Carpenter	History of Animals	22
Mr Brenan	Antique Lace	53
Mr Kilroe	Irish soils and subsoils	20
Mr Brenan	Modern Lace	53
Mr Carpenter	History of Animals	21
Mr Lister	Books old and new	44
Mr Sey	Genesis of the Dublin Mountains	46
Count Plunkett	Verocchio's Works	25
Mr Ussher	Irish Birds and their modes of life	43
Dr Pethybridge	Carnivorous and Parasitic Plants	27
Mr Seymour	Irish Minerals	20
Mr Westropp	Irish Silversmith's work	33
Mr Ussher	Irish Birds	36
Prof. Johnson	Seaweeds and their collection	16
Mr Barrington	Wild birds useful to farmers	30
Prof. Johnson	Trees in summer and winter	26

Bibliography

UNPUBLISHED PAPERS

Royal Irish Academy Manuscripts

Minute Books of Committee of Antiquities of the Royal Irish Academy (May 1785–March 1780).

Minute Books of the Council of the Royal Irish Academy (May 1785–December 1890).

Dublin Museum of Science and Art

Annual Reports of Directors
Annual Reports to the Department of Science and Art (1877–99)
Annual Reports of the Department of Agriculture and Technical Instruction (1899–1920)
National Museum of Ireland, Director's Reports (1927/8–1936)

Ceremonial of laying the first stone by the HRH the Prince of Wales 10 April 1885 (with reply of the HRH and statement by V. Ball Director), Dublin.

National Archives

Files relating to the Architectural Competition for the Dublin Museum of Science and Art.

National Museum of Ireland

National Museum of Ireland Scrapbook of Newspaper Cuttings.

BRITISH PARLIAMENTARY PAPERS

British Parliamentary Papers

Report of the Commissioners appointed to inquire into the facts relating to the Ordnance Survey Memoir of Ireland. Together with the Reports, minutes of evidence, appendix. 1844.XXX

Select Committee on Ordnance Survey (Ireland). Report, proceedings, minutes of evidence, appendix and index. 1846.XV

Report from the Select Committee appointed to inquire into the condition of the scientific institutions of Dublin which are assisted by government aid; together with the proceedings of the committee, minutes of evidence, appendix and index. 1864.XIII

Reports from Commission on the Science and Art Department in Ireland together with the minutes of evidence, appendix and index. 1868/9.XXIV

Reports from the Committees of Museums of the Science & Art Department. Report of the Select Committee appointed to enquire into and report upon the administration and cost of the Museums of the Science and Art Department. 1897.XII

Museums of the Science and Art Department. Minute by the Right Honourable the Lords of the Committee of the Privy Council on Education on the 2nd Report from the Select Committee (1898) on the museums of the Science and Art Dept with appendix. Presented to both houses of Parliament by Command of Her Majesty 1899. 1898.XI

Report of a Committee appointed by the Lords Commissioners of Her Majesty's Treasury to inquire into the circumstances under which certain Celtic Ornaments found in Ireland were recently offered for Sale to the British Museum, and to consider the relation between the British Museum and the Museums of Edinburgh and Dublin with regard to the acquisition and retention of objects of Antiquarian and Historic Interest, with evidence, appendices and index. 1899.LXXVII

Department of Science and Art Annual Reports 1854 to 1899.

The Parliamentary Debates (Hansard)

Parliamentary Papers, Irish Free State

Report of the Committee of Enquiry on the National Museum, 1927

NEWSPAPERS AND PERIODICALS

Dublin Penny Journal
Dublin Literary Gazette
Dublin University Magazine
Evening Herald
Freeman's Journal
Gaelic Journal
Hibernia
Irish Builder

Irish People
Irish Nation
Irish Penny Journal
Irish Times
Nation
News Letter
The Leader
United Irishman

COLLECTIONS OF ESSAYS AND ADDRESSES

Armstrong. E. C. R. (1920) *Catalogue of Irish Gold Ornaments in the Collection of the Royal Irish Academy*. Dublin.

Asbourne, Lord (1914) 'Irish Nationality', in J. Dunn and P. J. Lennox (eds), pp. 170–5.

Atkinson, Robert (1906) Presidential Address, *Proceedings of the Royal Irish Academy*, 26C, pp. 44–54.

Ball, Valentine (1892) *General Guide to the Science and Art Museum, Dublin*. Dublin: Her Majesty's Stationery Office. (3rd edn).

Bigger, Francis Joseph (1914) 'The Ruins of Ireland', in J. Dunn and P. J. Lennox (eds) *The Glories of Ireland*, pp. 89–94. Washington DC: Phoenix Ltd.

Bodkin, T. (1935) *The Importance of Art to Ireland*. Dublin.

Boyd, E. A. (1917) *Standish O'Grady. Selected Essays and Passages*. Dublin: The Talbot Press.

Chart, D. A. (1949) 'The Care of Ancient Monuments in Northern Ireland 1921–1948', *Journal of the Royal Society of Antiquaries of Ireland* LXXIX, pp. 182–5.

Clibborn, E. (1860) 'On the Gold Antiquities Found in Ireland', *Ulster Journal of Archaeology* 8, pp. 36–51.

Cochrane, R. (1892) 'Notes on the "Ancient Monuments Protection (Ireland) Act 1892" and the previous legislation connected therewith', *Journal of the Royal Society of Antiquaries of Ireland* 2(4) pp. 411–29.

Coffey, D. (1914) 'Irish Metal Work', in J. Dunn and P. J. Lennox (eds) pp. 78–83.

Crone, J. S. and F. C. Bigger (eds) (1927) *Articles and Sketches. Biographical, Historical, Topographical by Francis Joseph Bigger*. Talbot Press: Dublin.

D'Alton Canon (1914) 'The Island of Saints and Scholars', in J. Dunn and P. J. Lennox (ed) pp. 9–19.

de Blacam, Aodl (1921) *What Sinn Féin Stands For*. Dublin: Mellifont Press.

Dunn, J. and P. J. Lennox (eds) (1914) *The Glories of Ireland*. Phoenix: Washington DC.

Ferguson, M. C. (1896) *Sir Samuel Ferguson in the Ireland of his Day*. London.

Ferguson, S. (1847) 'Ireland's Claims to an Adequate Parliamentary Representative of Learning in a Letter to James MacCullagh ...; and a Letter to Lord Morpeth on the Formation of a Museum of National Antiquities in Dublin', Dublin.

(1882) 'Presidential Address', *Proceedings of the Royal Irish Academy* 2, pp. 185–200.

Fitz Gerald, W. (1891/5) 'Mullaghmast: Its History and Traditions', *Journal of the Kildare Archaeological Society* 1, pp. 379–90.

Flood, G. (ed) (1911) *The Spirit of the Nation. Ballads and Songs of the writers of 'The Nation' with original and ancient music.* Dublin: James Duffy & Co. (2nd edn).

Graves, Charles (1866) 'Address Delivered to the Royal Irish Academy on the Death of George Petrie', *Proceedings of the Royal Irish Academy*, 9, pp. 325–36.

Graves, C. L. (1914) 'Irish Wit and Humor', in J. Dunn and P. J. Lennox (eds), pp. 298–303.

Green, Alice Stopford (1908) *The Making of Ireland and its Undoing.* London.

(1911) *Irish Nationality.* London.

(1925) *A History of the Irish State.* London.

Gregory, A. (1901) *Ideals in Ireland.* London.

Griffith, A. (1914) *Thomas Davis, the thinker and teacher. The essence of his writings in prose and poetry.* Dublin.

(1918) *Resurrection of Hungry: a Parallel for Ireland with appendices on Pitt's Policy and Sinn Féin.* Dublin: Duffy & Co. (3rd edn).

Gwynn, S. (1912) *The Case for Home Rule.* Dublin: Maunsel and Co. (3rd edn).

Hackett, F. (1924) *The Story of the Irish Nation.* Dublin.

Hamilton, R. (1838) 'Presidential Address', *Proceedings of the Royal Irish Academy* 1, pp. 107–20.

Haverty, M. (1860) *The History of Ireland Ancient and Modern.* Dublin.

Hobson, Bulmer (1832) *Saorstát Éireann. Official Handbook of the Irish Free State.* Dublin: The Talbot Press.

Hyde Douglas (1901) 'What Ireland is Asking For', in A. Gregory (ed), pp. 55–61.

Irish Archaeological and Celtic Society (1857) *Report of Meeting Announcing the Archaeological and Celtic Society.* Dublin.

Irish Archaeological Society (1841) *Report of the first Annual General Meeting of the Irish Archaeological Society.* Dublin.

Jellett, J. H. (1870) 'Presidential Address', *Proceedings of the Royal Irish Academy*, 11, pp. 50–67.

Lloyd, H. (1846) 'Presidential Address', *Proceedings of the Royal Irish Academy*, 3, pp. 203–17.

Lynd, R. n.d. (*c.*1919) *Ethics of Sinn Féin.* Dublin.

(1936) *Ireland a Nation.* London: Grant Richards.

Macalister, R. A. S. (1925) *The Present and Future of Archaeology in Ireland.* Dublin: Falconer.

(1949) *The Archaeology of Ireland.* London: Methuen. (3rd edn).

MacCall, Seamus (1931) *And so Began the Irish Nation.* London: Longmans, Green & Co.

McKenna, J. E. (1909) *Irish Art.* Dublin: Catholic Truth Society of Ireland.

MacNeill, Eoin (1901) *Phases of Irish History.* Dublin.

(1921) *Celtic Ireland.* Dublin: Martin Lester Ltd.

(1932) 'History', in B. Hobson (ed), pp. 41–63.

MacSweeney, P. M. (1913) *A Group of Nation Builders. O'Donovan, O'Curry, Petrie.* Dublin: Catholic Truth Society.

Mahr, A. (1932) 'Archaeology', in B. Hobson (ed), pp. 212–32.

(1937) 'New Aspects and Problems in Irish Prehistory Presidential Address 1937' *Proceedings of the Prehistoric Society* III(2), pp. 262–436.

McAdam, R. (1853) 'The Archaeology of Ulster', *Ulster Journal of Archaeology* 1, pp. 1–8.

Moran, D. P. (1901) 'The Battle of Two Civilisations', in A. Gregory (ed), pp. 25–41.

Murphy, B. (1994) 'The First Dáil Éireann', *History Ireland* 1994(1), pp. 41–6.

O'Brien, William (1886) *The Irish National Idea.* Cork: Cork Young Ireland Society.

(1892) 'The Irish Language', *Gaelic Journal* 4(41), pp. 157–60 and 4(43), pp. 164–5.

(1893) *Irish Ideas.* London: Longmans, Green and Co.

Ó Conaire, B. (ed) (1986) *Hyde, Douglas. Language, Lore and Lyrics.* Dublin: Irish Academy Press.

O'Donoghue, D. J. (1914) *Essays Literary and Historical by Thomas Davis.* Dundalk: Dundalgan Press.

O'Driscoll, R. (1971) 'Ferguson and the Idea of an Irish National Literature, *Éire-Ireland* VI(1), pp. 82–95.

O'Carroll, L. E. (1914) 'Irish Manuscripts', in J. Dunn and P. J. Lennox (eds), pp. 84–8.

O'Connell, Daniel (1843) 'Speech at Mullaghmast', in Anon. *The Life and Death of Lord Edward Fitzgerald ... to which is added Mr O'Connell's speech at Mullaghmast on the Repeal of the Union*, pp. 99–104. Dublin: Grace.

O'Connell, John. (ed) (1846) *Life and Speeches of Daniel O'Connell.* Dublin.

O'Grady, Standish [pseud. Clive, A.] . (1876) 'Irish Archaeology', *Dublin University Magazine* 88(528), pp. 641–51.

(1881) *History of Ireland: Critical and Philosophical.* Dublin.

O'Hanlon, John (1888) *Report of the O'Connell Monument Committee.* Dublin: Duffy & Co.

O'Hegarty, R. S. (1918) *The indestructible nation. A Survey of Irish History from the English invasion.* Dublin: Maunsel.

O'Reilly, B. (1813) *A Catalogue of the Subjects of Natural History in the Museum of the Dublin Society, Systematically Arranged; also of the Antiquities, etc.* Dublin.

Pearse, Patrick H. (1952) *Political Writings and Speeches*. Dublin: Talbot Press.

Petrie, George (1837) On the history and antiquities of Tara Hill, *Transactions of the Royal Irish Academy* 18, pp. 25–232.

(1845) *The ecclesiastical architecture of Ireland, anterior to the Anglo-Norman invasion*. Dublin: Hodges and Smith.

(1970) *The Round Towers of Ireland*. Shannon: Irish University Press. (3rd edn).

Plunkett, George N. (1912) 'Presidential Address, delivered at the Museums Association Dublin Conference', *Museums Journal* 12(2), pp. 33–9.

Robinson, T. R. (1851) 'Presidential Address', *Proceedings of the Royal Irish Academy,* 5, pp. 101–11.

Rooney, J. J. (1914) 'The Sorrows of Ireland', in J. Dunn and P. J. Lennox (ed), pp. 145–52.

Russell, George (1901) 'Nationality and Imperialism', in A. Gregory (ed), pp. 15–22.

Sproule, J. (1854) *The Irish Industrial Exhibition of 1853. A Detailed Catalogue of its Contents*. Dublin.

Stokes, William (1868) *The Life of George Petrie*. London.

Talbot de Malahide, Lord (1866) 'Presidential Address', *Proceedings of the Royal Irish Academy,* 9, pp. 390–5.

Todd, J. H. (1856) 'Presidential Address', *Proceedings of the Royal Irish Academy*, 6, pp. 319–38.

Wakeman, W. (1848) *Handbook of Irish Antiquities*. Dublin.

Westropp, T. S. J. (1916) 'The Progress of Irish Archaeology,' Presidential Address, *Journal of the Royal Society of Antiquaries of Ireland* 46, pp. 2–26.

Wilde, W. (1840) *The Beauties of the Boyne and its Tributary, the Blackwater*. Dublin: McGlashan. (2nd edn).

(1857) *A Descriptive Catalogue of the Antiquities of Stone, Earthen and Vegetable Materials in the Museum of the Royal Irish Academy*. Dublin: Hodges & Smith.

(1861) *A Descriptive Catalogue of Animal Materials and Bronze in the Museum of the Royal Irish Academy*. Dublin: Hodges & Smith.

(1862) *A Descriptive Catalogue of the Antiquities of Gold in the Museum of the Royal Irish Academy*. Dublin: Hodges & Smith.

(1864) *Ireland, Past, and Present, the Land and the People*. A lecture. Dublin.

CONTEMPORARY BOOKS, PAMPHLETS AND ARTICLES

Alter, Peter (1974) 'Symbols of Irish Nationalism', *Studia Hibernica* 14, pp. 104–23.

Ames, Michael (1994) 'Cannibal tours, glass boxes and the politics of interpretation', in S. M. Pearce (ed.), pp. 98–106.

Anderson, Benedict (1983) *Imagined Communities. Reflections on the Origin and Spread of Nationalism.* London: Verso.

Andrews, J. H. (1975) *A Paper Landscape: the Ordnance Survey in Nineteenth Century Ireland.* Oxford: Oxford University Press.

Annis, S. (1986) 'The museum as a staging ground for symbolic action', *Museum* 38(3), pp. 168–71.

An Post (1992) *Postage Stamps of Ireland, Seventy Years.* Dublin: An Post.

Archer, Jean (1993). 'Geological Artistry: The Drawings and Watercolors of George Victor du Noyer in the Archives of the Geological Survey of Ireland', in A. Dalsimer (ed), pp. 133–44.

Atkinson, John A., Banks, Iain, & Jerry O'Sullivan (ed) (1996) *Nationalism and Archaeology.* Edinburgh: Cruithne Press.

Avgouli, Maria (1994) 'The First Greek Museums and National Identity', in F. Kaplan (ed), pp. 246–66.

Barrett, Cyril and Jeanne Sheehy (1996a) 'Visual Arts and Society, 1850–1900', in W. E. Vaughan (ed), pp. 436–74.

(1996b) 'Visual Arts and Society 1900–21', in W. E. Vaughan (ed), pp. 475–99.

Bartlett Tom and Keith Jeffrey (eds) (1996) *Military History of Ireland* Cambridge, Cambridge University Press.

Beckett, J. C. (1976) *The Anglo-Irish Tradition.* London: Faber and Faber.

Bell A. S. (ed) (1981) *The Scottish Antiquarian Tradition. Essays to Mark the Bicentenary of the Society of Antiquaries of Scotland and its Museum 1780–1980* Edinburgh: John Donald Publishers.

Bell, Jonathan (1988) 'Intelligent Revivalism: the First Feis na nGleann, 1904', in A. Gailey (ed), pp. 3–12.

(1996) 'Making Rural Histories', in G. Kavanagh (ed), pp. 30–41.

Bennett, Tony (1995) *The birth of the museum, history, theory, politics.* London: Routledge.

(1998) 'Speaking to the Eye. Museums, Legibility and the Social Order', in S. MacDonald (ed), pp. 25–35.

Boreland, Dorcas (1996) Anglophobes and Anglophiles: Some Early Accounts of Ireland', in J. A. Atkinson *et al.* (eds), pp. 104–10.

Bourke, M. (1993) 'Frederic Wm. Burton 1816–1900: Painter and Antiquarian', *Éire-Ireland* XXVIII(3), pp. 45–60.

Bourke, Thomas (1986) 'Nationalism and the Royal Irish Academy', *Studies* LXXV, pp. 196–208.

Bowler, Peter. J. (1989) *The Invention of Progress: the Victorians and the Past.* Oxford: Basil Blackwell.

Boyce, D. George (1988) '"One Last Burial": Culture, Counter Revolution and Revolution in Ireland 1886–1916', in G. D. Boyce (ed) *Revolution in Ireland 1879–1923*, pp. 115–36.

(1991) *Nationalism in Ireland* London: Routledge (2nd edn).

Boyce, D. George and Alan O'Day (eds) (1996) *The Making of Modern Irish History. Revisionism and the revisionist controversy.* London: Routledge.

Boylan, Henry (1998) *A Dictionary of Irish Biography.* Dublin: Gill and Macmillan. (3rd edn).

Boylan, P. J. (1995) 'Reflecting the State of the Nation', *Museums Journal* 95(2), pp. 24–5.

Bradshaw, Brendan (1989) 'Nationalism and Historical Scholarship in Modern Ireland', *Irish Historical Studies* 24, pp. 329–51.

Brady, Ciaran (ed) (1994) *Interpreting Irish History.* Dublin: Irish Academic Press.

(1994b) '"Constructive and Instrumental": The Dilemma of Ireland's First "New Historians"', in C. Brady (ed), pp. 3–31.

Breathnach, Edel (1997) 'Cultural identity and Tara from Lebor Gabála Érenn to George Petrie', *Discovery Programme Report* 4, pp. 85–98. Dublin.

Brett, David (1994) 'The Representation of Culture', in U. Kockel (ed), pp. 117–28.

(1996) *The Reconstruction of Heritage.* Cork: Cork University Press.

Bryson, L. and C. McCartney (1994) *Clashing Symbols? A Report on the Use of Flags, Anthems and Other National Symbols in Northern Ireland.* Belfast: Institute of Irish Studies, Queens University Belfast.

Buckley, Anthony D. (1988) 'Collecting Ulster's Cultures: are there *really* Two Traditions?' in A. Gailey (ed), pp. 49–60.

(1989) '"We're Trying to Find our Identity": Uses of History Among Ulster Protestants', in E. Tonkin, M. McDonald and M. Champion (eds), *History and Ethnicity*, pp. 183–97 London: Routledge.

(1994) 'Presenting a Divisive Culture: Two Exhibitions at the Ulster Folk and Transport Museum', in S. Pearce (ed), *Museums and the Appropriation of Culture. New Research in Museum Studies* 4, pp. 84–102. London: Athlone Press.

(1996) 'Why Not Invent the Past We Display in Museums?' in G. Kavanagh (ed), pp. 42–35.

Buckley, Anthony D. and Mary Kenny (1994) 'Cultural Heritage in an Oasis of Calm: Divided Identities in a Museum in Ulster', in U. Kockel (ed), pp. 129–48.

Buckley, Anthony D. and Rhonda Paisley (1994) *Symbols.* Belfast: Cultural Traditions Group of the Community Relations Council.

Cahill, Mary (1994) 'Mr Anthony's Bog-Oak Case of Gold Antiquities', *Proceedings of the Royal Irish Academy* 94c, pp. 53–109.

Cant, R. G. (1981) 'Davis Steuart Erskine, 11th Earl of Buchan: Founder of the Society of Scotland', in A. S. Bell (ed), pp. 1–30.

Champion, Timothy (1996) 'Three Nations or One? Britain and the National Use of the Past', in M. Díaz-Andreu and T. Champion (eds), pp. 119–45.

(1997) 'The power of the Picture. The Image of the Ancient Gaul', in B. L. Molyneaux (ed), *The Cultural Life of Images. Visual Representation in Archaeology*, pp. 213–29. London: Routledge.

Clarke, D. (1981) 'Scottish Archaeology in the Second Half of the Nineteenth Century', in A. S. Bell (ed), pp. 114–41.

(1996) 'Me tartan and chained to the past', *Museums Journal* (March), pp. 26–7.

Clogg, Richard (1985) 'Sense of the Past in Pre-independence Greece', in R. Sussex and J. C. Eade (eds), pp. 7–30.

Coffey, Petra (1996) 'A Victorian Exploration of the Irish landscape – the Work of George Victor du Noyer', *Archaeology Ireland* 10(2), pp. 26–28.

Collis, John (1996) 'Celts and Politics', in P. Graves-Brown *et al.* (eds), pp. 167–78.

Comerford, Patrick (1998) '1798 – The Lost Leaders', *Irish Times*, 10 January 1998.

Connolly, S. J. (1997) 'Culture, Identity and Tradition: Changing Definitions of Irishness', in B. J. Graham (ed), pp. 43–63.

(1998) *The Oxford Companion to Irish History*, Oxford: Oxford University Press.

Connor, Walker (1978) 'A Nation is a Nation, is a State, is an Ethnic Group', is a..., *Ethnic and Racial Studies* 1(4), pp. 379–88.

Cooney, Gabriel (1993) 'A Sense of Place in Irish Prehistory', *Antiquity* 67, pp. 632–41.

(1995) 'Theory and Practice in Irish Archaeology', in P. J. Ucko (ed), pp. 263–77.

(1996) 'Building the Future on the Past: Archaeology and the Construction of National Identity in Ireland, in M. Díaz-Andreu and T. Champion (eds), pp. 146–63.

Corlett, Chris (1998) 'Interpretation of Round Towers – Public Appeal or Professional Opinion?' *Archaeology Ireland* 12(2), pp. 24–7.

Cramb. A. (1996) 'Scotland's Touchstone Fulfils its Destiny', *Daily Telegraph*, 4 July 1996.

Crawford, W. H. (1995) 'Irish Linen Centre: "Flax to Fabric" Exhibition', *Museum Ireland* 5, pp. 61–6.

Crone J. S. (1937) *A Concise Dictionary of Irish Biography*. Dublin: Talbot Press.

Crooke, Elizabeth M. (1998) 'Exhibiting 1798. Three Recent Exhibitions', *History Ireland* 6(4), pp. 41–5.

(1999) 'Archaeology and Nationalism in Nineteenth Century Ireland', *Museum Ireland* 9, pp. 21–8.

Crossman, Virgina and Dymphna McLoughlin (1994) 'A Peculiar Eclipse: E. Estyn Evans and Irish Studies', *Irish Review* 15, pp. 79–96.

Crozier, Maurna (ed) (1989) *Cultural Traditions in Northern Ireland.*

Varieties of Irishness. Belfast: Institute of Irish Studies, Queen University Belfast.

(1990) (ed) *Cultural Traditions in Northern Ireland. Varieties of Britishness.* Belfast: Institute of Irish Studies, Queen University Belfast.

Cullen, L. M. (1980) 'The Cultural Basis of Modern Irish Nationalism', in R. Mitchison (ed) *The Roots of Nationalism*, pp. 91–106. Edinburgh: John Donald.

Dalsimer, Adele (ed) (1993) *Visualising Ireland. National Identity and the Pictorial Tradition.* London: Faber and Faber.

Davies, A. C. (1981) 'Ireland's Crystal Palace, 1853', in J.M. Goldstrom and L. A. Clarkson (eds) *Irish Population, Economy, and Society.* Oxford: Clarendon Press.

de Vere White, T. (1967) *The Parents of Oscar Wilde.* Hodder and Stoughton. London.

Díaz-Andreu, Margarita (1995) 'Archaeology and Nationalism in Spain', in P. Kohl and C. Fawcett (eds), pp. 39–56.

(1996) 'Constructing Identities Through Culture. The Past and Forging Europe', in P. Graves-Brown *et. al.* (eds), pp. 48–61.

(1997) Nationalism, Ethnicity and Archaeology – the Archaeological Study of Iberians Through the Looking Glass, *Journal of Mediterranean Studies* 7 (2), pp. 155–68.

Díaz-Andreu, M. and T. Champion (eds) (1996) *Nationalism and Archaeology in Europe.* London: Routledge.

Dickson, David (1987) 'Historical Journals in Ireland: The Last Hundred Years', in B. Hayley and E. McKay (eds), pp. 87–101.

Dietler, Michael (1994) '"Our Ancestors the Gauls": Archaeology, Ethnic Nationalism, and the Manipulation of Celtic Identity in Modern Europe', *American Anthropologist* 96, pp. 584–605.

Dillon, Myles (1967) 'George Petrie (1789–1866)', *Studies* LVI, pp. 266–76.

Dolley, M. (1972) 'Aspects of George Petrie III: George Petrie and a Century of Irish Numismatics', *Proceedings of the Royal Irish Academy* 72C, pp. 165–93.

Dube, Colleen (1996) 'Kilmainham Gaol "A potent blend of fact and fiction"', *Museum Ireland* 6, pp. 57–63.

Duffy, Patrick J. (1997) 'Writing Ireland: Literature and art in the representation of Irish place', in B. J. Graham 1997a. (ed.), pp. 64–84.

Dunleavy, J. E. and G. W. Dunleavy (1991) *Douglas Hyde: a Maker of Modern Ireland.* Berkeley Oxford: University of California Press.

Dunleavy, M. (1996) 'A Future for our Museums', *Museum Ireland* 6, pp. 31–9.

Edwards, Ruth Dudley (1979) *Patrick Pearse. The Triumph of Failure.* London: Faber and Faber. (2nd edn).

Elsner, John and Roger Cardinal (1994) *The cultures of collecting.* London: Reaktion Books.

Evans, E. E. (1968) 'Archaeology in Ulster Since 1920', *Ulster Journal of Archaeology* 31, pp. 3–8.

Evans, Gwyneth (1999) 'Emyr Estyn Evans and Northern Ireland' by Matthew Stout (Review Article), *Ulster Journal of Archaeology* 58, pp. 134–42.

Fleischmann, A. (1972) 'Aspects of George Petrie IV: Petrie's Contribution to Irish Music', *Proceedings of the Royal Irish Academy* 72c, pp. 195–218.

Foley, Tadhg and Sean Ryder (eds) (1998) *Ideology and Ireland in the Nineteenth Century*, Dublin: Four Courts Press.

Forgan, Sophie and Graeme Gooday (1996) 'Constructing South Kensington: the Buildings and the Politics of Huxley's Working Environments', *The British Journal for the History of Science* 29, pp. 435–68.

Foster, Roy (1987) 'Anglo-Irish Literature, Gaelic Nationalism and Irish Politics in the 1890s', in J. M. W. Bean (ed), *The Political Culture of Modern Britain*, pp. 91–110. London: Hamilton.

(1988) *Modern Ireland 1600–1972*. London: Penguin.

(1993) *Paddy and Mr Punch. Connections in Irish and English History*. London: Allen Lane. The Penguin Press.

Fowler, D. D. 1987. 'Uses of the Past. Archaeology in the Service of the State', *American Antiquity* 52(2), pp. 229–48.

Gailey, Alan (1986) 'Creating Ulster's Folk Museum', *Ulster Folklife* 32, pp. 54–77.

(1988a) (ed) *The Use of the Past*. Belfast: Ulster Folk and Transport Museum.

(1988b) 'Tradition and Identity', in A. Gailey (1988a), pp. 61–7.

(1992) 'Conflict-resolution in Northern Ireland: the Role of a Folk Museum', *Museum* 44(3), pp. 165–96.

Garvin, Tom (1981) *The Evolution of Irish Nationalist Politics*. Dublin: Gill & Macmillan.

(1987) *Nationalist Revolutionaries in Ireland 1858–1928*. Oxford: Clarendon Press.

Gathercole, Peter and David Lowenthal (1990) *The Politics of the Past*. London: Unwin Hyman.

Gellner, Ernest (1983) *Nations and Nationalism*. London: Blackwell.

(1987) *Culture, Identity and Politics*. Cambridge: Cambridge University Press.

Glandon, Virginia. E. (1976) 'Index of Irish Newspapers, 1900–22 Part 1', *Éire-Ireland* XI(4), pp. 84–121.

(1977) 'Index of Irish Newspapers, 1900–22 Part 2', *Éire-Ireland* XII(1), pp. 86–115.

Goldering Maurice (1993) *Pleasant the Scholars Life: Irish Intellectuals and the Construction of Nation State*. London: Serif.

Goodwin Mark (1990) 'Objects, Belief and Power in mid-Victorian

England: The Origins of the Victoria and Albert Museum', in S. M. Pearce (1990a), pp. 9–49.

Graham Brian (1994a) 'Heritage Conservation and Revisionist Nationalism in Ireland', in G. J. Ashworth and P. Larkham (eds), *Building a New Heritage. Tourism, Culture and Identity in a New Europe*, pp. 135–58. London: Routledge.

(1994b) 'The Search for the Common Ground: Estyn Evans' Ireland', *Transactions of the Institute of British Geographers* 19, pp. 183–201.

(1997) (ed), *In Search of Ireland. A Cultural Geography*. London: Routledge.

Graves-Brown, Paul, Siân Jones and Clive Gamble (ed) (1996) *Cultural identity and archaeology: the construction of European communities*. London: Routledge.

Greene David (1972) 'Aspects of George Petrie II: George Petrie and the Collecting of Irish Manuscripts', *Proceedings of the Royal Irish Academy* 72C, pp. 158–63.

Greenhalgh, P. (1989) 'Education, Entertainment and Politics: Lessons of the Great International Exhibitions', in P. Vergo (ed), *The New Museology*, pp. 74–98. London: Reakion Books.

Harbison, Peter (1976) *The Archaeology of Ireland*. The Bodley Head Archaeologies.

Hardman, R. and G. Jones (1996) 'The Stone of Scone Goes Home', *Daily Telegraph*, 4 July 1996.

Hayley, Barbara (1976) 'Irish Periodicals from the Union to the Nation', *Anglo-Irish Studies* ii, pp. 83–108.

(1987) 'A Reading and Thinking Nation: Periodicals as the Voice of Nineteenth Century Ireland', in B. Hayley and E. McKay (eds), *Three Hundred Years of Irish Periodicals*, pp. 29–48. Dublin: Irish Association of Irish Learned Journals.

Healy, T. (1995) 'The National Museum of Ireland: Its History and its Role in the Development of National Identity', Unpublished MA dissertation, Cortauld Institute of Art, London.

Heaney, Seamus (1993) 'The Sense of the Past', *History Ireland* 1(4), pp. 33–7.

Herity, Michael and George Eogan (1977) *Ireland in Prehistory*. London: Routledge and Kegan Paul.

Heuser, Barbara (1990) 'Museums, Identity and Warring Historians. Observations of History in Germany', *The Historical Journal* 33(2), pp. 417–40.

Hewison, Robert (1987) *The Heritage Industry*. London: Methuen.

Hobsbawm, E. J. (1990) *Nations and Nationalism Since 1780*. Cambridge: Cambridge University Press.

Hobsbawm, E. J. and T. Ranger (1983) *The Invention of Tradition*. Cambridge: Cambridge University Press.

Hodder, Ian (1984) 'Archaeology in 1984', *Antiquity* 58, pp. 25–31.

(1987) 'The Contextual Analysis of Symbolic Meanings', in S. M. Pearce (1994) (ed), p. 12.

(1991) *Reading the Past: Current Approaches to Interpretation in Archaeology*. Cambridge: Cambridge University Press. (2nd edn).

Hodder Ian, Michael Shanks, Alexandra Alexandri, Victor Buchli, John Carman, Jonathan Last and Gareth Lucas (eds) (1995) *Interpreting Archaeology. Finding a Meaning in the Past*. London: Routledge.

Hoffman, D. (1994) 'The German Art Museum and the History of the Nation', in D. J. Sherman and I. Rogoff (eds), pp. 3–21.

Hooper-Greenhill, Eilean (1992) *Museums and the shaping of knowledge*. London: Routledge.

Hroch, Miroslav (1985) *Social Preconditions of National Revival in Europe. A Comparative Analyses of the Social Composition of Patriotic Groups Among the Smaller Nations of Europe*. Cambridge: Cambridge University Press.

(1996) 'Epilogue', in M. Díaz-Andreu and T. Champion (eds), pp. 294–9.

Hudson, Kenneth (1987) *Museums of Influence*. Cambridge: Cambridge University Press.

Hutchinson, John (1987) *The Dynamics of Cultural Nationalism*. London: Allen and Unwin.

(1996) 'Irish Nationalism', in G. D. Boyce and A. O'Day (eds), pp. 100–19.

Impey, Oliver and Arthur MacGregor (eds) (1985) *The Origins of Museums: the Cabinet of Curiosities in Sixteenth and Seventeenth Century Europe*. Oxford: Clarendon.

Jackson, Alvin (1992) 'Unionist Myths 1912–1985', *Past and Present* pp. 164–85.

(1996) 'Irish Unionism', in G. D. Boyce and A. O'Day (eds), pp. 120–40.

James, Simon (1998) 'Celts, Politics and Motivation in Archaeology', *Antiquity* 72, pp. 200–9.

Johnson, N. C. (1993) 'Building a Nation: an Examination of the Irish Gaeltacht Report 1926', *Journal of Historical Geography* 19, pp. 157–68.

(1997) 'Making Space: Gaeltacht Policy and the Politics of Identity', in B. J. Graham 1997a. (ed), pp. 174–91.

Jones, M. (1995) 'From Haggis to Home Rule', *Museums Journal* 95(2), p. 26.

Jones, R. (1990) 'Sylwadu Cynfrodor ar Gor y Cewri; or a British Aborginal's Land Claim to Stonehenge', in C. Chippendale, P. Devereux, P. Fowler, R. Jones and T. Sebastian (eds), *Who owns Stonehenge?*, pp. 62–87. London: B. T. Batsford.

Jones, Sian (1996) 'Discourses of Identity in the Interpretation of the Past', in P. Graves-Brown, S. Jones and C. Gamble (eds), pp. 62–80.

(1997) *The Archaeology of Ethnicity. Constructing Identities in the Past and the Present*. London: Routledge.

Kaplan, Flora E. S. (ed) (1994) *Museums and the Making of Ourselves. The Role of Objects in National Identity*. Leicester: Leicester University Press.

Karp, Ivan and Steven D. Lavine (eds) (1991) *Exhibiting Cultures: the poetics and politics of museum display*. Washington; London: Smithsonian Institution Press.

Kavanagh, Gaynor (ed) (1996a) *Making Histories in Museums*. Leicester: Leicester University Press.

(1996b) 'Making Histories, Making Memories', in G. Kavanagh (ed), pp. 1–14.

Kearney, Richard (ed) (1997) *Postnationalist Ireland, Politics, Culture, Philosophy*. London: Routledge.

Kennedy, Brian P. (1990) *Dreams and Responsibilities. The State and the Arts in Independent Ireland*. Dublin: The Arts Council.

(1992) 'The Failure of the Cultural Republic: Ireland 1922–39', *Studies* 81(321), pp. 14–22.

Kilbride-Jones, H. E. (1993) 'Adolf Mahr', *Archaeology Ireland* 7(3), pp. 29–30.

Kim, Hongham (1998) 'Removing the Legacy of the Korean Past', *Curator* 41(3), pp. 178–86.

Kockel, Ulrich (ed) (1994) *Culture, Tourism and Development: The Case of Ireland*. Liverpool: Liverpool University Press.

Kohl, Philip L. (1993) 'Nationalism, Politics and the Practice of Archaeology in Soviet Transcaucasia', *European Journal of Archaeology* 1(2), pp. 181–8.

Kohl, Philip L. and Clare Fawcett (eds) (1995) *Nationalism, Politics and the Practice of Archaeology*. Cambridge: Cambridge University Press.

Lacey, Brian (1997) 'The National Museum of Ireland at Collins Barracks', *Museum Ireland* 7, pp. 80–1.

Lee, Joseph (1989) *Ireland 1912–1985*. Cambridge: Cambridge University Press.

(1992) *The Modernisation of Irish Society 1848–1918*. Dublin: Gill and Macmillan (3rd edn).

Leerssen, Joep (1996) *Remembrance and Imagination. Patterns in the Historical and Literary Representation of Ireland in the Nineteenth Century*. Cork: Cork University Press.

Leonard, Jane (1986) 'Lest We Forget', in D. Fitzpatrick (ed) *Ireland and the First World War*, pp. 59–67. Dublin: Trinity History Workshop.

Levine, Philippa (1986) *The amateur and the professional: antiquarians, historians and archaeologists in Victorian England 1838–1886*. Cambridge: Cambridge University Press.

Lewis, Geoffrey (1989) *For instruction and recreation: a centenary history of the Museums Association*. London: Quiller Press.

(1994a) 'Museums and Their Precursors: a Brief World Survey in J. Thompson (ed), *The Manual of Curatorship*, pp. 5–21. London: Butterworth.

(1994b) 'Museums in Britain: a Historical Survey', in J. Thompson (ed), *The Manual of Curatorship*, pp. 22–46. London: Butterworth.

Lohan, Rena (1994) *A Guide to the Archives of the Office of Public Works*. Dublin: Stationery Office.

Lowenthal, David (1985) *The Past is a Foreign Country*. Cambridge: Cambridge University Press.

(1990) 'Conclusion: Archaeologists and Others', in P. Gathercole and D. Lowenthal (ed), pp. 302–14.

(1993) 'Remembering to Forget', *Museums Journal* 93(6), pp. 20–2.

(1995) '"Trojan Forebears", "Peerless Relics": the Rhetoric of Heritage Claims', in I. Hodder *et al.* (eds), pp. 125–30.

Lucas, A. T. (1965) 'The Role of the National Museum in the Study of Irish Social History', *Museums Journal*, 65(2), pp. 112–21.

(1969) *The National Museum: Its Place in the Cultural Life of the Nation*. Dublin: National Museum of Ireland.

Lucas, Gareth (1995) 'Interpretation in Contemporary Archaeology: Some Philosophical Issues', in I. Hodder *et. al.* (eds), pp. 37–44.

Lyons, F. S. L. (1982) *Culture and Anarchy in Ireland 1890–1939*. Oxford: Oxford University Press. (2nd edn).

(1996) 'The Watershed 1903–7', in W. E. Vaughan (ed), pp. 111–22.

McAleese, M. (1998) *Remarks by President Mary McAleese at the Presentation of the Gulbenkian Foundation and Heritage Council Awards at Dublin Castle*. Office of the Secretary to the President. Dublin.

McCafferty, Kevin (1996a) 'Frae "Wile Norn Aksints" tae oor ain National Leid? Part 1', *Causeway* 3(1), pp. 39–44.

(1996b) 'Frae "Wile Norn Aksints" tae oor ain National Lleid? Part 2' *Causeway* 3(2), pp. 48–53.

MacCann, W. J. (1990) '"Volk and Germanentum": the Presentation of the Past in Nazi Germany', in P. Gathercole and D. Lowenthal (eds), pp. 74–88.

McColgan, John (1983) *British Policy and the Irish Administration 1920–22*. London: Allen and Unwin.

MacDonagh Oliver, W. F. Mandle and Pauric Travers (eds) (1983) *Irish Culture and Nationalism 1750–1950*. Dublin: Macmillan Press.

MacDonald, Sharon (1998) (ed) *The Politics of Display. Museums, Science and Culture*. London: Routledge.

MacDonald, Sharon and Gordon Fyfe (eds) (1996) *Theorizing Museums. Representing Identity and Diversity in a Changing World*. Oxford: Blackwell Publishers.

McDowell, R. B. (1967) *Alice Stopford Green*. Dublin.
(1985) 'The Main Narrative', in T. Ó Raifeartaigh (ed), pp. 1–92.
(1996) 'Administration and the Public Services 1870–1921', in W. E. Vaughan (ed), pp. 571–605.

McDowell, R. B. and D. A. Webb (1982) *Trinity College Dublin 1592–1952. An Academic History*. Cambridge: Cambridge University Press.

MacGaiolla Chroist, Diarmait (1996) 'Northern Ireland: Culture Clash and Archaeology', in J. A. Atkinson *et al.* (eds), pp. 128–34.

McKay, Enda (1987) 'A Century of Irish Trade Journals 1860–1960', in B. Hayley and E. McKay (eds), pp. 103–21.

McKillop, B. (1995) 'Seoul Searches for a New Image', *Museums Journal* 95(2), p. 27.

Malcolm, E. (1983) 'Popular Recreation in Nineteenth-Century Ireland', in O. MacDonagh *et al.* (eds), pp. 40–55.

Malty, A. and J. Malty (1979) *Ireland in the Nineteenth Century. A Breviate of Official Publications*. Oxford: Pergamon Press.

Malty, A. and B. McKenna (1980) *Irish Official Publications. A Guide to Republic of Ireland Papers, with a Breviate of Reports 1922–1972*. Oxford: Pergamon Press.

Maxwell, Constance (1946) *Trinity College Dublin 1591–1892*. Dublin: Dublin University Press.

Mazariegos, Oswaldo Chinchilla (1998) Archaeology and Nationalism in Guatemala at the Time of Independence, *Antiquity* 72, pp. 376–86.

Meenan, J. and D. Clarke (eds) (1981) *The Royal Dublin Society 1721–1981*. Dublin: Royal Dublin Society.

Meyer, A. B. (1905) *Studies of the Museums of the United States and Europe*. Washington: Government Printing Office.

Mitchell, G. F. (1985) 'Antiquities', in T. Ó. Raifeartaigh (ed), pp. 93–165.

Monk, M. and J. Sheehan (eds) (1998), *Early Medieval Munster. Archaeology, History and Society*. Cork: Cork University Press.

Moody, T. W. (1978) 'Irish History and Irish Mythology', *Hermathena* 124, pp. 7–24.

Nesbitt, N. (1979) *A Museum in Belfast*. Belfast: Ulster Museum.

Nutty, K. (1994) 'Irish Identity and the Writing of History', *Éire-Ireland* 29, pp. 160–72.

O'Brien, J. and D. Guinness (1994) *Dublin. A Grand Tour*. London: Weidenfeld and Nicolson.

O'Callaghan, M. (1984) 'Language, Nationality and Cultural Identity in the Irish Free State, 1922–7: the Irish Statesman and the Catholic Bulletin Re-appraised', *Irish Historical Studies* 94, pp. 226–45.

O'Conor, C. (1949) 'Origins of the Royal Irish Academy', *Studies*, pp. 325–37.

Ó Cuiv, B. (1969) 'The Gaelic Cultural Movements and the New

Nationalism', in K. Nowlan (ed), *The making of 1916*, pp. 1–27. Dublin: Dublin Stationery Office.

O'Halloran, Clare (1989) 'Irish Re-creations of the Gaelic Past', *Past and Present* 124, pp. 69–95.

(1991) 'Golden Ages and Barbarous Nations: Antiquarian Debate on the Celtic Past in Ireland and Scotland in the Eighteenth Century'. Unpublished PhD Dissertation. Cambridge University.

Officer, David D. (1995) 'Re-presenting War. The Somme Heritage Centre', *History Ireland* 3(1), pp. 38–2.

Ó Raifeartaigh, T. (ed) (1985) *The Royal Irish Academy, a Bicentennial History 1785–1985*. Dublin: Royal Irish Academy.

Ó Riain, M. (1998) 'Nelson's Pillar: a Controversy that Ran and Ran', *History Ireland* 6(4), pp. 21–5.

Ó Riordian, S. P. (1964) *Antiquities of the Irish Countryside*. London: Methuen (3rd edn).

O'Riordan, C. E. (1986) *The Natural History Museum, Dublin*. Dublin: The National Museum of Ireland.

O'Shea, Shane (1997) *Glasnevin Cemetery. An Historic Walk*. Dublin: Dublin Cemetery Committee.

O'Sulllivan, J. (1998) 'Nationalists, Archaeologists and the Myth of the Golden Age', in M. Monk and J. Sheehan (eds), pp. 178–89.

Ó Tuathaigh, G. (1990) *Ireland Before the Famine 1798–1848*. Dublin: Gill and Macmillan. (2nd edn).

Owen, T. M. (1988) 'The Role of a Folk Museum', in A. Gailey (ed), pp. 75–84.

Owens, G. (1994) 'Hedge Schools of Politics. O'Connell's Monster Meetings', *History Ireland* 2(1), pp. 35–40.

Parkes, S. (1996) 'Higher Education, 1793–1908', in W. E. Vaughan (ed), pp. 539–70.

Pearce, Susan M. (ed) (1990a) *Objects of Knowledge: New Research in Museum Studies* vol. 1. London: Athlone.

(1990b) 'Objects as Meaning; or Narrating the Past', in S. M. Pearce (ed), pp. 125–40.

(1994) *Interpreting Objects and Collections*. London: Routledge.

Perks, R. (1993) 'Ukraine's Forbidden History: Memory and Nationalism', *Oral History* Spring, pp. 43–53.

Philbin, E. M. (1985) 'Chemistry', in T. Ó Raifeartaigh (ed), pp. 275–300.

Piggott, Stuart (1983) 'Foreword', in K. Sklenár, p. v.

Pollak, A. (1998) 'History Made Again on Flanders Field', *Irish Times*, 12 November 1998.

Poole, M. A. (1997) 'In Search of Ethnicity in Ireland, in B. J. Graham (ed), pp. 128–48.

Puloy, M. G. (1996) 'High Art and National Socialism. The Linz Museum as Ideological Arena', *Journal of the History of Collections* 8(2), pp. 201–16.

Rafroidi, P. (1983) 'Imagination and Revolution: the Cuchulain Myth', in MacDonagh *et al.* (eds), pp. 137–47.

Raftery, J. (1972) 'Aspects of George Petrie I: George Petrie (1789–1866) a Reassessment', *Proceedings of the Royal Irish Academy* 72c, pp. 153–7.

Renfrew, Colin (1996) 'Prehistory and the Identity of Europe or Don't Lets be Beastly to the Hungarians', in Graves-Brown *et. al.* (eds), pp. 125–37.

Rowlands, Michael (1994) 'The Politics of Identity in Archaeology', in G. C. Bond and A. Gilliam (eds), *Social Construction of the Past. Representation as Power*, pp. 129–43. London: Routledge.
(1996) 'Memory, Sacrifice and the Nation', *Cultural Memory* 30, pp. 8–17.

Ruiz Zapatero, G. (1996) 'Celts and Iberians: Ideological Manipulations in Spanish Archaeology', in P. Graves-Brown *et al.* (eds), pp. 179–95.

Ryan, Michael (1995) 'The Way We Were and the Way We Tell It', *Museum Ireland* 5, pp. 31–42.

Sandahl, Jette (1996) 'Emotional Objects', *Museum Ireland* 6, pp. 17–30.

Shanks, Michael (1992) *Experiencing the past: On the Character of Archaeology*. London: Routledge.

Shanks, Michael and Ian Hodder (1995) 'Processual, Post-processual and Interpretative Archaeology', in I. Hodder *et al.* (eds), pp. 3–29.

Shanks, Michael and Chris Tilley (1992) *Reconstructing Archaeology, Theory and Practice*. London: Routledge (2nd edn).

Sheehan, Elizabeth (1991) 'Architecture as Destiny? Trinity College and University College, Dublin', *Éire-Ireland* XXVI(3), pp. 7–24.

Sheehy, Jeanne (1980) *The Rediscovery of Ireland's Past: the Celtic Revival, 1830–1930*. London:Thames and Hudson.

Shelton, A. A. (1990) 'In the Lair of the Monkey: Notes Towards a Post-modernist Museography', in S. M. Pearce (ed), pp. 78–102.

Sheridan, K. (1998) 'A Farewell to Arms', *Irish Times*, 13 June 1998.

Sherman, D. J. and I. Rogoff (ed) (1994) *Museum Culture. Histories, Discourses, Spectacles*. London: Routledge.
(1994b) 'Introduction: Frameworks for Critical Analysis', in D. J. Sherman and I. Rogoff (1994a) (eds), pp. ix–xx.

Sklenár, K. (1981) 'The History of Archaeology in Czechoslovakia', in G. Daniel (ed) *Towards a History of Archaeology*, pp. 150–8. London: Thames and Hudson.
(1983) *Archaeology in Central Europe the First 500 Years*. Leicester: Leicester University Press.

Smith, Angèle (1998) 'Landscapes of power in nineteenth century Ireland. Archaeology and Ordnance Survey maps', *Archaeological Dialogues* 5(1), pp. 69–84.

Smith, Anthony D. (1983) *Theories of Nationalism*. London: Duckworth. (2nd edn).

(1984a) 'National Identity and Myths of Ethnic Descent', *Research in Social Movements, Conflict and Change* 7, pp. 95–130.

(1984b) 'Ethnic Myths and Ethnic Revivals', *European Journal of Sociology* 15, pp. 283–305.

(1986) 'State-Making and Nation-Building', in J. Hall (ed), *States in History*, pp. 228–63. London: Blackwell.

(1988) 'The Myth of the "Modern Nation" and the Myths of Nations', *Ethnic and Racial Studies* 11(1), pp. 1–26.

(1991) *National Identity*. London: Penguin.

Smith, Laurajane (1994) 'Heritage Management as Post-processual Archaeology?' *Antiquity* 68, pp. 300–9.

Sørensen Marie-Louise Stig (1996) 'The Fall of a Nation, the Birth of a Subject: the National Use of Archaeology in Nineteenth-Century Denmark', in M. Díaz-Andreu and T. Champion (eds), pp. 24–47.

Stention, M. and S. Lees (1979) *A Who's Who of British Members of Parliament 1919–1945*. Brighton: Harvester Press.

Stevenson, R. B. K. (1981a) 'The Museum, its Beginnings and its Development. Part 1: To 1858', in A. S. Bell (ed), pp. 31–85.

(1981b) 'The Museum, its Beginnings and its Development. Part 2: The National Museum to 1954', in A. S. Bell (ed), pp. 142–211.

Stout, M. (1996) 'Emyr Estyn Evans and Northern Ireland: the Archaeology and Geography of a New State', in J. A. Atkinson *et al.* (eds), pp. 111–27.

Sussex, R. and J. C. Eade (eds) (1985) *Culture and Nationalism in Nineteenth Century Eastern Europe*. Columbas: Slavica Humanities Research Centre Australia National University.

Thompson, J. (ed) (1984) *Manual of Curatorship*. London: Butterworth.

Thompson, William Irwin (1982) *The imagination of an insurrection, Dublin, Easter 1916: a study of an ideological movement* (Mass.: Lindisfarne Press).

Thomson, D. (1969) *The Aims of History, Values of the Historical Attitude*. London: Thames and Hudson.

Tierney, M. (1998) 'Theory and Politics in Early Medieval Archaeology', in M. Monk and J. Sheehan (eds), pp. 190–9.

Tilley, Chris (1991) 'Interpreting Material Culture', in I. Hodder (ed), *The Meaning of Things. Material Culture and Symbolic Expression*. London: HarperCollins, pp. 185–94.

Trigger, Bruce (1984) 'Alternative Archaeologies: Nationalist, Colonialist, Imperialist', *Man* 19, pp. 355–70.

(1995) 'Romanticism, Nationalism and Archaeology', in P. Kohl and C. Fawcett (eds), pp. 263–79.

Turpin, John (1989) 'The Dublin Society and the Beginnings of Sculptural Education on Ireland, 1750–1850', *Éire-Ireland* 24, pp. 10–26.

Ucko, Peter J. (ed) (1995) *Theory in Archaeology. A World Perspective*. London: Routledge.

Urry, John (1996) 'How Societies Remember the Past', in S. MacDonald and G. Fyfe (eds), pp. 45–65.

Uzzell, David L. (1989) *Heritage Interpretation, Vol. 1, The Natural and Built Environment*. London: Belhaven Press.

(1996) 'Creating Place Identity Through Heritage Interpretation', *International Journal of Heritage Studies* 1(4), pp. 219–28.

Vaughan, W. (ed) 1996. *A New History of Ireland. Ireland Under the Union 1870–1921*. Oxford: Oxford University Press.

Walker, Brian (1996) *Dancing to History's Tune. History, myth and politics in Ireland*. Institute of Irish Studies: Queen's University Belfast.

Wallace, Patrick (1977) *The Dublin Museum of Science and Art*. Dublin: National Museum of Ireland.

Walsh, Aidan (1997) 'Planning and Developing a Museum Framework for Northern Ireland', in M. Fitzgibbon and A. Kelly (eds) *From maestro to manager: critical issues in arts and culture management*, pp. 97–110. Dublin: Oak Tree Press.

Walsh, Kevin (1992) *The Representation of the Past: Museums and Heritage in the Post-modern World*. London: Routledge.

Warner, Richard (1982) 'The Broighter Hoard: A Reappraisal and the Iconography of the Collar', in B. G. Scott (ed), *Studies in Early Ireland: essays in Honour of M.V. Duigan*. Association of Young Irish Archaeologists.

(1999) 'The Broighter Hoard. A Question of Ownership, in O'Brien G. (ed) *Donegal History and Society*. Country House Press, pp. 69–90.

Whelan, Kevin (1993) 'The Bases of Regionalism, in P. O'Drisceoil (ed), *Culture in Ireland Regions: Identity and Power*, pp. 5–63. Institute of Irish Studies. Belfast: Queens University Belfast.

(1998) *Fellowship of Freedom. The United Irishmen and 1798*. Cork: Cork University Press.

White H. B. (1911) 'History of the Science and Art Institutions, Dublin, *Museum Bulletin* 1(4), pp. 7–34.

(1912) 'History of the Science and Art Institutions, Dublin', *Museum Bulletin* 2, pp. 41–4.

Whitfield. N. (1974) 'The Finding of the Tara Brooch', *Journal Royal Society of Antiquaries of Ireland* 104, pp. 120–42.

Wilson, A. (1995) *A Review of Major Museums in Northern Ireland*. Department of Education for Northern Ireland.

Wilson, T. G. (1942) *Victorian Doctor. Being a Life of Sir William Wilde*. London: Methuen & Co.

Woodman, P. C. (1992) 'Irish Archaeology Today: A Poverty Amongst Riches', *Irish Review* 12, pp. 34–9.

(1995) 'Who Possesses Tara? Politics in Archaeology in Ireland', in P .J. Ucko (ed), *Theory in Archaeology*, pp. 278–97.

Wright, Philip (1996) 'Germany', *Museums Journal* (96)3, pp. 20–5.

Index

A History of the Irish State to 1014, 62
Abbey Theatre, 26, 146
Act of Union, 71, 106, 107
Adams, Mr, 142
Amateur, 74
And so Began the Irish Nation, 60–1
Anderson, Benedict, 20
Anglo-Celt, 86
Anglo-Irish Treaty 1921, 140
antiquarian activity, England, 68–9
antiquarians in Ireland, and cultural
    nationalism, 50–3, 68–82, 91–9
    and maintenance of the Union, 97
    reducing prejudice, 93–4
    reflecting the political context, 94–7, 99
    divisive rhetoric, 98
Antrim, County, 21, 30
archaeology, and nationalism, 11–22, 59,
    148–9
    under Nazi regime, 10
archaeology in Ireland
    as a national duty 50–2, 91–9, 103–5, 107,
    132–4, 139, 152
as a political/national symbol, 1, 17, 22–30,
    33–67, 69–81, 88, 93–9, 107, 129, 134, 145,
    148–55
    in Dublin Museum of Science and Art, 111
    interpretations of, 5, 4, 54–6, 83–6, 93
    maintenance of the Union, 96–7, 110, 112
    neglect during British rule, 45, 86, 147
    preservation of, 46, 47, 52, 110, 122
    reduce prejudice, 93–4
    sanctuary from politics, 73–4, 90, 93, 96–7,
    152
    superiority of Irish, 62–4, 88, 95–6, 132,
    143
Archer, Jean, 3
Architecture, 159
    British Museum 15
    meaning, 15–16, 119, 162–3
    Museum of Science and Art, Dublin, 66,
    115–22
Ardagh Chalice, 151, 159
    as a nationalist symbol, 42, 63–4
arts, 110
arts in Ireland, 85–6, 90, 101, 146
    negative impact of English rule, 86, 136
    sanctuary from politics, 30, 90
Atheneum, 79
Austria, 10

Ball, Valentine, 121, 175 (fn 68)
Belfast Museum, 141

    as Ulster Museum, 141, 161–2
Belgium, 160–1
Bell of St. Senan, 94
Bell, Jonathan, 30
Belleek, Pottery Co. Fermanagh, 109
Bennett, Tony, 14, 153
Berlin, 11
Bigger, Francis Joseph, 63–4
Bodkin, Thomas, 142, 146
Book of Armagh, 63
Book of Dimma, 63
Book of Durrow, 64
Book of Kells, 41, 63, 64, 151–2, 156
Book of Rights, 45
Boru, Brian, 36, 79, 101
Botanic Gardens, 135
Boyce, D. George, 19, 22, 72
Boyd, E. A., 55
Brinkley, Dr, 86
Bristol, 145
British Association for the Advancement of
    Science, 102, 145, 195
British Israelites, 156
British Museum, 15, 125, 129–34, 145
Broighter Hoard, 129–34, 140, 153
    Royal Irish Academy, 129–30
Buckingham Palace, 119
Buckley, Anthony, 157
Burton, Frederic, 40
Butt, Isaac, 128

cabinets of curiosities, 14, 70, 101–2, 128
Cambridge, 145
Cardiff, 15, 145
Carson, Sir Edward, 130
Catholic Association, 50
Catholic Emancipation, 87, 72, 73, 90
Catholic Rent, 50
Celtic Ireland, 60
Celtic Society, 23, 73
Church of Ireland, 106
Clark, Sir Ernest, 140
Clive, Arthur, 55
Clonmacnoise, 163
Coffey George, 62, 137
Coffey, Petra, 3
Cole, Sir Henry, 110–12, 114
collecting, in Ireland, 128
    as a national duty, 107, 113, 129–34
    individuals, 70–1, 82–99
    Dublin/National Museum, 123–5, 145,
    146–7
    political support for, 34, 45–8, 72–3

Royal Dublin Society, 101–2
Royal Irish Academy, 70, 73, 102–5, 110,
    113
Trinity College, Dublin, 101
Collins Barracks, 162
Collis, John, 148
colonialist archaeology, 59
Commissioners of Foods and Forests, 106
Cooney, Gabriel, 4
Cork Young Ireland Society, 33
Council of Ireland, 139
Craig, Sir James, 140
cross, as a nationalist symbol, 42, 87
Cross of Cong, 63, 64, 83, 94, 107
Cuchulainn, as a nationalist symbol, 62, 64,
    156
Cullen, L. M., 72
cultural nationalism, 22–31, 51, 71, 79, 99,
    104
    rejection of, 52–3
cultural revivalism, concept of, 22, 25, 30–1,
    99, 149
Cultural Traditions Group, Northern Ireland,
    158
Cumann na nGaedheal, 47

Dáil, 139
Dargan, William, 79
Davis, Thomas, 41, 45, 51, 68, 72, 92, 99, 104
    and archaeology, 50–2
    and education 95
    and nationalism, 26
    Ordnance Survey, 78
    reference to George Petrie, 51, 87, 92
Dawson, Charles, MP, 118
Day, Robert, 130
Dean Dawson, Collection, 103, 107, 153
Deane, T. N. & son, 118, 119
Denmark, 2, 10
Department of Agriculture and Technical
    Instruction, 135, 137
Department of Education (Irish Free State),
    143
Department of Science and Art, London, 6, 80,
    105–15, 117, 122–3, 136, 153
Derrinboy Armlets, 159
Dillon, John, 28
Dillon, Viscount, 130
Donnelly, Captain, 108
Du Noyer, George Victor, 3
Dublin Literary Gazette, 73, 90
Dublin Penny Journal, 24, 74–5, 81, 84–5,
    101
Dublin Review, 74
Dublin Museum, *see also* Museum of Science
    and Art, Dublin *and* National Museum of
    Ireland
Dublin University Magazine, 55–6, 74, 78, 87,
    96

Duffy, Charles Gavan, 152
Duffy's Hibernian Magazine, 41
Dunamase Food Vessel, 159
Duke of Leinster, 101

Early Christian Period, as a nationalist symbol,
    60, 87–8, 94
education, 79, 106, 123, 143
    and Irish nationalism, 94–5
    legislation, 105–6
    National Board of Education, 108
Education for Mutual Understanding, 158
Elgin Marbles, 13
emigration, 98
Enlightenment, concept of, 70
Esmonde, Sir Thomas, 133
Eucharistic Congress, 145
European Union, 10
Evans, Estyn, 4, 141
Evans, Gwyneth, 4
Evening Herald, 132
Exhibition, Cork 1852, 79
Exhibition, Dublin 1853, 79
Exhibition, Great, London, 1851, 79

famine,79, 98
Farwell, Justice, 130
Fenians, 52 *see also* Irish Republican
    Brotherhood
Ferguson, Samuel, 30, 71, 92, 98, 114
    and education policy, 95
    and maintenance of the Union, 96
    Ordnance Survey, 78
    and revivalism, 23
Finland, 19
First World War, commemoration, 159–61
Foster, Roy, 81
France, 10, 42
Freeman's Journal, 1

Gaelic Journal, 38, 47, 60
Gaelic League, 23–4, 30, 36–7, 47, 60, 115,
    137
    and archaeology, 36
    and cultural nationalism, 26
Gaelic Society, 23
Gellner, Ernest, defining nationalism, 18–9,
    21, 23
General Museum of Economic Geology,
    London, 105
Geological Survey, 112
George II, statue, 162
Georgian Dublin, Preservation of, 163
Germany, 10–11, 67
    Nazi regime, 10
    archaeology and museums, 10
Gibson, Joseph, 130
Gladstone, William, 121
Glasnevin Cemetery, 87, 89

Golden Age, and nationalism, 19, 32–3, 42, 151, 153, 163
Government of Ireland Act (1920), 139, 140
Graham, Brian J., 3–4
Graves, Arnold, 135–6
Graves, Charles, 94
  accolades to George Petrie, 83
  on Irish antiquarians, 84
Gray, Edmund Dwyer, MP, 118
Greece, 2, 9, 13
Green, Alice Stopford, 60–1, 62, 63, 64
Griffith, Arthur, 24, 27, 47, 59, 68
Guatemala, 9
Gulbenkin Foundation and Heritage Council Awards, 148

Hamilton, George Alexander, 108
Hamilton, Sir William, 71, 92, 97
Handbook of Irish Antiquities, 92
Hardiman, James, 123
harp, as a national symbol, 42, 65, 66, 74, 101
Haughton, Rev. Samuel, 108
Haverty, M., 42, 43
Hewitt, John, 158
Hibernia, as a nationalist symbol, 41–2, 44
Hibernia, 117, 137
  reference to George Petrie, 87
Hibernian Magazine, 41
Hitler, Adolf, 10
Hobsbawm, Eric, 18, 20, 32, 68
Hodson, Sir George, 116
Home Rule, 59, 68, 128, 132, 136, 140, 151
Home Rule, Bill, second, 128
Home Rule, Bill, third, 56, 80
House of Commons Debates, 117–8
House of Lords, Dublin, 70
HRH, Prince of Wales, 121
Hroch, Miroslav, 18, 24
Hudson, W. E., 123
Hungary, 47
Hutchinson, John, 23–4, 71–2
Huxley, Prof. T. H., 108
Hyde, Douglas, 25, 27, 29, 48, 151
  and collecting, 47
  and cultural nationalism, 26
  reference to George Petrie, 87

Iberno Celtic Society, 23
iconography, 65, 74, 149
  and archaeology, 39–42
identity, *see* national identity
Illustrated London News, The, 35
imagination, 54, 149
  and archaeology, 37–8, 49, 64
imagined community, 32, 49
industry, 79, 123, 135, 154
Ireland a Nation, 60
Irish Archaeological and Celtic Society, 73
Irish Archaeological Society, 51, 73, 93

Irish archaeology, cultural nationalism, 22–30
Irish Art, 63
Irish Builder, 48, 117, 119, 120, 122, 123
  about Tara Hill, 36
Irish Charity Commissioners, 135
Irish Free State, 141, 147
Irish identity, concept of, 22
Irish language, 157
  and education, 28–9
  and politics, 27, 29
Irish Literary Theatre, 26, 134
Irish Nation, 42, 56–7, 59, 65, 138
  on collecting, 46
  about Tara Hill, 36
Irish nation, definition of the concept, 96, 99, 138
Irish National Magazine, 42, 73
Irish Nationality, 62
Irish nationalism, 62
  and invention of tradition, 21
  defining the concept, 57–8
Irish Parliamentary Party, 27–9
  and cultural nationalism, 22, 29
Irish Penny Journal, 74, 81, 84
Irish People, 52–3
Irish Quarterly Review, 74
Irish Republican Brotherhood, 29, 52–3, 98, 128
  and culture, 22
Irish Times, 1, 133–4
Irish traditions, 20
  concept of, 22
Irish Volunteers, 60

Japan, 15–16
Jellett, Rev. J. H., 104

Kane, Sir Robert, 116
Kaplan, Flora, 2, 154
Kilmainham Gaol, 162
King Edward VII, 130
King William III, statue, 162

Laffan, Colonel, 108
landscape, and nationalism, 32–4, 64
language, 20, 22, 28–9, 48, 51, 65, 69
  and Irish nationalism, 23, 25–6, 28–9, 34, 51, 87, 139
  Ulster Scots, 157
  Irish 27–9, 87, 93, 157
Leader, The, 27
Leerssen, Joep, 69, 72
Leighton, Stanley, 133
Leinster House, 101, 115
Lisburn Museum, Irish Linen Centre, 156
literary revivalism, 54
literature, nationalist, 60
Lithberg Enquiry, 141–7, 153
Lithberg, Professor Nils, 142

Liverpool, 15, 110
Londonderry, 76
Louth Advertiser, 86
Lowenthal, David, 13, 163
Lynd, Robert, 64–5
Lyons, F. S. L., 72
Lucas, A. T., 3

Macalister, Robert, 58, 67, 139, 151
MacNeill, Eoin, 57, 60, 138–9, 151
MacSweeney, Patrick, 80
  on Irish antiquarians, 81, 84
Mahr, Dr Adolf, 146
manuscripts, 83
Marquis of Kildare, 108
Maxwell, Constance, 101
Mayor Dublin, Lord, 108, 116
McAleese, Mary, 148, 159
McCurdy, Mr, 116
McKenna, J. E., 63
McNeill, Charles, 142
McSwiney, P.P., 109
memorials, concept of 152
  First World War, 159–61
  O'Connell, 87–90, 161
  1798 Rebellion 161–2
memory, 13, 109, 159–61, 163
  and archaeology, 36, 54, 62, 149, 154–5
  and nationalism, 33, 109
Merrion Square, 115
Meyer, A. B., 127
Mitchel, John, 51
Monasterboice, and nationalism, 36
Moran, D. P., 27
Morpeth, Lord, 95
Moyer, Dr, 116
Mullaghmast Rath, 36, 152
  and nationalism, 37
Murphy, Dr P. A., 142
Museum Act (Northern Ireland) 1961, 141
Museum of Economic Geology, 100
Museum of Practical Geology, London 106
Museum of Irish Industry, 80, 100, 105, 106,
  112
  collections of, 106
Museum of Science and Art, Dublin, 6, 80,
  112, 128, 134–6, 144, 153–4, 154
  architectural competition, 115–23
  Art and Industrial Division, 123–5
  Antiquities Division, 123, 125
  catalogues, 125, 144, 181–3
  collections, 62–4, 124–5, 136, 138
  director's reports, 144–5
  management of, 109–12, 122
  naming of, 115, 137–8
  as National Museum of Ireland, 3, 6, 141–7,
  162
  national symbol, 64–6
  Natural History Division, 123

  politics, and, 109–12, 122, 136
  public lectures, 125, 184
Museum of Science and Art, Edinburgh, 112,
  125–7
Museum of Science and Art, South
  Kensington, London, 108, 111; *see also*
  Department of Science and Art, London
museums,
  and politics, 9–16
  and politics in Ireland, 1, 65, 109–12,
  117–19, 121, 122–3, 128, 129–34, 152–3,
  155–63
  concept of Dublin Museum, 45, 63–5,
  109–12
  definition of purpose, 143
  Austria, 10
  Germany, 10–11
    under Nazi regime, 10
  Northern Ireland, 140–1
  UK, 15, 145
Museums Association, UK, 1, 2, 138, 145
myths, 32, 41, 54, 59–60, 67

narrative, nationalist, 58–67
nation defining the concept, 48–9, 68–9
Nation, 17, 37, 41, 45, 46, 50–1, 58, 72, 86,
  104
  on archaeology, 36–7, 41, 52, 72
  and Irish language, 29
  George Petrie's round towers essay, 92
  and meeting at Tara Hill, 36
  Ordnance Survey, 77
National Academy (proposed), 139
National Education Board, 72, 73, 94
National Gallery, 115, 140, 146
national identity, 48, 149
national identity in Ireland, 22–31
  and archaeology, 33–67, 132–4, 161
  and museums, 109, 118, 128, 147, 148, 149,
  154–5
  Northern Ireland, 155–7
National Library, 119, 135, 140
National Museum of Ireland, 3, 6, 141–7,
  153–4, 162
  see also Museum of Science and Art,
  Dublin
National Museum of Irish Antiquities and
  Historic Monuments (proposed), 113
National Society of Cork, 45
National University, 29
nationalism, concept of, 17–21, 68–9, 91, 96
nationalism in Europe, 17–18
nationalism in Ireland,
  and museums and archaeology, 1, 32–67,
  93–4, 149, 152–3
  see also cultural nationalism
Nationality, 59
Natural History Museum, 80, 100, 102, 105,
  108, 112, 115, 123

Nelson's Pillar, 162
New Grange, 45
Newry Examiner, 86
newspaper publishing, 86, 117, 132
    and politics, 58–9, 73–4
Normans, 42, 64, 85
Northern Ireland, 140–1, 155–9, 163
numismatics, 82, 125

O'Brien, Dermod, 142
O'Brien, William, 38, 123, 151
    and archaeology, 33, 45
    Irish Ideas, 38
O'Brien, William Smith, 73
O'Connell, Daniel, 22, 29, 34, 37, 73, 90, 161
    and archaeology, 50
    and George Petrie, 83, 87
    and meeting at Tara Hill, 34, 36, 72
    memorial to, 87–90, 161
O'Conor, Charles, and antiquarians, 72
O'Curry, Eugene, 54–5, 73, 84
    concept of the nation, 81, 87
    Ordnance Survey, 76
O'Donovan, John, 55, 73, 84
    concept of the nation, 81, 87
    Ordnance Survey, 76, 78
O'Driscoll, Robert, 30
Office of Public Works, 115, 119
O'Grady, Standish, 30, 53–6
    and interpretation of archaeology, 54, 56
O'Halloran, Clare, 85
O'Halloran, Sylvester, influence on Standish
    O'Grady, 53, 55
Ordnance Survey, 46, 52, 73, 75–8, 81, 96
    George Petrie, 76–8, 82
    memoirs, 76
    Nation, 77
    Parliamentary Commission, 77
    William Wakeman, 76, 78
Ossianic Society, 23
Otway, Caesar, 74
ownership, 149, 150–1
    and archaeology, 71, 114, 129, 134
    and nationalism, 67

Parnell, Charles, 121, 137
Partition, 57
    impact on museums and archaeology,
    139–141
patriotism, 86, 91, 134
    concept of, 104
    archaeology and, 33, 104
    Royal Irish Academy and, 121
    Eighteenth Century, 69–70
    Ordnance Survey, 78
Pearce, Susan, 12
Pearse, Patrick, 24, 27–8, 156
    culture and, 28
    education and, 95

Pembroke, Lord, 115
penny journals, 58
Petrie, George, 3, 7, 51, 74, 82–91, 94, 98–9,
    114, 149–50, 153, 157
    accolades to, 38, 82–4, 91
    and revivalism, 23
    biography, 83
    collecting, folklore, 82
    collecting, music, 82
    collecting, numismatics, 82
    contribution to nation-building, 81
    cultural revivalism, 90
    Ecclesiastical Architecture of Ireland, 82
    Fine Arts Essay, 85–6, 90
    interpretation of, 85
    landscape artist, 82
    Memorial to Daniel O'Connell, 87–90, 161
    On the History and Antiquities of Tara Hill,
    82
    Ordnance Survey, 76–8, 82
    Papers to Royal Irish Academy, 82
    politics of, 85–90
    revivalism and, 23
    Round Towers, 83
    Royal Irish Academy Catalogue, 82
Phases of Irish History, 60
Philosophical Societies, 70
Physico-Historical Society of Ireland, 70
Piggott, Stuart, 11
Pim, Jonathan, 109
Playboy of the Western World, 26
Plunkett, Colonel, 131–2, 134–7, 175 (fn 68)
Plunkett, Count George Noble, Address to
    Museums Association, UK, 1, 138
    as Director of the Dublin Museum 137–9,
    175 (fn 68)
    political activity, 137–8
    renaming of the Dublin Museum 137–8
Plunkett, Horace, 30–1, 135, 137, 152
Plunkett, Joseph, 138
political nationalism, 25–7, 29, 31, 51
    concept of, 29
    culture and, 22
Popular History of Ireland, 42
postage stamps, 159
Powerscourt, Lord, 116, 117, 121
Prague, 15
Protestants, 50–1, 74, 149, 161–2
    cultural nationalism and, 50–1, 71–2
    cultural revivalism and, 30–1
    identity and, 71–2, 156–7
Proto-national bonds, 20, 32
Public Record Office, Dublin, 140
Public Records Act (NI), 140
Puloy, Monika, 10

Queen Victoria, 97, 102
    statue, 162

Rebellion, 1798, Commemoration, 161–2
Recess Committee, 135
Redmond, John, MP, 130, 133
    and political nationalism, 28
religion, and nationalism, 50
Renan, Ernest, 55
Repeal Association, 34, 36, 39, 74
    and archaeology, 37
    and meeting at Tara Hill, 34
revival, 1780s, 22, 24
revival, 1830s, 23–4
revival, 1890s, 24, 56
revival, Gaelic, 134
Rising 1798, 22, 161–2
Rising 1916, 60, 162, 138–9, 141
Robinson, Rev. T. R., 92, 97
Robinson, Sir John, 130
Roman invasion, 64, 86, 95, 132
Romantic nationalism, 45, 85, 92, 103
Round Towers, 74, 159–61
    and George Petrie, 83
    interpretation of, 83
    and nationalism, 33, 42, 49, 60, 87–8
Royal College of Science, 106, 112, 119
Royal Commission, 1851, 101
Royal Commission, 1864, 107–8
Royal Commission, 1868, 111, 128
Royal Commission, 1897, 135
Royal Commission, 1898, 130, 135
Royal Dublin Society, 46, 69–70, 80, 101,
    105, 107–8, 112, 115, 122
    Collections of, 71, 100–2, 104
    Exhibition, Dublin 1853, 79
Royal Hibernian Academy, 82, 84
Royal Institute of Science and Art (proposed),
    79
Royal Irish Academy, 3, 5, 46, 51–3, 68, 70,
    80–1, 92, 107–8, 117, 121–3, 128, 130, 144,
    149–50, 153–4
    and 1780s revival, 22
    and 1916 Rising, 138
    Antiquities Committee, 102, 104
    collections, 55–6, 71, 82, 102, 104, 110,
    112, 149
    Department of Literature and Antiquities,
    92
    Exhibition, Dublin 1853, 79
    Museum, 86, 100
    Ordnance Survey, 77
    Presidential Addresses, 92
    treasure trove, 102

Royal Irish Institute (proposed), 109
Royal Society of Antiquaries of Ireland, 58,
    85, 137, 151
Royal Society of Arts, London, 69
Royal Institute of Science and Art (proposed)
    79
Royal Society of Edinburgh, 69
Russell, George, 26
Russell, Rev. C. W., 108

Sandon, Lord, 112
Saorstat Eireann, 60
Saunders Newsletter, 86, 103
Science and Art Museum, Act 1877, 3, 80, 115
Science and Art Museum, South Kensington,
    80, 108
Scotland, 2, 13, 106, 108, 110, 126–7, 130
Scottish Society of Antiquaries, 126
Sexton, Mr, MP, 117, 118
Sinn Fein, Support for, 47, 59, 138
Sklenar, Karl, 9
Smith, Anthony, defining nationalism, 18–19,
    21, 23
Society for the Preservation of Irish Language,
    23
Society of Antiquaries of Scotland, 2, 126
Society of Antiquaries, London, 126, 130
Somme Heritage Centre, 156
South Korea, 15–6, 162
Spain, 2, 9
spirituality, and Irish nationalism, 47, 63
St. Patrick's Bell Shrine, 64, 94, 159
St. Patrick's College Maynooth, 80, 108
Statues, Preservation of, 162
Steele, William Edward, 175 (fn 68)
Stephens, James, 53
Stokes, William, 90, 94
Stone of Scone, 13
Stonehenge, 19, 43
Stout, Matthew, Evans, 4
symbolism, 49, 75, 79, 134
symbols, 149
    and archaeology, 34, 38–42, 134
    harp, 65
    museums as, 115, 128, 147
    shamrock, 65
    Tara Brooch, 42, 63–4
Symbols Exhibition, Northern Ireland, 158
Sweden, 142

Talbot de Malahide, Lord, 92–3, 113, 148
Tara Brooch, 49, 86, 94, 151, 153, 159

as a nationalist symbol, 42, 63–4
Tara Hill, 34, 45, 50, 62, 78, 94, 149, 152, 156, 159
  and Repeal Association meeting, 35–6
  and patriotism, 37
Tara Torques, 83
Tara, paramilitary group, 156
Technical Educational Association of Ireland, 135
The Archaeology of Ireland, 67
The Beauties of the Boyne and the Blackwater, 92, 97
The Glories of Ireland, 63
The Indestructible Nation, 60
The Making of Ireland and its Undoing, 62
The Story of the Irish Nation, 60
'the troubles', 163
Thompson, Sir Edmund, 130–1
Thompson, William, 78
Tilley, Chris, 12
Times, The, 79
Todd, Rev. James, 77, 93, 94, 113
  Ordnance Survey, 77
Tower Museum, Derry, 157, 158
traditions, concept of national, 34
traditions, 48
traditions, invention of, 55
treasure trove, 130, 140–1
Trigger, Bruce, 59
Trinity College Dublin, 70, 108, 146, 152
  Museum, 100–1

Ulster Folk and Transport Museum, 3, 157–8

Ulster Journal of Archaeology, 92
Ulster Museum, 3, 141, 161–2
Ulster-Scots language, 157
Unionism, 30, 90, 96–7, 110, 139–40, 156
United Irishman, 45
  on antiquarianism, 52
University College Dublin, 60
University Education (Ireland) Act 1881, 105

Vereker, John Prendergast, 109
Victoria and Albert Museum, 147 *see also* Science and Art Museum, London

Wakeman, William, 96
  and cultural nationalism, 92
  Handbook of Irish Antiquities, 92
  Ordnance Survey, 76, 78
Wales, 106
Webb, Sir Aston, 119
Westminster Hall, London, 119
Westropp, T. S. J., 85, 149–50
Whelan, Kevin, 21
White, H. Bantry, 3
Wilde, Sir William, 4, 94, 95–6, 113, 123
  politics of, 97–8
  catalogue 1853, 92
  and Irish archaeology, 96
  The Beauties of the Boyne, 92, 97
Wilson, Alistair, 148
Worsaae, J. J. A., 105

Young Irelanders, 17, 24, 74, 152
  concept of the Irish nation, 49–52, 87